T0303374

THE HARLAN RENAISSANCE

THE HARLAN RENAISSANCE

STORIES OF BLACK LIFE IN APPALACHIAN COAL TOWNS

William H. Turner

WEST VIRGINIA UNIVERSITY PRESS
MORGANTOWN

Copyright © 2021 by William H. Turner
All rights reserved
First edition published 2021 by West Virginia University Press
Printed in the United States of America

"I, Too, Am an Appalachian" © 1970 by Edward J. Cabbell. Reprinted by permission of Melissa Rolan.

ISBN 978-1-952271-20-5 (cloth) / 978-1-952271-21-2 (paperback) / 978-1-952271-22-9 (ebook)

Library of Congress Cataloging-in-Publication Data
Names: Turner, William Hobart, author.
Title: The Harlan renaissance : stories of black life in Appalachian coal towns / William H. Turner.
Other titles: Stories of black life in Appalachian coal towns
Description: First edition. | Morgantown : West Virginia University Press, 2021. | Includes bibliographical references and index.
Identifiers: LCCN 2021009493 | ISBN 9781952271205 (cloth) | ISBN 9781952271212 (paperback) | ISBN 9781952271229 (ebook)
Subjects: LCSH: Turner, William Hobart. | Turner, William Hobart—Family. | African Americans—Appalachian Region—History—20th Century. | Children of coal miners—Kentucky—Lynch—Biography. | Appalachian Region—History. | Appalachian Region—Race relations. | Appalachian Region—Social conditions. | Harlan County (Ky.)—Social life and customs. | Lynch (Ky.)—Biography.
Classification: LCC E185.912 .T87 2021 | DDC 976.9/154 [B]—dc23
LC record available at https://lccn.loc.gov/2021009493

Book and cover design by Than Saffel
Cover image: Turner siblings as stairsteps, Peggy, Marie, Irvin, Evelyn, Bill, 1952. Photo by Robert "Smokypipe" Rutherford. William H. Turner Collection.

Contents

Foreword

BILL TURNER and I have been friends for a good many years and fellow workers in Appalachian and Black studies. Yet I did not fully understand him until I read portions of his memoir. His problem with Appalachian studies is that in most of the books and articles that have been written about this place, little or no mention is made of Black people. His view is that his people have been here in substantial numbers while writers have dwelt only on White people—some of whom always focus on and even brag about their Scottish, Scots-Irish, English, German, or whatever ancestry, as if that makes them somehow more special than others. It dawned on me that I am culpable in this matter also, for I have written quite a bit about Appalachian people, and I have even gone to Wales to understand why so many Welsh Baptists and coal miners wound up in Appalachia.

Dr. Turner became acquainted with Alex Haley when Haley joined the Berea College board. Haley was the writer of the blockbuster book *Roots*, which won the Pulitzer Prize and was made into a movie. Haley was also a friend of John Rice Irwin, who received a MacArthur genius grant for his development of the sixty-five-acre Museum of Appalachia in Norris, Tennessee, with its many pioneer buildings and artifacts and an Appalachian hall of fame. The museum is an affiliate of the Smithsonian Institution. Irwin had helped Haley to purchase a tract of land near the museum to build his estate after the success of *Roots*. On one of Bill Turner's frequent visits to his estate, Haley took him to visit the Museum of Appalachia. Turner was eager to see what Irwin had collected about Blacks in Appalachia. He found nothing. Then Haley told Turner that it was up to him to tell his story of Blacks in the region with a memoir about his own family, one of many who had moved into the central Appalachian coalfields from the Deep South—from central Alabama, in particular. His grandfather, father, and one brother were miners. Turner grew up in Lynch, Kentucky, a model mining town built from scratch by US Steel with decent houses, a hotel, department stores, other amenities, and respectable wages after the United Mine Workers of America (UMWA) won a contract. Turner had pleasant memories of his life there. Haley promised to help him shape his book. He also promised to help in any way he could, and he did until the time of his death in 1991.

I grew up on a farm in far western North Carolina where the only Blacks were in the county seat some fifteen miles away. I became aware of them when I noticed this little yellow bus going to and fro on the highway between Hayesville and Murphy, the latter of which was in the next county. When I inquired about the bus, I was told that it was transporting Hayesville's Black children from our county, which had no colored school, to the colored school in Murphy.

I don't remember my parents ever talking about Black people except my mother saying that her family, the Morgans and Weathermans, had taken in a Black orphan child during the Civil War to rear with their own children and that all the children slept in the same bed. However, when I asked, she said she did not know what happened to that person. The first Black family that I got to know was when I trained horses at the Urquardt Stables in Flat Rock, North Carolina, before going to college. They groomed and fed the horses. Eddie, the father, would wake me almost every morning, singing hymns and spirituals as he fed the horses. We became friends.

When I talked of going to college, Marguerite Bidstrup, the director of the John C. Campbell Folk School in my village of Brasstown, said, "If you are going to college, you should go to Berea." I applied and was accepted, and then I learned that it was a school founded by the Kentucky abolitionist John G. Fee in 1855 to help free and educate slaves and their families. Fee and his associates were forced out of Berea during the Civil War, but when Fee heard that the Union army was recruiting slaves into the army at Camp Nelson in nearby Nicholasville, Kentucky, and that their families were following them to the camp, he prevailed upon Union officials to build shelter for them, and then he set up a school for these women and children. When the Civil War was over, he led some of these people to Berea, where he hoped to build an interracial village.

Berea College operated as an interracial and coeducational work-your-way-through, no-tuition school until 1904 when the Day Law, named for a mountain-area representative in the Kentucky legislature, was passed to make it illegal to educate the two races together. The Black graduates of the school argued that since Reverend Fee's main purpose was to free and educate Black people, Berea should become a colored school. However, the president of the college, Dr. William G. Frost, had just announced his discovery of another group of needy people. Influenced by a trip through eastern Kentucky mountains, Frost deemed these (White) people "our contemporary ancestors in the Southern Mountains" in his eponymous 1899

Loyal Jones, founding figure of Appalachian studies at Berea College, with Bill Turner in Black Mountain, NC, 2019. William H. Turner Collection.

article in *Atlantic*. Thus, during the college's segregated years, the southern mountains became Berea's primary recruiting region. The Berea trustees voted to maintain its emphasis on the southern mountains but also to split its endowment, raise additional funds, and build a new school for Black students. This school became the Lincoln Institute in Shelby County, Kentucky, just outside Louisville.

The Day Law was amended in 1950, and I was in the first reintegrated class at Berea College. There were only a few Black students that first year, but Jesse Reasor (later Zander) from Appalachia, Virginia, and I became lifelong friends. Much later, she invited me to come to Phoenix, where she was a distinguished teacher, to speak at a gathering of Berea College alumni living in Arizona.

There were no Black teachers at Berea while I was a student, but we frequently had notable Black chapel speakers such as Dr. Benjamin Mays and his student Rev. Dr. Martin Luther King Sr. I am grateful for my educational experience at Berea College.

After graduate school and military service, I worked ten years for the Council of the Southern Mountains (CSM). Founded in 1913 by John C. and Olive Dame Campbell, the CSM had an integrated membership, and the first Black members came mainly from the Tuskegee Institute and other Black schools. Much later, in the 1960s, we received War on Poverty and other federal grants to improve the lives of poor Appalachian people, and I visited and advised in several Black communities, including McDowell County, West Virginia, with its 28 percent Black population. The CSM was one of the casualties of the War on Poverty, but McDowell County's poverty programs, also named the "Council of the Southern Mountains," are still active with several integrated programs.

In 1970, Willis D. Weatherford Jr., president of Berea College, invited me to join the college staff and establish an Appalachian Studies Center, the first in the region, and teach classes as well as develop other programs to support Berea College's commitment to Appalachian people. That's when I met Bill Turner. When the University of Kentucky added an Appalachian Studies Center in 1977, John B. Stephenson was chosen to run it. A professor of sociology, Dr. Stephenson was a mentor to Bill and was supportive in getting him a fellowship to do graduate work at the University of Notre Dame. Dr. Stephenson and I often conferred, and one day we discussed the need for a book on Appalachian Black people. I mentioned that I had a friend, Edward Cabbell. In 1975, while in town to perform at the Celebration of Traditional Music, Ed opened the trunk of his 1965 Chevrolet to show me this great pile of material he had collected about Blacks in Appalachia. John then told me about Bill Turner, his bright former student who had just earned his doctorate in sociology from Notre Dame. We then conspired to get the two of them together. They were two very different personalities. Ed grew up on a farm in McDowell County and sometimes dressed in overalls, while Bill, despite his coal-camp raising, was a more elegant, bowtie-wearing, three-piece-suit man. But they agreed to accept the task of doing the book. I found financial aid to support Ed, John got money to support Bill, and they went to work and produced *Blacks in Appalachia* (1985). The book was well reviewed by scholars and has been about the only reliable book on the subject.

Not only is Bill Turner's life story well told in this book, but it affirms what I heard many times while talking to my Black Berea students who grew up in other central Appalachian coal camps. *The Harlan Renaissance* will confirm, once again, Bill's reputation as the primary, essential, and most down-to-earth scholar where Blacks in Appalachia are concerned. I am proud to call Bill my dear friend.

Loyal Jones

Acknowledgments

IF THIS is considered a good book by families such as those I grew up in the midst of in Harlan County, Kentucky, in the middle of the twentieth century, and if it is appreciated for its frankness and truthfulness, it belongs to all of us. But if it shames or degrades even a single person from such communities, it belongs to me. I make no claim that this book describes the lives of a whole class of Black Appalachians in coal camps. I do, however, make assertions that I think, with certainty, apply to the critical mass of them. The personal experiences and anecdotes in these pages connect to wider—worldwide—social relations and understandings. William Earl Turner, my father, is acknowledged as the brainwave behind this book. Born in 1916 and always called by his middle name "Mr. Earl" by the kids, he was from a family of eleven in Coeburn, Virginia. He was a coal miner from the time he was fourteen—in 1931—when he followed his father's carbide light to a coal seam in what he called "a dog hole" mine along Tom's Creek in Wise County, in what is still called "Far Southwest Virginia." When his father died in 1930, Dad left the seventh grade at the Old Colored Methodist School to go into the coal mine to help his mother feed the family. My father died in 1987.

Angular, lanky, nimble, high-cheeked, chocolate, modest, self-effacing, and recognized as well-read, wise, and really smart by all who knew him, Dad provided dependably for ten of us during fifty years of marriage to Naomi Miller Randolph Turner, who was best known as "Punkin." They were married in 1939 when she turned sixteen and he was twenty-one.

He worked the mine in Lynch for four decades inside Black Mountain—Kentucky's highest peak—for US Steel. Growing up around our dinner table, I swallowed whole cloth the bits and pieces of the family ethic that he fed us. Daddy talked about the moral obligation disadvantaged people had to challenge authority and to seek equality and justice by taking action to confront a condition rather than just reacting or responding defensively to it. He taught us not to wait for the goodwill of the powers that be. It came as a surprise to no one when Dad became the lead plaintiff in a class action employment discrimination lawsuit filed on behalf of several Black coal miners in Lynch by the Kentucky Commission on Human Rights in 1970. The suit was initiated while I was working as a field representative for the commission in the summer of 1968. Four months before he died, he told a reporter for the Louisville *Courier-Journal* in 1987:

> Being black held me back. Everybody knows that. I should have been a mine foreman 25 or 30 years before anybody was. I was capable of being one. I had my papers. Some white boys came up and got the job. One day the mine superintendent came right up in my face and said, "Earl, take this young white boy and make a mine foreman out of him . . . but Earl, we can't give you that job cause there ain't no black foremen." . . . He was the damn superintendent . . . telling me that. What are you going to do?

Tom Metcalf and William Earl Turner. William H. Turner Collection.

Within a few years of the suit, thirteen Black men, including Dad, were promoted to the rank of foreman.

Dr. Alessandro Portelli, professor of Anglo-American

literature at the University of Rome La Sapienza, worked out his interest in comparing how Italian and American workers felt about labor conflict by conducting a long and drawn-out oral history project in Harlan County, Kentucky. He profiled and interviewed our father, mother, brother (Irvin), and grandmother for his award-winning book *They Say in Harlan County*, in which he interviewed more than 150 Harlan County women and men who told their stories that covered pioneer times up through the intense labor wars of the 1930s (around Evarts) and into the 1970s, when miners took strike action at the Eastover Coal Company–owned site in a section of Harlan County known as Brookside. During the thirty years Portelli spent conducting interviews in Harlan County, he was a frequent overnight guest in my parents' home in Lynch.

Dad mesmerized me with his knowledge of history and his first-rate storytelling. He was a folklorist, really, who told us traditional stories and folk tales, and he was unusual—among the Black people—for his use of Appalachian sayings and the local talk, tongue, phrasings, and dialect. A most convivial fellow, he was charming and talkative and most receptive to listening to peoples' problems. He could spin a yarn with the best of them. His constant companion from the time that I could walk, I learned a lot from my father, and he deliberately took me along when he was with his fishing and hunting buddies. Dad bought me a twenty-gauge, single-barrel Stevens shotgun—three feet, five inches in length—for a Christmas present in 1956 when I was ten.

I took a full course in Shit-Talking 101 before I was a teenager with Dad's outdoor buddies: Messrs. Jimmy Gaines, Peddy Reynolds, Dan Deadwyler, Jack Thomas, and Coleman "Muletrain" Washington. While accompanying them on fishing trips in the spring, summer, and fall of the year, and on rabbit- and squirrel-hunting trips in the winter season, I lent a close ear to their speech patterns, which were a combination of Alabama African American Vernacular English and just plain countrified Black men shooting the shit. They were certainly letting off coal-mining steam on their weekends away from the drudgery of their work, the densely packed neighborhoods, and their noisy homes that were customarily "full of chillum." These men, in another life, would have been tree-hugging environmentalists, only with coal dust under their fingernails and with their lungs full of silica. Constantly, it seemed when we were outdoors, one of these men would be coughing and hacking up a mass of murky phlegm. I developed a habit of spitting regularly for no reason based on biology. An instance of minor sees miners, minor does what miners do. It was only natural.

I also listened quite attentively to women in our house: to Mama, my older sisters, as well as the clusters of women who frequented Mama's kitchen. The space was hospitable and gossipy, especially on Friday and Saturday nights when Mama, an enterprising, though bootlegging, hairdresser, did hair for seventy-five cents a head while simultaneously hosting bid whist card parties fueled by glass quarts of Budweiser or Miller High Life beer served in paper cups. On any given Friday or Saturday, starting after supper, there would never be less than a dozen women and teenage girls rotating in and out of our kitchen; in cool and winter weather, they would be packed around our potbellied coal-burning stove. A foglike layer of pungent smoke deflected back from the ceiling just above the light bulb that hung from a single wire, the smell of which was a combination of smoldering cigarettes and the aroma of Black hair singed by hot curlers fuming in Posner's Bergamot, Sulfur-8, Dixie Peach, and Royal Crown Hair Dressing. Phrases such as *a good grade of hair*, *straight*, *wavy*, and their opposite, *kinky*, *nappy*, *wooly hair*, entered my vocabulary during this time. Mama's kitchen on weekends was quite like the porch where Alex Haley said he listened to the women folk in his family tell stories. I certainly learned a lot from my seat on the kitchen floor, in the corner, behind Mama.

Mama also had a rare gift: she was a mind-blowing cook. It is a mystery why none of us are stout or overweight. Everyone who knew her talked about "Punkin's cooking," which explained why we had so many visitors so frequently. Her swap-gossip skills and splendid foodstuffs made people feel right at home. Some people, like Reverend Gabriel and Reverend Middlebrooks, came to our house purposely, regularly, and predictably, just to eat Sister Punkin's food.

I wonder if our mama would not have allowed things to wrack her nerves so badly—or wracked others' nerves—had she known that stress is one of the main causes of alopecia, or spot baldness. The condition causes hair to stop growing or to be lost from some or all areas of the body—in Ma's case, the entire head. Mama always wore a headscarf around the house and in the yard where she hung clothes on a line and tended her flowers and garden. I witnessed her countless times as she would sit at the kitchen table with a mirror and prepare for bed by installing rollers and curlers in her wig, then don her night scarf. When she went out in public—to attend church or to shop or whatever—she wore a wig.

I was fifty-four the first time I saw my mother's uncovered head. She was a month or so from dying when my wife, Vivian, along with my sisters Peggy and Evelyn, removed Ma's ever-present scarf and wig while bathing her. No pun intended, but the sight of Ma's bald head was a glaring reminder to me of her countless warnings to us about hair images in terms of what was adequate and desirable for Black women. Certainly, kinky, curly, or nappy hair was "bad," not "good," hair. In a small way, the now multibillion-dollar Black hair industry played out in our kitchen in the 1950s, and I saw firsthand how Black women had different types of hair with different characteristics. The hairdos carried, for some, painful treatments to relax the naps and curls without being burned. I watched as Mama endured Vivian's Afro style when they met in the summer of 1968. Ma told Vivian that she could not understand why Vivian would deliberately "go away from such pretty long hair, which many colored women would die to have." When Mama embraced our dreadlocked daughter Kisha at her graduation from Spelman College in Atlanta—where at least three dozen of our family members convened in 1993—she said, "I sure hope I get to fix your hair myself before I leave this world." Ma could not believe the title of bell hooks's 1999 children's book *Happy to Be Nappy*. But by the time she died in 2001, Ma had, of necessity, accepted braids, coils, cornrows, locks, weaves, twists, and twirls in the hair of Black women—and men—in Harlan County.

Scattered like pellets from a shotgun are references throughout this book to the teachers I had at the Lynch Colored Public School. From Mr. Charles "Chief" Cross—the janitor, for whom I worked as an assistant janitor from the sixth to the eleventh grade—to the strict and dignified principal, Mr. John V. Coleman, I am particularly and tremendously thankful. These teachers—and teachers at schools just like ours throughout central Appalachia—gave their students such distinctive and extraordinary preparation that I compare them to the central characters in that well-known tale from Greek mythology about Achilles. Thetis, his mother, dipped him in the River Styx to make him invulnerable because it had been predicted that he would die young. The teachers at these colored schools immersed us into a stream

William H. Turner and mother, Naomi, 1987. Photo by Jessica Boyatt. William H. Turner Collection.

of knowledge and self-respect that provided an impenetrable layer of protection against the damage of racism.

Such teachers were the waters of the river; they touched us all over. Most parents, like mine, were not high school graduates, so they threw us to the mercy and magnanimousness of these trusted teachers. I still carry around in my head the voices and antics and high achievements of many former classmates and students—before and after me—with whom I shared the Lynch Colored School, also known as Lynch West Main High School. In the format of the *Reader's Digest* examples that Dad and I would discuss, I could write volumes on "The Most Unforgettable Characters I Ever Met," even after leaving that sacred schoolhouse more than a half century ago. Most of the students from that school—and similar ones—were unconquered by life's ups and downs. The weaknesses and vulnerabilities of our lives—those parts that were covered by the hands of our families as we were being enfolded by life's vicissitudes—were offset by exposure to a wide-ranging set of experiences we had *before* we left the otherwise isolated and insulated mountains of Appalachia. The victim mentality went down the river.

When I left Harlan County at age twenty and chanced upon the late Dr. John Bell Stephenson—my teacher and academic advisor at the University of Kentucky from 1966 to 1968—I was ready for Freddie, or more than prepared. John—who founded the Appalachian Center and the Appalachian studies program at the University of Kentucky (UK) in 1977—constantly advised me, from the time he learned that I was from Harlan County, to study analytically and methodically what my father had taught me to appreciate about Appalachia and about *being* Appalachian. John and I were close friends and associates until he died in 1994, while he was president of Berea College. Next to my father, there is no person who influenced me more than John Bell Stephenson. It was John, along with Doris Y. Wilkinson, an African American and another of my UK sociology professors, who guided my career. Doris reminded me of my mother and grandmother—full of motherly wit, only with a PhD.

Dr. Ronald D. Eller, who succeeded John as the director of the Appalachian Center and Appalachian studies program at UK, is the author of *Uneven Ground: Appalachia since 1945*, among other groundbreaking Appalachia-themed books and articles. Ron has assisted in all phases of virtually every idea I have formed or entertained about Appalachia over the past four decades. Professor Eller is also the best fly-fishing coach and all-around fishing buddy one could ever have.

Every person who writes a book—whether self-published or the imprint of Simon & Schuster or Random House—is pushed off the cliff of hesitancy and delay by someone who encourages them, igniting the fuse of self-confidence. Thirty years ago, Ernie Pitt, the publisher of the *Winston-Salem Chronicle*—a Black weekly—opened his pages for my op-ed column "Lift Every Voice." Thanks goes to Ernie, and to his wife, Elaine, who sent me the fifty dollars each week for the column. A few years after settling into my popularly accepted status as a thought leader in the Winston-Salem community, I found myself sitting across a table—in a Confederate-themed restaurant—from Ken Otterbourg, a calmly brilliant writer and editor for the daily White newspaper, the *Winston-Salem Journal*. More than anyone, it was my dear friend Ken, who is the godfather of my grandson Hodari Jr., who convinced me to take myself seriously as a writer, even using the label *raconteur*. He is simply the best. A Black man from Harlan County, Kentucky, and a Jewish man born and raised in New York City, twenty years apart in age, walk into a Confederate-themed eatery in a North Carolina town after which two major cigarette brands—Winston and Salem—were named. There is a great joke in there somewhere.

Elizabeth Catte, editor-at-large for West Virginia University Press and author of *What You Are Getting Wrong about Appalachia*, guided me superbly over a two-year period in developing this book. Michael Jauchen, a freelance editor, did the proofreading and copy editing. I can't thank both of them enough for the many aha moments they gave me, making me write and rewrite, my writing measurably better than it was before I met them.

I also appreciate, immeasurably, master teacher Loyal Jones, one of the founders of Appalachian studies. In association with John Bell Stephenson, Loyal connected me to Edward Joseph Cabbell in 1979, by which time Ed had spent a decade solidifying his place as the father of Black Appalachian studies. I keep a photo above my desk of Ed—he's wearing bib overalls—next to one of John Stephenson and Alex Haley, the author of *Roots*. Ed and I coedited the collection of readings titled *Blacks in Appalachia*, which was published in 1985. More than three decades later, Amazon still advertises the anthology with a bit of enthusiasm:

> Although southern Appalachia is popularly seen as a purely white enclave, blacks have lived in the region from early times. Some hollows and coal camps are in fact almost exclusively black settlements. The selected readings in this new book offer the first comprehensive presentation of the black experience in Appalachia.
>
> Organized topically, the selections deal with the early history of blacks in the region, with studies of the black communities, with relations between blacks and whites, with blacks in coal mining, and with political issues. *Blacks in Appalachia* focuses needed attention on a neglected area

of Appalachian studies. It will be a valuable resource for students of Appalachia and of black history.

Dr. Patricia A. Smith read the first draft of this manuscript-in-progress in 2015. We met in 2012, just after Vivian and I moved to Texas, where I started lecturing at Prairie View A&M University, fifty miles northwest of Houston, where Patricia was a professor of education. Patricia was "coming through," as the idiom goes, a life-threatening experience with cancer. Her head-on resilience through that fight was truly inspiring. Patricia constantly reminded me to keep it real so everyday folk, like our grandmothers, will know this special story about this distinctive group of people—Black Appalachian coal-mining families. Patricia, just fifty years old when she died in January 2020, introduced me to Tim McGraw's hit "Live Like You Were Dying." If truth be told, Patricia showed me how to live more audaciously.

To Vivian Love Turner, my wife, I thank you for always showing me how superior intellect thinks and how dignified character acts, and for sparking a long-enduring, loving, and complementary relationship. Our connection has been marked by mutual encouragement and support, and I am most thankful that you have, according to most of our family and friends, "put up with Bill" now for more than fifty-two years.

To our ideal sons, Will—and his wife Maisha and their children, Amani and Lucien—and to Hodari—and his wife Lillian and their offspring, Africa and Hodari Jr.—and to our beloved daughter, Kisha, my starkly precise historian and fact-checker, this book is dedicated to you guys collectively as well as to all of our extended family. When my brother Karl read the first draft of this book, he called our surviving siblings—Marie, Evelyn, Tony, and Jeff—and said, "Our late mama and daddy and our sister Peggy and brother Irvin will approve of what Bill has written."

There has always been a debate among child psychologists and family counselors about whether opposite-sexed siblings should share a bedroom and, if they do, for how long. In our house, and in the houses of most of all our neighbors in our coal camp, no matter the specific ages or how dissimilar their developmental stages, opposite-sex siblings slept in the same bedroom. Our house had only two bedrooms.

That Peggy, Marie, Irvin, Evelyn, and I slept in the same bedroom—from 1946 until Peggy left home after graduating from high school in 1958—is the rhyme and reason why we were, and are, to this day, so profoundly devoted to each other as brothers and sisters. In turn, as the older ones left the nest, a bed spot opened. For example, by the time baby sister Evelyn graduated from high school and moved out in 1963, bed spots opened for the younger ones who came along—Tony, Karl, and baby brother Jeff. When I chose to attend the local community college—because Dad thought, "We should fish a couple more years with your little brothers before you leave for good"—I became the first one in our family to stay in our parents' house after graduating high school. Until I was twenty, I continued to live in the same space with my younger brothers: Tony, Karl, and Jeffery, the baby child, who is thirteen years my junior. As siblings, our visits to the homeplace were sustained until Mama died in 2001. By then, we were very close-knit as a family, our family tree tighter than Dick's hat band, or tighter than the bark to a tree.

Since Earl and Naomi married in 1938, their eight children, three of whom hold college degrees, brought into being for them, as it were, sixteen grandchildren, half of whom hold college degrees; nineteen great-grandchildren; and five great-great-grandchildren. All these Turners hold each other in high

Turner siblings as stairsteps, Peggy, Marie, Irvin, Evelyn, Bill, 1952. Photo by Robert "Smokypipe" Rutherford. William H. Turner Collection.

esteem; we love each other unconditionally and are in touch constantly. I am grateful for the insights and corrections I got when I talked to them, seeking to confirm my memories. I look forward to talking with my siblings and nieces and nephews about this work when it is finished, trusting that each of these highly critical and opinionated relatives, all of whom also favor each other, will forgive me for any shortcomings. Our friends and neighbors said of our family, "You can tell a Turner anywhere, but you can't tell 'em anything!"

Finally, I am hugely grateful to countless numbers of people in the space I call WestVaTucky, where southern West Virginia, southwest Virginia, and eastern Kentucky come together, both physically and culturally. I have been the guest in homes where some I hardly knew chatted with me for hours in formal, recorded interviews. I am appreciative to these salt-of-the-earth people for the many meals and drinks and for the dialogues in their parlors, on their porches, by phone, email, and letter, and at their kitchen tables, on walks and rides together, in juke joints and pool rooms, during family reunions, in places of worship, and in cemeteries during Memorial Day rites. They doled out accounts, chronicles, descriptions, lies, narratives, whoppers, and yarns, all of which allowed me to learn about the past and to put my own stories into a comparative perspective. The tenacity, spirit, and cordial hearts of those who helped me, especially by passing on their enduring belief in the value of education and the equality of all humans, showed me not only the kindness of the human spirit but also the eagerness of people to tell their stories and the path on which one should travel to achieve once-unspeakable goals in the face of unrelenting hard times.

Introduction

I WOULD not have chosen to be born in Harlan County, Kentucky, a year after World War II ended, except that is where my mother was. In fact, she was born in Harlan County, in Benham, two decades earlier and was fixed firmly there to her parents, both of whom were among the first group of Black people to migrate in great numbers to the county in the Roaring Twenties. Mama's two older sisters were also born in Benham, Kentucky.

Naomi Randolph married William Earl Turner (born in nearby Wise County, Virginia) when she was sixteen, in 1938. My four older siblings—Barbara (who was born in 1939), Marie, Irvin, and Evelyn (who was born in 1945)—whom she birthed before she was twenty-two, were all born in Harlan County. Starting four years after I was born in 1950, Mama had three more children—Mark, Karl, and Jeffery—the last one born sixty years ago, and all of them in Harlan County. Our parents adopted the sons of our sisters Barbara and Marie, who both divorced when their sons were younger than five. Our father believed that children, especially boys, should grow up, if possible, with a man in their lives. Richard and Frederick forever referred to their grandparents as "Ma" and "Daddy" and to their mothers by their first names.

A critical mass of us African Americans lived throughout the span of the twentieth century in the heart of Appalachian coal country—in our case in Harlan County, Kentucky—right along with the small numbers left from the Indigenous populations, the settler pioneers (the so-called native Whites), the European immigrants, and the recently arrived Hispanics. Our sense of belonging in Harlan County was realized over almost a century, but it remains unbreakable. Our sister Marie, seventy-eight at the time of this writing and widowed twice, thought so much of the place where she was born and raised that she returned there to be married—her third time—when she was seventy. She and her husband Billy wanted to celebrate their vows "with lifelong friends at home," not with the people they knew in Detroit, where Billy had migrated after high school in Benham.

Our connections to this land attached us to it like chocolate-colored railroad crossties atop crushed white gravel. We were spiked down and anchored in place there, able to carry heavy loads and perform a balancing act on life's narrow steel rails, our arms outstretched the way an acrobat holds a stabilizing pole while on a high wire, looking up and moving forward, one step at a time, gingerly. Even though I never traveled far beyond Lynch during my first twenty years, I read enough magazines like *Jet*, *Ebony*, *Look*, *Life*, *Reader's Digest*, *National Geographic*, and the *Saturday Evening Post* to appreciate its relatively well-designed and orderly surroundings and the durability, toughness, and graciousness of the people. That said, I never went around humming the state song, "My Old Kentucky Home," as though the place was that charming, picturesque, and serene. We seemed to know, intuitively, that our Appalachian coal-town hollow was a temporary stopover to some other promised land.

The Commonwealth of Kentucky became the fifteenth

state in 1792. In 1819, a county was carved out of a tract of land in the southeast portion of the commonwealth and was named after Silas Harlan, a Revolutionary War soldier, surveyor, and pioneer who died in the famous Battle of Blue Licks fighting alongside Daniel Boone in what was one of the last battles of the American Revolutionary War. Harlan County—the key setting of this book—is one of the most well-known and legendary counties in Kentucky in the heart of coal country. The county was destined for distinction and fame when J. P. Morgan, one of the world's foremost financial notables, used the resources of one of his companies, US Steel, to buy land and begin surveys of what would become the town of Lynch. Morgan also owned International Harvester and General Electric.

Mable Brown Ellis, in an article titled "Children of the Kentucky Coal Fields," published in *Child Magazine* in 1920, wrote of the origins of Lynch: "[Then] in 1917 the greatest corporation in the world was creating a city overnight, blasting its streets into the side of the mountains, moving a river from one side to the other side of the valley, erecting a metropolitan hotel where stood a log cabin barely two years before." George D. Torok, in *A Guide to Historic Coal Towns of the Big Sandy Valley* (2004), tied the 1917 emergence of Lynch to production efforts for World War I, revealing how the coal reserves on the fourteen-thousand-acre site were designated for use in US Steel's massive mills in Gary, Indiana, long before a single car of coal was loaded. Less than five years after ground was broken to bring Lynch into existence as a coal town, its workers set the world record for coal production in a nine-hour shift when 12,820 tons were mined, enough to fill 256 cars in six trains. Big bucks also left Lynch during this time in the form of money orders mailed to foreign countries: $400,000 in 1923 alone.

Lynch was a model company town, among the first planned communities in the mountains of the South. The engineers estimated that there was enough coal to stay in business for a century, so they, by design, constructed the business, mining, recreational, health care, and residential structures of the most durable materials. All municipal services were first-rate. By mid-September 1917, the year of my father's birth, three hundred cars of materials had been unloaded, and the building of the town began. A mine was opened, and rail tracks were extended from Benham, which was owned by International Harvester, another of J. P. Morgan's companies. The new town was named after Thomas Lynch, the president of US Steel, who had passed on three years earlier.

Within the blink of an industrial eye, between 1917 and 1920, the population of Lynch increased dramatically to seventy-two hundred. The first nonnative residents in Lynch were Italian and Hungarian stonemasons brought directly from Ellis Island by the company; these robust souls were the first line of laborers who carved out what became a colossal coal camp, carved into the wilderness. By 1940, Harlan County's population (75,275) was exceeded in Kentucky only by the counties of Jefferson (Louisville) and Fayette (Lexington).

Lynch and towns like Harlan, Hazard, Jenkins, and Wheelwright (in eastern Kentucky); Big Stone Gap, Grundy, and Stonega (in southwest Virginia); and Gary, Keystone, and Beckley (in southern West Virginia) were as racially and ethnically diverse—each group living in their neighborhoods and with traditions openly displayed—and as booming and blooming as New York City. Harlan County was to Kentucky Black coal-mining families in the 1920s through the 1940s what Harlem was to Black New Yorkers in the same period. It was the cultural and social epicenter of the region for Blacks, and as "the blackest town for mountains around," Lynch was equivalent to 125th Street in Harlem—the school was our Schomburg Center for Research in Black Culture, and the Pool Room was our Apollo Theater.

The influx of Blacks—primarily from central Alabama—into the coalfields of central Appalachia reached its peak in the 1920s, the exact same time during which the Great Migration of Black Americans took place from the Black Belt South to the urban North. The section of New York City known as Harlem became ground zero for an African American cultural rebirth and resurgence that was labeled as the New Negro Movement or the Harlem Renaissance. America's cultural gatekeepers—the mainstream journalists, critics, and publishing houses—had not, until the influx of Blacks to New York City in the 1920s, paid any attention to African Americans as far as literature, music, art, and politics were concerned. At this point, still, a critical mass of entertainers, such as Appalachian (Chattanooga) blues vocalist Bessie Smith, writers, and musicians exploded onto Harlem's performance spaces and in newspaper and magazine pages around the world. Not only did some of the top artists, like Duke Ellington, make highly publicized forays during this period into coal camps such as Lynch and Bluefield, West Virginia, but Maceo Pinkard, a Bluefield native, although not well known, also composed "Them There Eyes."

When I went away to college in Lexington to the University of Kentucky at the age of twenty in 1966, my initial observation, my version of cultural shock, was made by phone to my parents: "I've never understood why they say there are no Black people in our neck of the woods. I have never seen this high a concentration of White people in my whole life!"

Fact is the counties in Kentucky's coal-producing regions—Bell, Floyd, Harlan, Knox, Laurel, Letcher, Perry, and Pike—were among the state's most populous counties at the onset of World War II, and the percentage of Blacks in those counties was uniformly higher than in other parts of the state. Coal was king, and throngs of people moved into the region during the first four decades of the twentieth century to make their living serving the emperor. In 1940, Lynch's population hovered around eleven thousand—about 14 percent of the county—and with some 4,500 employees working its mines, the US Steel plant there was, per capita, one of the state's largest employers.

The social and civil engineers of US Steel developed a business plan designed to extract an amount of coal, by the ton, that would require two thousand men. Drawings from 1917 show how the designers laid out a way to efficiently house the workforce, deciding that two rooms per man employed should be constructed, which resulted in four thousand rooms in roughly one thousand houses, which averaged four rooms each. These thousand-plus dwellings included five boarding houses plus a hotel; four neighborhood-based, company-owned retail shops; and a massive four-story department and general store called "the big store," as in "I owe my soul to the company store," the hook line of "Sixteen Tons," a Merle Travis–written song made famous in 1955 by Tennessee Ernie Ford. By January 1918, fifteen hundred men were on the payroll, and the population of Lynch grew to sixty-five hundred. In these early days of its formation, most of the laborers lived in rough bunkhouses and were fed in two company kitchens. In 1926, two years after our mother was born in the neighboring town of Benham, *Success* magazine carried the following line in its profile of the metropolis-like, but otherwise isolated, rural settlement where I was born two decades later: "Lynch is the melting pot of the Cumberlands. Thirty-two nationalities help season the pot that boils in this vastness of these American mountains and bring forth

Fourth of July celebration in Lynch, KY, 1929. Southeast Community College Appalachian Collection, Cumberland, KY. Used with permission.

a mixture more deliberately American than can be found on the long-populated eastern coast."

By 1940, Lynch boasted of its 133-room hotel, which contained a kitchen, two dining halls, a shoe shop, a clothing store, a soda-water fountain, a cigar store, four bowling lanes, a billiard room, a reading room, a parlor, a spacious lobby, a beauty shop, and various other service rooms. Only Whites could spend a restful night at the Lynch Hotel and leisurely eat the meals prepared by Black hands.

Our family was among the nearly four thousand Black people living in Lynch at the time. Life in Lynch in the middle of the twentieth century moved with a great display of energy, and it teemed with something—what the French called *je ne sais quoi*, an undefinable, elusive, and rather pleasing quality. It bustled with lots of people, many unforgettable characters, and all sorts of activities, both the sacred and the profane. I started this chapter off by joking that "I would not have chosen to be born in Harlan County, Kentucky, a year after World War II ended, except that is where my mother was." That remark, which my father would have called "smart-alecky," was an inflated perversion of the stereotypical view of an Appalachian coal town. To the contrary, as far as the lifestyles of working-class people across the United States could be compared between the two world wars, Lynch was a self-contained world of export and commerce.

The mythical reputation of Harlan County, especially the "Bloody Harlan" tag, is linked to several major events in the struggle to unionize coal miners, which took place in the mid-1930s. The boom times of the forties faded into what became the awful fifties, when major changes hit Lynch like the caving in of the roof of a mine, wrought on by the weight of the ever-increasing mechanization of coal mining. Machines marginalized and then replaced men, and migration out of the area cleared people out of it just as the in-migration a half century earlier had filled it. US Steel sold its Lynch works to Arch Minerals of St. Louis in 1963, the same year the Lynch Colored School was closed. In 1960, there were nine hundred coal-mining and related workers in Lynch. The losses and the proof of displacements were intense and evident. Yet by 1982, the Lynch mines, moving toward their lowest employment numbers, set another record for production of coal in one year—two million tons. A decade later, the last coal was removed from a seam in Lynch; it wasn't done by coal miners but through strip-mining, which requires very few laborers. On the north face of Black Mountain, the vegetation was cleared, the soil was removed, holes were drilled and blasted with dynamite, and the coal was "stripped" from the naked and exposed mountainside. The area has not yet been reclaimed. When the last Lynch mine was closed and sealed—literally—it invoked the feeling one gets at a burial site when the preacher says, "Earth to earth, ashes to ashes, dust to dust." The mine opening was like a source of life, like a dear brother or sister, now departed, recommitted unto itself—the mountain.

The demise of the coal towns of central Appalachia never caused a collective sense of future shock. After all, the changes did not come like the COVID-19 crisis of 2020. There were plenty of signals, spread over the decades since 1950. It is not like people were stupid or foolish, thinking that the good times would last forever. Losing work was one thing, but the loss, the destruction of entire communities—physically and psychologically—was yet another. Acknowledgment of the new realities (coal ain't coming back), resilience, and flexibility are the captions of the next chapters in the story of Appalachian coal towns, yet to be recorded.

This picture of Black families in the heart of Appalachia, a kind of time-lapse exposure, is not the ordinary photo, the one taken with a typical White lens. This picture is meant to transform those ordinary depictions of Appalachian coal camps by bringing readers right up close to a Black insider's view, my lens zooming in and out between personal memory, family, community, and regional history, and facts about the environment, some pretty well known, some not so much. If indeed light is to photography and filmmaking what sound is to music, I have tried to cast light, detailed clarifications onto some of the words, expressions, and practices that exist mainly in those dark and blurred and concealed regions of a culture known only to, and noticeable only by, those with the lived experiences of it. Some of it, what I have seen in the Black coal camps of Appalachia, is almost certainly distorted by this account, this glimpse, this view, just the way ultra-wide-angle shots distort photographs. And because I move between specific contexts—which are both fixed and past tense—and dynamic memory, I have tried to steady the images, freeze the frame, so to speak, and when fitting, I have sought to concentrate on the foreground, then blur the background, and vice versa. At heart, from my heart, this book is a series of stories: stories that are personal, narratives that were told to me, and things I heard and observed, as well as participated in, personally. Other peoples' stories and tales about families I knew merge into both personal and community cultural identity narratives, all combining to make the lives of Black people in Appalachian coal camps meaningful and unique.

This book is a personal as well as a group biography, framed inside a wide-ranging summary of the history and culture of Black people who have been embedded for most of the past century in the coal-producing zones of the central Appalachian Mountains where (eastern) Kentucky, (southwest) Virginia, and (southern) West Virginia come together. From the late nineteenth century into the first three decades of the twentieth century, multiple thousands of Black men—in the form of a massive and portable labor force, followed by their families—moved from the Black Belt, mainly from central and northern Alabama, into the central Appalachian coalfields.

Blacks—especially Black coal miners—were unseen from the earliest times that coal was mined in central Appalachia, despite the fact that thousands of them worked underground in the coalfaces of Alabama around Jefferson County (Birmingham) and in the nearby counties of Walker and Tuscaloosa long before the Civil War. A century earlier, Blacks worked in the first coal mines to operate in the United States—in Virginia, along the James River—not far from where the

Turner siblings, Christmas 1967. Photo by Robert "Smokypipe" Rutherford. William H. Turner Collection.

first enslaved Africans entered the United States of America in 1619, near Hampton, at Old Point Comfort.

"Working in a Coal Mine," a song made popular in 1966

by Lee Dorsey, spoke to how work for the men in coal towns fluctuated like the ebb and flow of sea tides: high tide then low tide, rhythmic, boom then bust. By the time Dorsey's tune was listed at number nineteen on the Billboard Hot 100 singles of 1966, the layoffs—brought on mainly by automation—had already been in full swing for a decade. The level of anxiety as to whose daddy would be next on the out-of-a-job list was at an all-time high.

Each ton of coal that the backbreaking labor of men produced—primarily with picks and shovels in the first decade of mining in Lynch, starting in 1917—added resources to US Steel's research and development coffers, which, in turn, brought into being the laborsaving machinery that disproportionately replaced Black miners. The Black people who had left Alabama and entered these coalfields between 1890 and 1940 knew firsthand the experiences of their parents when machines transformed agricultural production. After all, their grandparents had been slaves in Alabama. Slavery lasted just sixty years after Eli Whitney invented the cotton gin.

Just as the cotton gin transformed the manner—and especially the speed—with which seeds could be separated from cotton, coal-mining machines such as the Joy Loader modernized the efficiency—and especially the speed—with which coal could be separated from the mountains that encased it. By the time I was born—twenty years after the founding of the Lynch Colored Public School—machines were replacing men in the mines of Lynch.

Chilling scenes filled with deep emotions pack my memory as families all around us began to move out in droves. The names of men scheduled for unemployment were posted on the door of the lamp house where the men checked in for work. These notifications were mirrored in the vestibule of our church, where a list revealed each week how much each member gave in church the previous week. As the number of names on the company cutoff list increased, the number of names on the church membership offerings list decreased. The company giveth, the company taketh away. The last days, even for churches, have already come to pass in many once-bustling coal towns like my birthplace, Lynch, which was described in a US Steel corporate press release in the year of my birth, 1946, as "The World's Greatest Coal Town." Not one person has worked in a coal mine in Lynch in the twenty-first century.

In the mid-1960s, the central Appalachian coalfields were popularized as a "White" space in the United States. Although many parts of the geographical area known as Appalachia were and are predominantly White, the region, like most of the United States, has never been entirely White. The inhabitants of the central Appalachian coalfields have always represented racial and ethnic diversity. But despite that, the music, arts, and crafts that have traditionally represented Appalachia are often presented to—and are therefore perceived by—the public as the exclusive province of White people.

Whitesburg, Kentucky, in neighboring Letcher County to the northwest, shares Black Mountain with Harlan County and is but what we called a hop, skip, and a jump from where I grew up. Historian and lawyer Harry Caudill, in 1962, published his groundbreaking work *Night Comes to the Cumberlands* from his residence in this town that locals pronounce as "Wattsburg." In the same year, through some unusual act of karma, Michael Harrington, a founding member of the Democratic Socialists of America, published *The Other America: Poverty in the United States*. Together, these books became the forces behind President Lyndon Baines Johnson's signature antipoverty initiative, the War on Poverty. Some would call it the War on White Poverty.

One academic, John C. Belcher, also writing in 1962 in *The*

Southern Appalachian Region: A Survey, edited by University of Kentucky sociologist Thomas R. Ford, who was under contract to the Ford Foundation, concluded, "the number of Negroes" in the Appalachian region was "such a small proportion of the total population, the social consequences [of their presence and migration] are not likely to be of any great [significance]."

J. D. Vance's *Hillbilly Elegy: A Memoir of a Family and Culture in Crisis*, published in 2016, was the latest in a long line of writing that advanced extremely negative and damaging stereotypes about White Appalachian people. Vance positioned unemployment and the opioid crisis in central Appalachia at the feet of the people themselves, going so far as to imply that even government assistance does not alleviate these issues because the so-called Scots-Irish heritage of the people predisposed them to self-destructive conduct.

Many White-lens views that focused on Appalachia—the literary, social science, historical, and, especially, Hollywood versions of the region that were forerunners to Vance's work—depicted White people as too closely related, banjo-strumming, backward, toothless, religious fundamentalist hillbillies who were uneducated, mean-spirited desperados. The movie based on *Hillbilly Elegy*, directed by Ron Howard (Opie of *The Andy Griffith Show*), will have been released by the time this book is published. Many have already predicted that Howard's depiction of Appalachian people, if it is true to Vance's script, will not stray far from the portrayal of the region and its people as shown in the 1972 box office hit *Deliverance,* which starred Burt Reynolds and Jon Voight.

My account of Appalachia falls closer to a look back at my people and our culture—one that not only counters the social science and literary representations of central Appalachia as a racially and ethnically homogenous space but one that also celebrates Black people from the region who made great strides, despite both racist customs and governmental negligence. Here, readers will see an assortment of specific examples of places, people, and events that enlarge the view of Appalachia's diversity. I am thankful to the editors of *Appalachian Reckoning: A Region Responds to* Hillbilly Elegy—Anthony Harkins and Meredith McCarroll—for inviting me to contribute to the collection of voices they assembled in 2019. I titled my piece "Black Hillbillies Have No Time for Elegies." From the highly acclaimed 1993 book of essays on moral authority, *Race Matters,* by Cornel West to the Black Lives Matter movement, there is hardly any mention of Blacks in Appalachia, some of whom live in the poorest counties in the United States.

Blacks in central Appalachian coal camps are the most historically marginalized of the subcategories and subgroups within the national African American population, even as compared, for example, to the Black underclass in urban areas or the Blacks in the Mississippi Delta. There is no one-size-fits-all or across-the-board "sameness" when it comes to the history of African American subgroups, nor of personal accounts within those groups. That is one of the main reasons why this book matters. These Black Appalachian mountain stories are also important and significant, and they make a difference because the history of Blacks in central Appalachia has been lost to the generations following mine.

There is also what I consider to be an assault on the integrity and self-determination of Blacks in Appalachia coming from some non-Appalachian Black poets and cultural workers who, in the past generation, have literally retitled—given new names to and branded—Blacks in Appalachia and are marketing performances and services on Facebook, Snapchat, Instagram, and Twitter. The 2020 forty-third annual Appalachian

Studies Association Conference, planned for the University of Kentucky but canceled due to the coronavirus, was billed as "the largest African American gathering of an ASA conference." Almost two dozen Black-themed panels planned for the conference were labeled, categorized, and trademarked with stickers such as "Affrilachian," "Afrolachian," and "Blackalachian."

For many years, since the late 1970s at least, I have had an abundance of personal contentment driving the ridges and valleys and hollows of eastern Kentucky, southwest Virginia, and southern West Virginia, walking narrow streets and pathways, sitting on porches and at kitchen tables, going to church services and civic club meetings, visiting hospitals and rest-home bedsides, talking with older people who told me stories and opened their piano stools and the boxes kept in closets to share with me photos and documents such as obituaries. The memories shared with me by these close-knit and interrelated families, with their common experiences, are the heart and soul of this quasi-group biography.

Throughout this book of memory, I have blended personal and common experiences and used the pronoun *we* to substitute for other nouns (*Blacks*, *Whites*) that identify classes of people. I have also used noun phrases, such as *Black women*, to modify a reference to something about the experience of Black women that is separate and distinct from the experience of Black men, while *Black people* refers to either, always contextually understood.

The use of *we* sometimes refers specifically to my extended family, and then again, contextually, it is used as an allusion to all the Black people in the area in which I grew up; after all, all Blacks had comparatively similar experiences in central Appalachian coal camps, where they have occupied precise and unique geographical, economic, historical, political, and cultural spaces. Blacks in central Appalachia exist as a racial minority group in the midst of a marginalized—White—cultural minority. Where commonalities across racial and class lines intersect, *we* also refers to all of us, as in, "We are all Appalachians; all of us are Americans."

Dr. John Henrik Clarke, the distinguished African American historian, professor, and a pioneer in the creation of Pan-African and Africana studies, reminded us:

> History is a clock that people use to tell the political time of day. It is also a compass that people use to find themselves on the map of human geography. History tells a people where they have been and what they have been. It also tells a people where they are and what they are. Most importantly, history tells a people where they still must go and what they still must be.

I have tried to keep at the core of this book a clock, a compass, and a timetable. It is the clock that ticks in these pages, one that I want readers to hear, and see, the repetitiveness of the ticking, its regularity, and the predictable rhythms that walled in, like the mountain, the people and places described here—how they look, what they did, where they were, and where they still are on the map of human geography.

Dr. Clarke's clock allegory is also quite appropriate for this synopsis of Black people in central Appalachian coal towns because it helps to show where they were before coming to the region and what happened to them while they were there, and it depicts their activities insofar as what they made happen, where they are today, and what they will need to do in order get where they wish to be in the future. The experiences of Blacks in Appalachian coal towns have benefits for people everywhere.

CHAPTER 1

Alex Haley—The Taproot

I DECIDED *how* to write this book many, many years after I decided *to* write it.

Author's grandsons William Lucien ("Muletrain") and Hodari Jr. ("Junebug") at Alex Haley Heritage Square, Knoxville, TN, 2019. William H. Turner Collection.

"Bill, nobody can write the *right* book about Black people in Appalachian coal towns except you. Nobody will. You've got to want to write it and know just *how* to write it."

Mr. Alex Haley, the writer of *The Autobiography of Malcolm X* and *Roots: The Saga of an American Family*, gave me that piece of advice in 1990 as he smiled and convincingly jabbed his right index finger into my chest. We were sitting in a swing on the wraparound porch of his white, colonial-designed, fantastically stylish farmhouse on the parkland-like 157-acre Haley Farm near Norris, in the Appalachian foothills of East Tennessee, twenty-five miles north of Knoxville. The Haley Farm—now home to the Children's Defense Fund—is not far from the Museum of Appalachia, which was founded in 1968 by his friend John Rice Irwin and is described on the museum's website as "a living history museum that interprets the pioneer and early 20th-century period of the Southern Appalachian region."

Mr. Irwin told me in the company of Alex that the museum was a monument to his "devotion to preserving the history of our people's struggle in Appalachia." I marked Mr. Irwin's words, his specific reference to "our people's struggle." After a personal tour of the Museum of Appalachia led by Mr. Irwin, I commented to Alex that very little about the museum was Black, whether in the form of works of art—not even photographs—or the presence of "living actors," who led the tours. One simply had to guess that Blacks ever existed in southern Appalachia after walking about the grounds of the museum. Alex responded, pokerfaced, "It is your topic to explore and to expand upon what Ed Cabbell has started. It is your void to fill, your problem to solve. You are responsible for building and maintaining Appalachian African American museums. It is not John Rice Irwin's responsibility."

Mr. Haley and I talked about a book titled *Blacks in Appalachia* that I had coedited in 1985 with Edward Joseph Cabbell. "You don't want anything else you write about Appalachia, about our people, to be in that sterile, antiseptic, academic voice," said Alex. "Write it so that your mama—and her friends—can read it and will sit on the porch and talk about it!"

Alex inspired millions of Americans—especially African Americans—to seek and appreciate their ancestral origins with his larger-than-life book and movie *Roots*. Unveiled during the nation's bicentennial observation in 1975, *Roots* won the Pulitzer Prize for literature. Alex's dear friend and fellow story writer James Baldwin wrote in 1976:

> *Roots* is a study of continuities, of consequences, of how a people perpetuate themselves, how each generation helps to doom, or helps to liberate, the coming one—the action of love, or the effect of the absence of love, in time. It suggests, with great power, how each of us, however unconsciously, can't but be the vehicle of the history which has produced us. Well, we can perish in this vehicle, children, or we can move on up the road.

Roots carried readers and viewers "on up the road," through the predicaments in the lives and family ties that were lost—beginning in the Gambia, in West Africa—because of the slave trade. Alex's—and vicariously, the roots of African Americans in general—branched out in the United States as he retraced the details of the bonds and footprints remembered through stories told to him by Queen Jackson Haley. Alex's paternal grandmother and other women in his extended family, in west Tennessee, on the Mississippi River hamlet of Henning, spent untold hours talking about their roots and branches, within his earshot, just sitting on the front porch. Young Alex—enthralled and fascinated—absorbed the tiniest details in the stories.

My friendship with Alex started when the telephone rang at my home in Lexington, Kentucky, at 9:25 in the evening in February 1980 as I was starting my journey to uncover and to write the broad outline of my family history. I had sketched the borders of our family's journey inside the everyday experiences of other Blacks like us in central Appalachian coal towns—doing so in the manner that Haley had chronicled in *Roots.*

Vivian yelled from the top of the stairs on that cold night: "Bill," she shouted, "some guy who says he's Alex Haley is on the phone." Although I had never heard Mr. Haley's voice directed to me, I knew immediately that it was him, his soft, unique voice carrying over the phone as distinctively as the whip-poor-wills I had listened to as a boy. After all, I had seen him on television and listened intently to countless interviews with him. By then, I had used *The Autobiography of Malcolm X* and *Roots* in my classes at Fisk and Howard University.

"Bill," he said warmly, as though we were old friends, "your buddy John Stephenson of Berea College gave me your number after I read copies of the newsletter you publish called *Sojourner* out of the Center for Appalachian Studies at the University of Kentucky. I am extremely impressed with what you are doing, concentrating on Black people in Appalachian coal towns, something I never read or thought about that much."

"I'm interested in . . ." he continued slowly, like he was measuring—and writing—his words. I listened intently, weighing each syllable, as he continued, speaking deliberately, "I'm very much interested in writing a book about Black people in Appalachia, and I want your help as advisor and research assistant. I see you live in Lexington, about two-and-a-half hours from my place just north of Knoxville. When can you come down to talk?" I replied, without dillydallying, "Is tomorrow too soon?" We both laughed at the same time. "See you tomorrow, buddy," he giggled. I was speechless, stunned, and awestruck.

The next afternoon was an unusually warm day in East Tennessee. Alex and I sat for two hours talking and laughing frequently before lunch on a stylish wooden bench inside a fifty-foot circular-shaped pergola built out over a lake the size of three football fields. "I checked you out," he told me, "by talking to two of your best friends and admirers—C. Eric Lincoln and John Hope Franklin." At the time, both were professors at Duke University.

Alex had known both famous professors for decades, consulting with Dr. Franklin while he penned *Roots*. Dr. Franklin was the world's premier authority on the history of Blacks in the United States, having served as chairman of the history department at the University of Chicago and having authored the highly acclaimed text *From Slavery to Freedom*, which he published in 1947. Alex and C. Eric (both insisted I call them by their first names) hung out in Harlem together while Alex was working on *The Autobiography of Malcolm X* and Lincoln was busy finishing up *The Black Muslims in America*. I always knew when in the presence of any one of them, or sometimes all three of them together, that I was an extremely fortunate fellow. However, I could never bring myself to call Dr. Franklin "John Hope," as they did, even when just he and I were on the frequent crappie fishing trips that we took together at Lake Jordan, outside Durham. We lived in Winston-Salem, North Carolina, from 1985 until 2002. I visited with Dr. Franklin and Dr. Lincoln often. We were fishing buddies.

I had met both Dr. Franklin and Dr. Lincoln twenty years

earlier, in 1971, when I was on the sociology faculty as Fisk University in Nashville, Tennessee. Dr. Lincoln was on leave from Duke University and writing and lecturing at Fisk. I used to sit in on his classes. Dr. Franklin was in and out, a frequent visitor to Fisk in his capacity as chairman of the board of trustees. Fisk was also his alma mater, and Dr. Lincoln held a master's degree from Fisk.

Dr. Lincoln called himself "a proud but invisible Black Appalachian"—this title owing to his origin in Athens, the county seat of Limestone County, Alabama, twenty miles west of Huntsville. I cherished telling him about a US Steel labor recruiter known widely in Harlan County as "Limestone." It was Mr. Benjamin P. Limestone, a White man, who ferried hundreds of Black men from Alabama, often with their wives and children, in a big truck, often laden with watermelons, some farm animals, and vegetables, to jobs in the coal mines of Harlan County, specifically Lynch, between 1917 and 1930.

I was blissful when Alex told me that both Dr. Franklin and Dr. Lincoln considered me "a longtime fishing buddy," a prestigious ranking that I considered right up there with being son to my parents and husband to my wife.

Through stops and starts over the following two days, Alex moved seamlessly between time with his guests who arrived at his beehive-like retreat and quiet time with just me. I learned a lot about *Roots*, including how Alex felt about the controversial lawsuit—and subsequent settlement—of plagiarism charges levied against him by Harold Courlander, a highly respected folklorist and anthropologist who had published widely on the cultural connections between African Americans and their retentions of African customs. Implying that he was a more prolific writer than Courlander, Alex, in reference to why he allowed his attorneys to settle, said, "I like what Thomas Edison, who had more than a thousand patents, once said in reply to a lawsuit over patent infringement: 'I really didn't invent a lot of things,' he said, 'I simply improved on a lot of things.'" That was good enough for me. For that matter there is not much that is new about what I have written in this book. I believe, however, that I have improved on a lot of things.

It was dreamlike to hear Alex talk about his relationships with people like Malcolm X, James Baldwin, Oprah Winfrey, Muhammad Ali, Lou Gossett, Maya Angelou, Miles Davis, Toni Morrison, and other luminaries in the world of Black entertainers, creatives, and the intelligentsia. He told me stories about the lead actors in the *Roots* television series, as well as about the ordinary folks, the lowbrows and hangers-on, like I was considered in later years on visits to the Haley Farm by some of the stars in Alex's galaxy, when he would invite me to his frequently held over-the-top parties and gatherings, which, he said, were "just like Jimmy [Baldwin] used to hold in Saint-Paul de Vence, his place in the South of France."

On one such occasion—a lavish birthday party for poet and actress Maya Angelou—I found myself circling around the much-too-congested driveway that led to the farm. Instead, I negotiated a rutted road off the main highway that led to the back of Alex's property. It was no big deal because Alex and I had traveled the road once for the reason, as he put it, just so he could "see what was back here." After parking my four-wheel-drive Isuzu Trooper, I walked through the woods a short distance and exited into a clearing on the far side of the lake from where I could see—and be seen by—the crowd gathered in front of the house and on the pergola. It looked like a cheery scene from *Gone with the Wind*, only it was inhabited by at least two hundred all-Hollywood-dressed-up Black people, some of whom had arrived from the Knoxville airport by helicopter. Not more than a dozen or so White people could be seen, one of whom was the governor of Tennessee, Mr. Lamar Alexander. The rest of the Whites I knew by sight because they worked for Alex as cooks, housekeepers, groundsmen, or security officers.

Heading unhurriedly toward the assembled swarm, I was entranced with the extraordinary scene. That is, up until two White county sheriff's deputies started running toward me. I recognized both because I had by then seen them numerous times; they moonlighted guarding Alex's stuff. I did not think much of it and smiled self-consciously once they explained their hurried presence. The closer we got to the main house—with me between them—the more I could tell that there was some buzz and curiosity and a bit of uneasiness on some of the extravagant partygoers' faces, and it was all focused on the dark-skinned stranger dressed in all white who was being escorted by two uniformed White county sheriff's deputies.

"Oh, hell, that's Bill, he's my mountain-man friend; he knows all the secret entrances to this place," Alex yelled to anyone within earshot while embracing me. Otherwise, Dr. Maya Angelou, the guest of honor, was giving me a very cold-shouldered look, one that only she could give to someone who was otherwise crashing her classy, invitation-only birthday bash. Alex had not informed his guest of honor that he had invited me.

Roots remains unparalleled, to this day, as an application of skillfully detailed narration of a Black family's pilgrimage through the chaos of enslavement to the solid ground of partially recovered connections. The subtitle of the book—*The Saga of an American Family*—was like the green background in a television studio; almost any Black family in the United States could stand in the same foreground. Mine, and that of the people I know in coal towns, certainly could and did.

Roots is celebrated as a classic of American ambition: for many Black people of my generation, the book reflected our collective strivings as we swam, held on to each other, dog-paddled, and otherwise waded through the treacherous waters of America's racist excesses. Wade in the water, children!

Alex shared with me, often in late-night talks over snacks of peanut butter on rice cakes that I washed down with glasses of Jack Daniels (he used to drink the same stuff), the back-story of how he found his home village, Juffure, located in the Gambia, West Africa, nineteen miles inland on the north bank of the River Gambia and the home of Kunta Kinte, the main character in *Roots*. I held artifacts from the Mandinka tribe and handled the Emmy Awards and Chicken George's hat from the record-breaking television miniseries. From his library shelves, I pulled each copy and flipped through the pages of the thirty-seven languages into which *Roots* was translated. To touch and read the original handwritten letters from Malcolm X to Alex was heavenly sublime and awe inspiring.

Roots revealed how each generation can overcome challenges—the ravages of racism—through undying family loyalty; the acquisition of education, skills, and crafts; and decisive, positive actions: all self-driven and purposive activities. In those revelatory moments with him, I felt as though God had directed my steps into Alex's path for me to learn how to best tell the story of Blacks' history in Appalachian coal camps, from start to end.

What kept me from writing this book before now is something I cannot make sense of, but I can easily recall Alex saying, only half-jokingly, that he'd like to read the book before he died. I said to myself repeatedly, between then and now, that I had *better* write this book.

On Sunday, October 9, 1988, I was at my father's bedside

in the Appalachian Regional Hospital in Harlan, Kentucky. He had been diagnosed a year earlier with acute myeloid leukemia. Dad, but five years removed from retiring after nearly a half century as an underground coal miner, described himself as feeling "lower than a snake's belly in a wagon track" that day. The nurse said, "Pick up the phone, Mr. Turner. It's Mr. Alex Haley," whom she called "that rat'er." Her Harlan County, from-the-middle-of-nowhere accent had trained her to pronounce *writer* as "rat'er." She was very impressed that I knew Alex Haley personally. "I just loved that *Roots* movie!"

Alex had called Vivian in Winston-Salem, who gave him my parents' home number in Lynch. Mama, in turn, gave Alex the hospital's number in Harlan. As though a dazzling light-emitting diode (LED) came on in his dark and drug-fuzzed brain, Dad, without pause, after realizing it was Alex, sat up and went into a rant about President Ronald Reagan. "I've seen a picture of you and that damn fellar together," Dad said disparagingly, in his own backwoods accent. "I know you're a good man and you might be a Republican, but I thank you for helping Bill, but don't you forget how Reagan is destroying unions!"

I was not embarrassed at all, and I relished in the back-and-forth as they talked for at least twenty minutes. Frozen in time and in my mind forever, I drove back to North Carolina the next day—by way of Alex's farm—to thank him in person for putting up with my old man's bluster. In his usual aw-shucks manner, Alex looked me in the eyes, grasped me by both shoulders, and said, "I sure hope your daddy lives until I can get to Harlan County to meet him and your mama personally." Dad, as he himself would put it, kicked the bucket three weeks later. Alex sent what had to be the biggest spray of flowers ever seen in a Harlan County funeral.

At the time of this writing, I am three years past the age Alex was when he died after issuing his fear that he would not live to see this book published. Dad also died when he was seventy-one. Alex "croaked," another of Dad's expressions for death, on February 10, 1992, almost a decade, exactly, from the day we met. I spoke to him by phone the day before, February 9, from Keystone, in McDowell County—one of West Virginia's many model coal towns. Keystone—then and now—has the highest percentage of Blacks in its total population among all places in central Appalachia. It has a rich and colorful history.

"Take some notes, interview somebody in Keystone," he implored me from where he was to speak in Seattle, Washington. "See how they compare to your people in Lynch." He said again, only half-jokingly, that he was there "representing the man who wrote *Roots*," the last thing he ever said to me, which he had said many times before. He did not have the time, or maybe he simply did not take the time, not anymore, to write—much—after penning *Roots*.

I attended Alex's funeral in Memphis, Tennessee, and his interment on the grounds of his boyhood home in nearby Henning. I sat next to, as fate and intentions required, Dr. John Bell Stephenson and his wife, Jane—the couple who had practically adopted me when I was twenty and new to the University of Kentucky and who had introduced me to Alex ten years earlier.

I inhaled the same time as John did when Bishop William H. Graves, presiding prelate of the Christian Methodist Episcopal Church, noted that "*Roots* was a godsend to America and to the world." His text for the eulogy, Psalms 78:2–8, spoke clearly and precisely of the life destiny, the calling, and the mission of Alex Haley:

> O my people, listen to my teaching. Open your ears to what I am saying. For I will show you lessons from our history, stories handed down to us from former generations. I will reveal these truths to you so that you can describe these glorious deeds of Jehovah to your children and tell them about the mighty miracles he did. For he gave his laws to Israel and commanded our fathers to teach them to their children from generation to generation.

Through *Roots*, a deservedly celebrated work, Alex not only lionized himself, but, more importantly—surely to Alex—he had also captured the essence of the experiences of his beloved country's most visible, though reluctant, immigrants: Americans of African descent.

Thus, starting from the moment that Omoro and Binta Kinte decided on the name "Kunta," and ending when Alex was lowered into the ground just spittin' distance from the porch of his boyhood home where his maternal kin told the stories to him, this world is a better place for the fact that he passed this way.

Alex Haley Heritage Square, in Knoxville, Tennessee, is the site of a thirteen-foot-high statue of Alex that is the focal point of Morningside Park in one of the city's oldest Black neighborhoods. I was honored to watch as the nearly five-thousand-pound figurine—designed by sculptress Tina Allen and cast in bronze in New York City—was unveiled on the occasion of the Tennessee bicentennial celebration in June 1996. Alex chose Tennessee as his home, his final living and burial place. "I'm sure," he once told me as we rode on a wagon pulled by an old tractor around his farm, "my people passed through this part of Tennessee on their way to Henning—I can tell!" Vintage Alex.

Alex was fascinated by Appalachia, particularly as he saw it through the lens provided by the native eyes of East Tennessee old folk, Black and White, as well as through his connection with John and Jane Stephenson and the Berea College family. Appalachia, East Tennessee, for Alex—a man with deep rural roots—became his replacement twist on the title of a book by Thomas Wolfe: You can go home again.

It is fitting that Alex Haley died during African American History Month. He was so spiritual and dramatic that I must believe he would have wanted it that way. But, far beyond most people, Alex stands tall, and not only as an indelible icon within the manmade category of his race. In his life, and now in his death, Alex's consummate work *Roots* mirrors poet Henry Wadsworth Longfellow's dictum from his classic poem, "A Psalm of Life": "Lives of great men all remind us/We can make our lives sublime,/And, departing, leave behind us/Footprints on the sands of time."

Those who really knew Alex Haley remember him most for the twinkle in his eyes, his simplicity, his total altruism, his self-effacing humility, and his sharp-edged sense of humor. No one should set out to try to do what he did, but there are a few things we can all do that would personify the qualities of the Alex Haley whose life I shared personally for a few fleeting and precious moments. The path I shared with Alex Haley is that principal nucleus—the taproot—that grew vertically downward and from which my inspiration to write this book is embedded.

CHAPTER 2

Between Alex Haley, W. E. B. Du Bois, Ed Cabbell, and the Affrilachian Poets

THE BLACK experience, for most Blacks—whether country or cosmopolitan—reveals a divided identity, a "double-consciousness," according to W. E. B. Du Bois, a leading scholar of the Black experience in the twentieth century and one of the founders of the National Association for the Advancement of Colored People (NAACP).

A Fisk University graduate with a Harvard-awarded doctoral degree in history, Dr. Du Bois explained his reference to Black Americans' psychosocial division in his 1903 book *The Souls of Black Folk*:

> It is a peculiar sensation, this double-consciousness, this sense of always looking at one's self through the eyes of others, of measuring one's soul by the tape of a world that looks on in amused contempt and pity. One ever feels his two-ness, an American, a Negro; two souls, two thoughts, two unreconciled strivings; two warring ideals in one dark body, whose dogged strength alone keeps it

Edward Joseph Cabbell, coauthor of *Blacks in Appalachia* and founder of John Henry Memorial Festival in Pipestem, WV, at Concord College, 1969. West Virginia and Regional History Center, WVU Libraries.

> from being torn asunder. The history of the American Negro is the history of this strife—this longing to attain self-conscious manhood, to merge his double self into a better and truer self. In this merging he wishes neither of the older selves to be lost. He does not wish to Africanize America, for America has too much to teach the world and Africa. He wouldn't bleach his Negro blood in a flood of white Americanism, for he knows that Negro blood has a message for the world. He simply wishes to make it possible for a man to be both a Negro and an American without being cursed and spit upon by his fellows, without having the doors of opportunity closed roughly in his face.

That Blacks in Appalachian coal camps are both Black *and* Appalachian—a deep space where race and class intersect—is an underlying theme in this book. In an interview titled "Alex Haley at Home in the Hills of East Tennessee," published in September 1992 in *Appalachia: Journal of the Appalachian Regional Commission*, Alex was asked by journalist Ann Hawthorne, "Do you see blacks in Appalachia identifying themselves as 'Appalachians'?"

Echoing W. E. B. Du Bois's double-consciousness theme, Alex answered by saying:

> No, they don't because that is superseded, if not drowned, in being black. Probably the most Appalachian man I've met is Bill Turner, a professor at Berea College. Bill is a scholar on blacks in Appalachia, but I've never heard Bill refer to himself as an Appalachian. I think the most you would get from any of these people is that they would say they are blacks *in* Appalachia. I would say the same of myself. I'm not an Appalachian. I wasn't born and brought

> up here. But I am a black in Appalachia—by choice. I've never heard a black refer to himself as Appalachian. And I know that what I've told you is why. If you deal with being black, you really don't have the time to deal with being Appalachian.

Black people in the communities I know in central Appalachia did not look at themselves through the eyes of others, certainly not through the White lens that distorted and reduced their humanity. We did not see ourselves as "they" saw us, but to survive, we watched, as in kept an eye on, White people in general. Whites in Appalachia, to us, were not "Appalachians," they were White people. Period.

That White people in greater Appalachia (the valley and ridge country of north Alabama and Georgia, western North Carolina, upland South Carolina, eastern Tennessee, eastern Kentucky, southwest Virginia, and West Virginia) were violent, incestuous, and ignorant had much more currency among so-called mainstream Whites than it did among Blacks. This is what Haley meant when he noted that Blacks in Appalachia do not identify themselves as "Appalachians," certainly not in the everyday, stereotypical references to Appalachian culture and values.

If the Black people in greater Appalachia—and also in the coal camps of central Appalachia—paid a lot of attention to the class-based bigotry that Whites in the American mainstream visited upon White Appalachians, then that would be what Toni Morrison called "one more thing" for them to decode and, ultimately, just another distraction. Indeed, it would be yet another level of consciousness for Black people in Appalachia, a degree beyond Du Bois's double-consciousness concept.

In *The Souls of Black Folk*, Du Bois describes the inner

tension that so-called inferior groups—Blacks, for example—experience at the hands of the "superior" group in America, the White supremacists. The psychological challenge involves constantly, subconsciously, "always looking at one's self through the eyes of a racist white society" and "measuring oneself by the means of a European-dominated nation that looked back [at Blacks] in contempt." The social inequality experienced by women living in patriarchal societies is another illustration of double-consciousness. What of the case of being Black and Appalachian and female—"inferior" on three levels? For one, it means Blacks could never rely on the government—or the foundations or the liberal White activists—to recognize and act on their concerns in the same way that White women could and do.

To the extent that identity is rooted in culture, Blacks and Whites in Appalachia practice a lot of the same elements of culture, particularly the rural-based varieties and ways of preparing food. Even today, one can go to any number of rural places in Appalachia, to coal towns, and sit at tables that are "bicultural" when it comes to the production and consumption of food. Pinto beans, pork chops, chitterlings, sweet potatoes, hog maw, fried potatoes, okra, fish, fat back, barbecue, poke salad (salat or sallet), potato salad, yeast-based rolls, kale, collard and turnip greens, and cornbread adorn dinner tables across central Appalachia, across racial lines. Families locked into similar economic positions in common geographical spaces tend to have similar diets. Soul food enjoyed by all souls. I have a baseball cap inscribed with the acronym GRITS: Gentleman Raised In The South.

My homeboy, whom I have always known only as "Buck" Andrews, Black, sixty-six, who now lives in East Bernstadt near London, Kentucky, is much, much more alike in his way of speaking, in his values and worldview, and in what anchors him emotionally to most of his White neighbors than he is to a Black man his age on the west side of Louisville, a world away from where he was born and raised. But still, Buck told me recently that he "watches," and "keeps an eye on," White people in general. Thus despite being a "good ole Black boy," Buck knows that he is not the same kind of "Appalachian" as his White hunting and fishing buddies.

And then there is the symmetry in the values orientations as can be observed, but not measured quantitatively, between Blacks and Whites in Appalachia, the oft-mentioned first one of which is "love of the land." Thomas A. Dorsey was inclusive when he wrote the song "There Will Be Peace in the Valley." After all, mountains and valleys go hand in hand, so to speak, with serenity, calmness, relative quietude, breathtaking beauty, stillness, the sounds of silence, fresh mountain air, and streams—outside the extraction zones. These natural elements are daily experiences for all rural, mountain, Appalachian people, no matter their color or ethnicity.

From their experiences on the land as tenant farmers or sharecroppers in Alabama to their lives in central Appalachia, Black families brought their attachment to and love for the land, even if most of them never owned any of it, unlike a critical mass of their White mountain neighbors. Despite that, in the coal camps, many Black men kept livestock such as pigs and chickens, and along with their wives and children, they cultivated gardens in their yards and carved out spots for growing vegetables on the edge of the woods. These transplanted Black industrial workers in mountain mining towns also went back and forth to Alabama as often as possible, visiting with their families, which also facilitated the retention of their rural customs and culture and their unique dialects. Their belief in, and the value they placed on, strong family ties—another widely recognized Appalachian value—framed family-focused manners of conduct, which always surpassed the needs of the individual. Same for the valuing of religion, hard work, and a sense of justice.

In 1973 and 1974, members of the United Mine Workers of America went on strike against the powerful and influential Duke Power Company at the Brookside mine in Harlan County, Kentucky. The Brookside Mine Strike has since become illustrative of an Appalachian David-versus-Goliath story. Lesser known, a year earlier, Blacks in the county took on local, state, and federal agencies who dismissed the loss of their homes as a "natural disaster." What Mrs. Mattye Guy Knight—my eleventh-grade teacher at the Lynch Colored Public School—did was an object lesson in how to achieve social justice, and it was a pivotal victory for the Black Appalachian Commission, then in its embryonic stages.

A week and a half before Christmas in 1972 marked nearly seventy years since a small group of Black families—then numbering four dozen—had staked out homesteads along a razorback-like ridge above the town of Cumberland known as Sanctified Hill. Mrs. Knight, high school teacher, church pianist, and a highly revered community leader, was the only professional person, man or woman, who lived in the nearly all-Black enclave, which was populated mainly by elderly Black widows and retired Black coal miners, many kith and kin. After an extended rain, like a soft, layered chocolate cake that was imploding, Sanctified Hill slid down its dirt roads and tangles of footpaths onto the White neighborhood below as the honeycombs of mining tunnels beneath it caved in. The city, county, and state government agencies immediately sided with the insurance companies who called it an "act of God" to relieve themselves of accountability to these potential litigants, mostly Black people.

The Black Appalachian Commission—founded in 1969 in

Chester Kyle, a coal miner for forty-five years in Benham, KY. William H. Turner Collection.

response to claims that the 1964-established federal Appalachian Regional Commission ignored the problems of Blacks in Appalachia—stepped in to support the leadership of Mrs. Knight in the fight to restore the life's work and savings of the

Sanctified Hill community. The fight ended on Capitol Hill in Washington, where financial aid and technical assistance resulted in a study that determined the cause of the slide and set the conditions for the relocation, rebuilding, and renaming of the community. A planned community—less than two miles away—emerged, which was christened Pride Terrace. This event, and the process of redress, was an example of a group of Black Appalachians valuing social justice, resilience, dignity, and self-respect in the same manner of the mainly White group that took on Duke Power Company.

"Appalachian values," a concept popularized in 1970 by Professor Loyal Jones, founder of the Appalachian Center at Berea College, is the catchall wording he used to describe the pride, endurance, resilience, sense of humor, honesty, patriotism, love of place, and family-centeredness of Appalachian people. These same beliefs and standards—the core ethos and belief systems—pertain to Black residents of coal towns as well in places such as Sanctified Hill and its successor, Pride Terrace. These folks carried over their "Alabama values."

The late Edward J. Cabbell (1945–2018), who was to Black Appalachian studies what Dr. Carter G. Washington was to African American studies in general, put the dual consciousness of African American Appalachians in poetic, almost whimsical, terms in a poem published in 1970 titled "I, Too, Am an Appalachian":

> I, too, am an Appalachian
> For years, I have breathed fresh mountain air
> traveled dusty mountain roads
> drank cool mountain stream water and fought the yearly
> autumn fires between
> hog killing, game hunting, mule hitching, soil tilling,
> harvest gathering, syrup making, berry picking,

home canning, feast tasting, banjo, guitar, and fiddle
picking and quilt making
and all kinds of weaving and liquor still watching and
church revival going times.
Yet to many folks I am not here
My most visible hue makes me invisible.
I move swift and silent through these hills
Nobody sees me, and nobody hears me
This is my assurance of acceptance and survival so
universally understood that I am not even a subject
heading in an index.
Still, I, too, am an Appalachian
I dream, and I wonder as I wander and ask myself: When
will Appalachia see me as I see Appalachia?
When will she recognize her long lost sons and daughters
who have toiled on her soils,
laid steel through her mountains
and crawled into her bowels to retrieve her beautiful
black diamond overload that shakes the chill from all
her children?
When will she tell my long-neglected story
While accompanying herself on the lute
drum instrument that I long ago taught her to frail while
singing in drone-like rhythms in celebration of her
beauty?
When will Appalachia see me as I see Appalachia
When will she open her arms and take me to her breast,
truly understanding that I, too, am an Appalachian?

Ed Cabbell was writing and publishing poetry from McDowell County, West Virginia, just as the Black Arts Movement was getting off the ground, represented best in 1965 when Dudley F. Randall founded Broadside Press in Detroit, which was devoted to printing, distributing, and publicizing the works of Black poets and writers like Gwendolyn Brooks, Nikki Giovanni, Sonia Sanchez, Sterling Plumpp, Audre Lorde, and Don Lee (Haki Madhubuti). Randall compared Ed Cabbell favorably to these poets, going so far as to say that Ed's poetry and literature "is as a voice of the African-American Appalachian experience immortalizing it in a way comparable to Langston Hughes of the Harlem Renaissance."

To flesh out Cabbell's "I, Too, Am an Appalachian" and mine down into it with an eye on critical explanation and interpretation reveals how Du Bois's concept of the dual consciousness of Black Americans applies to Blacks in Appalachia; only it becomes a triple presentation: American, Appalachian, and Black.

Twenty years after Ed Cabbell distinguished himself as the light that brightened the way to the study and appreciation of what he called the "invisible" history and culture of Blacks in Appalachia, Frank X Walker, African American and a poet at the University of Kentucky, fastened himself onto Blacks in Appalachia. But Mr. Walker did not like that classification—Blacks in Appalachia—so he renamed them "Affrilachians." Getting quickly to my downbeat response to Walker's entrée, I have christened him and most of his colleagues, the Affrilachian Poets, strangers in Appalachia with some inapplicable poems. Full transparency: despite my opinion, "Affrilachian" became an entry in the *New Oxford American Dictionary* shortly after Walker came up with the word in 1991.

According to Dr. Theresa L. Burris, chair of Appalachian studies and director of the Appalachian Regional and Rural Studies Center at Radford University in Virginia, writing in *An American Vein: Critical Readings in Appalachian Literature*, Mr. Walker "forged a space for himself in his native Appalachia, because he was tired of African Americans' exclusion

Martha Clark, the author's paternal great-aunt, in Tom Biggs Hollow, Letcher County, KY, 1986. William H. Turner Collection.

from Appalachian literature and he sought to eliminate their marginal status within the scholarship." Other scholars in Appalachian literature, such as Dr. Sylvia Bailey Shurbutt, director of the Center for Appalachian Studies and Communities at Shepherd University in West Virginia, enlarged Walker's bona fides as the voice for Appalachian Black people. Said

Dr. Shurbutt of Walker and his neologism while celebrating volume six of Shepherd University's *Anthology of Appalachian Writers*, which featured Walker's work, "It's a great term and a great phrase and it certainly is very descriptive. Frank deserves a lot of credit I think, through that word showing how diverse Appalachia really is."

Fact check: Effie Waller Smith, Black, born in 1879 and raised in Pike County, Kentucky, and a graduate of the Colored State Normal School at Frankfort (now known as Kentucky State University), published poetry in the early 1900s in *Harper's Magazine*. David Deskins released three volumes of Waller's poetry, *Rhymes for the Cumberlands*, *Rosemary and Pansies*, and *Songs of the Months*, in 1987, 1988, and 1989. Ed Cabbell published poetry that was situated in his lived experiences in Appalachia (mainly McDowell County, West Virginia) in *Black Diamonds*, a magazine published under the sponsorship of the John Henry Memorial Foundation, in 1978. Why those works of poetry were not recognized by Mr. Walker—and the gatekeepers of Appalachian letters—remains a mystery to me. In the cases of some historians, many journalists, so-called local color writers, popular culture playwrights like Robert Schenkkan (*The Kentucky Cycle*), and screenwriters, like those who created television shows such as *The Beverly Hillbillies* and *Justified*, these same upholders of Appalachian authenticity have been quick to apply such scathing categorizations as "culture vultures" and "outsiders appropriating culture." But in the case of Mr. Walker's novel term for Black people in Appalachia—which he grounded on the premise that nothing of literary significance existed in the Black Appalachian sphere until he coined the term *Affrilachia*—the caretakers of Appalachian culture required no answers or explanations. Maybe Affrilachian disciple and passionate Walker devotee Ms. Marie Cochran summed up best the panache of Walker's term in a 2019 essay titled "I Pledge Allegiance to Affrilachia": "Affrilachia is a clever term that is short enough for a tweet and long enough for a bumper sticker."

The renaming of Black people in Appalachia by Mr. Walker, who was born in central Kentucky, is reminiscent of how Christopher Columbus renamed the resident people whom he encountered when he landed in the Antilles. Columbus christened the New World location where he went ashore in the Caribbean Sea the *Indies,* the medieval name for Asia, then widely thought of as the rough equivalent to modern-day India. As you would have expected, by fault of logic, Christopher Columbus called the Antilles inhabitants he encountered *Indians*, and the label has stuck in various European languages ever since.

In a similar way, Mr. Walker's new term for Black people in Appalachia—*Affrilachians*—became quite popular; the phrasing and jargon having considerable currency among academics, expressly among specialists in Appalachian literature, many of whom gather annually in the name of the Appalachian Studies Association. This network of scholars and activists quickly lit into the book *Hillbilly Elegy* for being dismissive and damning of people in the region and issued a rejoinder in the form of a book, *Appalachian Reckoning: A Region Responds to* Hillbilly Elegy. However, that same group of Appalachian devotees has no arguments with Walker's problematic branding and labeling of Black people in the region. In 2019, the history department at Eastern Kentucky State University carried a course titled "Affrilachia," but the main text was *Blacks in Appalachia*, which I coedited with Ed Cabbell more than thirty-five years ago. Mr. Walker has served as writer-in-residence at several colleges throughout the Appalachian region, such as Shepherd University in West

Virginia in 2013, the same year he was named the Commonwealth of Kentucky's poet laureate. And, as he points out on his website, he has lectured, conducted workshops, read poetry, and exhibited (all focused on "Affrilachia") at more than three hundred conferences and universities. He has also been the recipient of countless awards, including the NAACP Image Award. In September 2020, Mr. Walker gave the keynote address at the Appalachian Festival at Frostburg State University in Maryland, titled "Affrilachian Lives Matter, Too!"—perhaps in a twist, although quite warped, on the "All Lives Matter" retort to "Black Lives Matter." Affrilachian shtick, gimmicky.

Mr. Walker coined the term *Affrilachia* in 1991, billing and branding himself and his network, the Affrilachian Poets, as *the* creative innovators and influencers where the identity of African Americans in Appalachia was concerned. Mr. Walker, in a masterful, social media-driven promotion, declared on his website that his new term "unified Appalachian identity and the region's African-American culture and identity." In an interview in 2012, Mr. Walker said, "I recently became a board member of the Appalachian Studies Association. I hope to use the opportunity to further promote our ideas about inclusiveness in the region." Like most professional organizations in higher education in America, the Appalachian Studies Association is especially wary of being perceived as an all-White organization, which it would be, for all practical purposes, save for the inclusion of writers such as the Affrilachian Poets. Over a period of almost a half a century, I can still count on my hands the number of researchers who have immersed themselves professionally in the study of Blacks in Appalachia. On the other hand, I am surprised at how many people I have known for decades in the Appalachian Studies Association network who now use the term *Affrilachian* as though it is an official US Census racial category. When the perfect vacuum is filled with just the right cleverness, the phrase "You can't make this stuff up" is more than appropriate.

Practically all the Black academics, activists, and researchers who have published about Black life and culture in Appalachia—starting with Ed Cabbell and certainly including me—see the term *Affrilachia* as little more than a contrivance, a thingamajig, a crafty means to turn Black people in Appalachia into a commodity. Black Appalachian culture for sale.

Gurney Norman, professor of creative writing at the University of Kentucky for nearly four decades—and Mr. Walker's undergraduate advisor—had a heavy hand in seeding Affrilachia into the fertile ground of Appalachian literary circles. Understandably, Mr. Norman was one of the first to endorse, validate, and legitimate Affrilachia: "If the dominant culture does not recognize you, refuses you space within its coterie, then create your own niche," he advised his protégé, as noted by Theresa Burris in her 2005-dated dissertation, "A Voice of Their Own: The Affrilachian Authors." Mr. Norman holds a deservedly high place in Appalachian literary circles. A reviewer for Library Thing of Norman's 1977 classic *Kinfolks: The Wilgus Tales*—which won the Weatherford Award for nonfiction from the Appalachian Studies Association—called *Kinfolks* "one of the great unknown gems of contemporary literature," christening Norman "the Mark Twain of Appalachia!" Mr. Norman and his wife Nyoka Hawkins own Old Cove Press, which published Mr. Walker's first volume of poetry, *Affrilachia*, in 2000, a year after they founded the publishing company, which "focuses on poetry, fiction, and art from Kentucky and its surrounding region." On the back jacket of *Affrilachia*, the marketing blurb reads, "Frank X Walker's pathbreaking book of poems *Affrilachia* is a classic of Appalachian and African-American literature. Walker created the word 'Affrilachia' to help make visible the experience of African Americans living in the rural and Appalachian South. The book is widely used in classrooms and is one of the foundational works of the Affrilachian Poets, a community of writers offering fresh ways to think about diversity in the Appalachian region and beyond." The assertion that Blacks were not visible in Appalachia prior to the publication of *Affrilachia* in 2000 is an outstandingly appalling example of selfish overindulgence and intellectual dishonesty.

Professor Norman's stamp of approval on *Affrilachia* is reinforced by the fact that he was born in Grundy, Virginia, grew up in the southern Appalachian Mountains, and was raised alternately by his maternal grandparents in southwest Virginia and his paternal grandparents in eastern Kentucky. What Mr. Walker does not have in terms of a connection to the land, the man whom he calls his literary father does. On the observation of the tenth anniversary of the Affrilachian Poets, in 2001, Walker said, "UK Professor Gurney Norman, a white man, has been there from the beginning. He has advised and supported us over the years, so we made him an honorary member." Surely Mr. Norman—whom I conversed with numerous times when we both joined the UK Appalachian Center as faculty in 1979—knew from the time he met Mr. Walker that there were critical masses of Blacks in the coal camps of Grundy, Virginia, and Jenkins, Kentucky. It is a mystery why Professor Norman did not say to his student in 1991, "Frank, there *are* and *always have been* Black people in my part of Appalachia; Bill Turner, who coedited the book *Blacks in Appalachia*, is from Lynch, in Harlan County, where there were thousands of Black people. Don't believe what you saw in the dictionary." Mr. Norman may wish to return a favor to the poet he trained and make Mr. Walker an honorary Appalachian.

Despite his hubris and excessively confident assertions, the bulk of the works of Mr. Walker—as well as the poetry and published essays of the vast majority of the members of his collective of self-described "renegade poets"—are neither specific to any part of the Appalachian region, nor do these mostly Appalachian-absentee writers reproduce anything in their writings that is unique about, or applies to, the history and culture of Black people in the Appalachian region, specifically central Appalachia. Said one member of the Affrilachian Poets, Shayla Lawson, a Lexington native and the writer-in-residence at Amherst College, "I don't write/live in Appalachia and I think very few, if any, of the Affrilachian poets actually do."

The Appalachian region, as defined by the 1964 congressionally designated Appalachian Regional Commission, includes parts of a 205,000-square-mile region that follows the spine of the Appalachian Mountains from southern New York to northern Mississippi, including all of West Virginia and parts of twelve states: Alabama, Georgia, Kentucky, Maryland, Mississippi, New York, North Carolina, Ohio, Pennsylvania, South Carolina, Tennessee, and Virginia. To the extent that the term *Affrilachia* could possibly be mapped into factual geography, it can be easily demonstrated that Affrilachian Poets are Appalachian in name only.

In an essay titled "Claiming Literary Space," published in *An American Vein: Critical Readings in Appalachian Literature*, Theresa Burris claims Mr. Walker "turned to poetry to relieve his frustration" because he was "tired of African Americans' exclusion from Appalachian literature and sought to eliminate their marginal status within the scholarship."

Burris anchors the acceptability and authenticity of Affrilachian poetry as a model of cultural hybridity, making her case around both Walker's and poet Nikky Finney's "Appalachian experiences." Finney, who grew up in the South Carolina low country, often visited her grandfather's farm in the foothills of Appalachia from where she "could see the tips of the Great Smoky Mountains way off in the distance." Burris continues to paint Walker as an Appalachian—despite the fact that he was not born and raised there and has never lived anywhere in the Appalachian region—when she analyzes his poem titled "Statues of Liberty," in which "he recognizes the black Appalachian women in his life." But the logic stops when Burris locates Walker's upbringing "in the foothills of the eastern Kentucky mountains," Danville, Kentucky, a space Walker called "very urban" because he "grew up in the housing projects . . . the one image you don't get when you think of Appalachia." Again, not only is Danville, Kentucky, in the everyday language, *nowhere near* the Appalachian foothills of eastern Kentucky, it appears, through this tangled web of deception, that Walker would be quite surprised to learn that public housing projects have existed for decades in the innermost regions of central Appalachia: in Big Stone Gap, Virginia, and Lynch, Cumberland, and Hazard, Kentucky, not to mention actual Appalachian urban areas like Huntington and Charleston, West Virginia, and Bristol, Johnson City, Kingsport, and Knoxville, all in East Tennessee.

The now-popular word is in mainstream use by many in the literary network of the annual conferences of the Appalachian Studies Association (ASA). Now in its fifth decade, the ASA, for the sake of diversity and inclusion, might well continue to go right along with this Black literary deceit. That the teachers and students of literature in the ASA could not do without Affrilachia is perhaps captured best in the well-known words of French philosopher and writer Voltaire: "If God did not exist, it would be necessary to invent him."

It could be that Affrilachia is Mr. Walker's way of showing the overlap between different people's social identities, known as intersectionality. Looked at in Walker's way, the experiences—the historical and material conditions—of Black Appalachians operate on the same level as that of all Black people; that is, he, without a lived experience in the region, can "relate to" and "identify with" them, a set of Black "others." Black Appalachians were, essentially, to Walker, no different than the residents of the housing project where he grew up in the Bluegrass section of Kentucky, in Danville, thirty-five miles southwest of Lexington. Geography, not to mention topography, does not matter to Walker, who simply adjusted his environmental lens and blurred the image of Black Appalachians, making them his alternate background. The mountain setting became a unique framework for his self-reflection as a person and creative artist. To Walker, apparently, most of Kentucky is Appalachia, including his campus base at the University of Kentucky in Lexington. Sadly, to some "outsiders," some on the coasts, for example, Walker is correct.

Affrilachia, as a brand name and symbol, does have considerably more cachet—distinguishing marks—than whatever appellation Mr. Walker could have conjured up based on Black life and culture in his central Kentucky homeland. With all due respect, Kentucky's Bluegrass region is dull, by comparison, to central Appalachia, given the image of Black poverty and marginalization required for Walker's creative hook to have a sharp barb. Not a single Black person with a lived experience in a central Appalachian coal town has a voice in Mr. Walker's 2001 documentary titled *Coal Black Voices*, described as "a web-based study guide and teaching curriculum to help learning communities explore, understand, and honor contemporary African American culture and celebrate regional expressions of the African Diaspora through the works of the Affrilachian Poets." Virtually nothing about coal or coal mining or Black coal-mining families is mentioned in this film, which was assertively marketed to high school literature teachers. Much ado about the Harlem Renaissance, but not anything about Harlan. *Coal Black Voices*, now almost two decades on the market, is still available for $350 on the website of the Cincinnati-based Media Working Group. Cultural appropriation, pure and simple. Coal sells.

Ms. Marie Cochran of Toccoa, Georgia, is the founding curator of the Affrilachian Artist Project, which, as described on the 2019 website of the Center for Craft in Asheville, North Carolina, "celebrates the intersection of cultures in Appalachia—specifically nurturing a network of African American creatives and welcoming anyone committed to the sustainability of a diverse region." I find Cochran's view both patronizing and stigmatizing concerning Black people native to the region, growing primarily out of her acceptance of Mr. Walker's false impression and his self-confessed lack of knowledge about Appalachia. The Appalachian region was racially and ethnically diverse before Mr. Walker's word *Affrilachia* claimed that it was not, but by coming into use, the word would make it so. Walker's logic begins with what he intended to end with.

No matter how "woke," progressive, or intersectional Mr. Walker is, he can neither walk in the shoes of nor genuinely understand the world of Blacks in Appalachia, especially not in central Appalachian coal camps. He is entitled, as is anyone else, to identify with Black people native to Appalachia, but there is nothing he can write or say or do to make of himself a Black Appalachian; nor do any of his poems make Blacks in Appalachia *Affrilachians.*

In my experiences in the region, it is the academicians and poets like Mr. Walker—not the people native to the region—who use the term *Appalachia.* I have traveled countless times through and visited a small coal town named Appalachia, in Wise County, Virginia. Appalachia, a town of fifteen hundred presently, lies at the foot of Black Mountain, halfway between where I was born in Kentucky and where my father was born in Coeburn, Virginia. In Appalachia, I never heard anyone refer to themselves as an Appalachian, as in the manner that a resident of Harlem identifies as a New Yorker.

I raised questions about the soundness and reliability of Walker's terminology in a 2012 essay titled "Affrilachia as Brand" printed in *Appalachian Heritage.* I quoted Ms. Betty Robinson, African American, now seventy-eight, and one of the first women—White or Black—to be a coal miner in her native Harlan County, Kentucky, who said, when I asked her if she identified as an Appalachian in an interview thirty years ago, "Now Bill, you know darn well I'm a Baptist."

The realism of Mr. Walker's Affrilachia is about as precise as the hidden fairyland known as Oz was to Omaha, Nebraska. The problem is that many (White) academicians and creatives, like Berea College poet and writer Silas House, choose, without asking why, to follow Mr. Walker's invitation and refer to Black people in Appalachia as "Affrilachians." I asked more than 150 Black people over a two-year period (2017–2019), "Have you heard the term *Affrilachia* as applied to Black people in the Appalachian region; and if so, do you refer to yourself as an Affrilachian?" If not an emphatic no as the answer to both questions, I was met with blank stares, as in, "What in the world are you talking about? I don't understand what you are asking me."

In late 2019, the group Friends of the Smokies (FOTS)—a 501(c)(3) organization which assists the National Park Service (NPS) in its mission to preserve and protect the Great Smoky Mountains National Park by raising funds and public awareness—used both the term "Affrilachian" and "African Americans in Appalachia" while promoting a new program "in honor of Reverend Dr. Martin Luther King Jr." The Friends initiated a fundraising campaign to finance a project titled "The Great Smokies Affrilachian Cultural Experience" to "support research efforts to collect untold oral histories, personal experiences and family stories of African Americans in the Great Smoky Mountains National Park."

In a series of email exchanges with FOTS officials and the NPS's Great Smoky Mountain National Park administrative office, I pointed out the inconsistencies and incoherence that results when they use both "Affrilachia" and "African Americans in Appalachia" at the same time, interchangeably. The officials, without any conflict, dropped the usage of "Affrilachian," deleting the reference from their website and signage.

In January 2020, I contacted Kiran Singh Sirah, president of the International Storytelling Center (ISC) of Jonesborough, Tennessee, after his agency used the tag "Affrilachia," again interchangeably with "African American," while marketing on its website a National Endowment for the Humanities–sponsored program focused on "African Americans in Appalachia." In the span of one week following my calls and emails, Mr. Sirah purged the website of the reference to "Affrilachia."

I was joined in the conversation with Mr. Sirah by Andrew Baskin, the founder of the Carter G. Woodson Center of Berea College; Ronnie Carson, creator of the Appalachian African-American Cultural Center in Pennington Gap, Virginia; Dr. Cicero Fain, author of *Black Huntington* (2019); Wayne Riley, originator of the Laurel County African American Heritage Center in London, Kentucky; and Dr. Darin Waters, founder and convener of the annual African Americans in Western Carolina and Southern Appalachia Conference, hosted by the University of North Carolina–Asheville. Each of these persons have publicly rejected the term.

Over the past decade, social media has become relatively flush with references to "Affrilachian Artists," and Mr. Walker's journal, *pluck!*, subtitled *The Journal of Affrilachian Art and Culture*, is published twice a year by the University of Kentucky. Professor Nikky Finney, who describes herself as "a 'Geechee girl' from South Carolina" and an "Affrilachian simultaneously," is the most famous of the Affrilachian Poets. A cofounder of the group while she was a professor at the University of Kentucky with Walker, Finney returned home to become the John H. Bennett Jr. Chair in Southern Letters and Literature at the University of South Carolina. In 2011, her fourth book, *Head Off and Split*, won the National Book Award for Poetry. Finney expressed her excessive pride as a member of the Affrilachian Poets this way: "Being an Affrilachian poet means that these black poets have founded a country where we might stand, stake a flag, and hear each other."

That as-yet-unfurled flag is staked as far away from anywhere in the Appalachian region as Texas by Louisville, Kentucky, native Yunina Barbour-Payne, who recently founded a performance genre in Austin known as Affrilachian Memory Plays, which, she says, "highlights the archived experiences of people of color in the Appalachian region." The geographical space in which the Affrilachian flag to which Professor Finney refers need not be logical, as in the case of Makalani Bandele, one of the most recent inductees into the Affrilachian Poets, who "considers himself a third- or fourth-generation Appalachian poet." A third- or fourth-generation Appalachian poet. Third or fourth, it doesn't seem to matter. Mr. Bandele, who grew up in Louisville, Kentucky, stated in a May 2020 interview that he spent part of his childhood in his father's hometown of Needmore, Kentucky, which is the same hometown as Frank X Walker's mother. However, Needmore is within Ballard County, in far west Kentucky, near a town called Monkey's Eyebrow, just across the Ohio River from Illinois, a part of the Paducah, Kentucky–Illinois Standard Metropolitan Statistical Area. There are four hundred miles between Paducah and Pikeville, Kentucky, which is in the Appalachian subdivision of the state. Midway between these two vastly different places in Kentucky is the section known as "the Bluegrass," Frank X Walker's home.

Dr. Kelly Norman Ellis, a Chicago State University-based Affrilachian Poet, wrote a poem titled "Affrilachia: For the Black Appalachians" in which she referred to Mildred Jeter, Black, and her childhood sweetheart Richard Loving, White, in a context that suggested their quandary was illustrative of something Appalachian. The Lovings won a case heard in 1967 by the US Supreme Court, which struck down Virginia's anti-miscegenation laws, recognizing their interracial marriage. The only problem—the missing step—in terms of realism and validity is this: where Mildred Jeter and Richard Loving lived in Virginia is a bit more than an hour directly south of Washington, DC—on I-95—in Caroline County, near Fredericksburg, which is *nowhere near* any of Virginia's Appalachian counties. I was given a handsomely framed copy of Ms. Ellis's Appalachian name-dropping poem—Bill Withers, Nina Simone, Booker T., Elvis, Bessie Smith, and Roberta Flack—when the Affrilachian Poets presented me with their Carter G. Woodson Lifetime Achievement Award during the collection's twentieth-anniversary symposium in 2011. I tripped over this abominable blooper: to use the Lovings as a best-case illustration of the Black Appalachian experience is an outstandingly shocking geographical misstep. That is like mistaking Harlan in Kentucky for Harlem in New York City, a twist on Mark Twain's legendary quip: "The difference between the almost right word and the right word is really a large matter. 'Tis the difference between the lightning bug and the lightning."

Regional humanities scholars—particularly the gatekeepers and interpreters of the Appalachian literary space—have been conspicuous for their lack of concern that Mr. Walker and the Affrilachian Poets, for the most part, do not write about the land, the mountain sites, the scenes, and those distinct backgrounds and situations of the Black people and their communities in central Appalachia, particularly in the region's heart: eastern Kentucky, southern West Virginia, and southwest Virginia. "The new word he came up with, Affrilachia," Burris notes, helped Walker to "relieve his frustration." That only three of the more than three dozen Affrilachian Poets listed on the collective's website in 2020 have a lived experience in the Appalachian region is a point worth raising. That fact alone might explain, at least in part, why the Appalachian region is a nonentity in the works of the vast majority of those listed as—and who self-identify professionally as—Affrilachian Poets. Unless it is fictional, most writers write about what they know. Black Appalachian people are real people. Like the person in the first lines of Ralph Ellison's *Invisible Man*, "I am not a spook like those who haunted Edgar Allan Poe; nor am I one of your Hollywood-movie ectoplasms. I am a man of substance, of flesh and bone, fiber and liquids—and I might even be said to possess a mind."

Mr. Walker conflates the whole of "Affrilachia" into a comprehensive and all-inclusive physical space when he blends and compresses together otherwise geographically and culturally distinct areas of Kentucky, as he does, for example, in the poem "Kentucke": "I too am of these hills / my folks / have corn rowed / tobacco / laid track / strip mined / worshipped & whiskied / from Harlan to Maysville."

Even the creative versifier in Mr. Walker should concede that "from Harlan to Maysville" is a very strenuous embellishment. These two very different places in Kentucky are four hours or 215 miles apart, and one (Harlan) is in the Appalachian Regional Commission–designated Appalachian region, while the other (Maysville, on the Ohio River) is not in an ARC-designated county. Maysville, sixty miles north of Lexington, is known as an important stop on the Underground Railroad. Author Harriet Beecher Stowe watched a slave auction there in 1833, which she included in her influential novel *Uncle Tom's Cabin*. However imaginative, lyrical, or poetic, this hogwash is not even suitable to make cheap tripe. I seriously doubt if Mr. Walker—given the combination of his nonrural Appalachian background and his extremely limited knowledge about Appalachia itself—knows the difference between tripe and chitterlings. Those who can stomach this and praise it have a different standard than I for the link between art and geographic paths and trajectories, or especially the link between spoken words and geological formations. Coal has never been strip-mined in Maysville, Kentucky. That is nonsense.

These lines from "Kentucke," which anchored *Affrilachia*—Mr. Walker's groundbreaking collection of poems—are prodigious examples of punning, but to leave the impression that "Affrilachia"—a physical space—covers, sincerely and credibly, a swath of the Bluegrass State "from Harlan to Maysville" is more than poetic aggrandizement; it is shrewdly misleading—and not just geographically. Appalachian borders matter. Reality is defiled when art distorts it.

When Mr. Walker handed me an autographed copy of his 2006 *Black Box Poems*, I was bothered, to say the least, when the opening lines in "Great Day in Harlan" described Black coal miners who "stood there at the mouth of shaft number five." That is a significant misleading detail: in my native Harlan County, I never heard my grandfather or father talk of the mantrip taking them to the mouth of a shaft mine. That is an elevator-like entrance, which contrasts starkly from the drift mines, where the mine opening coasted, on a long slope, to the face of the coal. One might need to be from there to know that; if not, one—even a creative poet like Mr. Walker—should have done the research. On his website, *Black Box* is described as a "powerful collection of poems . . . that continues the autobiographical, political, and literary journey of *Affrilachia*, Walker's groundbreaking book of poems about growing up black in the Appalachian south." The pushers of Mr. Walker's poetry situated his place of birth and raising in "the Appalachian South," despite the fact that Danville, Kentucky, is, again in everyday spoken Appalachian slang, *nowhere near the Appalachian South*!

It seems that when Mr. Walker and his coterie of Affrilachian writers—a self-described "marginalized community"—leaned their collective ladder against the side of the mountain that separated central (Lexington) from eastern Kentucky, they looked over the ridges and identified with and dedicated their writing to what they imagined to be the political, social, and economic struggles of the Black people whom they visualized to occupy the Appalachian region. What they really did was to project their own private selves, and the cheeky and invented world they call Affrilachia, on top of a place peopled by some inhabitants who look like them, at least some of them.

As a blackface variety of the all-White stereotype of the

Appalachian region that he intended to challenge, Mr. Walker's creative brand Affrilachia reduces the Appalachian region to a kind of Wakanda, that mythical country somewhere on a make-believe version of the African continent that the creators of the movie *Black Panther* brought into existence. *Affrilachia*, however ingenious a term, refers to an imaginary place. If it remains unchecked, Frank X Walker and his Affrilachian Poets might also completely fictionalize Black life and culture in the Appalachian region.

Walker's creative invention Affrilachia has sprouted copycat trademarks. African American Daniel White, who grew up in Shiloh, the historic African American neighborhood in Asheville, North Carolina, dubs himself—through a mouth full of gold teeth—"the Blackalachian," while hawking his tour-guide services along the Appalachian Trail, mainly to naive White tourists. "This is how they want us to look," said a member of the Cherokee nation in the North Carolina city of the same name when I pointed out to him that his outfit of head-to-foot feathers, the magnet for his take-a-photo-with-me business, was more in the style of the Plains Indian than the Eastern Band of Cherokee Indians.

Affrolachia—a recent entry in the vocabulary that is applied to African Americans in Appalachia—was founded inside the Duke University Center for Documentary Studies by Ms. Vonnia Davis, who, according to her website, is a documentary filmmaker and photographer. Affrolachia "confirms the contributions and historical presence of Indigenous Africans, Afro Americans, and African American's throughout Appalachia; we are Black Appalachians trademarked for the development of a culturally competent and culturally sensitive world and to promote those who fight replacement and displacement of communities, health inequities suffered by marginalized women, and systematic economic deprivation of poor people." Ms. Davis was scheduled to present a paper titled "What's My Name? Ontological and Identity Inquiries in Naming (Re) Construction" at the 2020 Appalachian Studies Association Conference at the University of Kentucky on a panel that Mr. Walker was to host, but the conference was canceled out of extreme concern for the coronavirus disease COVID-19.

Clearly, Mr. Walker intended for the word *Affrilachia* to trigger people to recognize the presence of Black people in the Appalachian region, primarily because it patches together stereotypical images of Africa and Appalachia. However, Walker, in the FAQ section of the Affrilachian Poets website, runs that image together with a more indefinite—and confusing—description of his brand: "Affrilachian Poets" represent "a myriad of ethnicities, from all around the world, Africa, Europe, Asia, South America, and the Caribbean." The website goes on to say, "Affrilachia plays host to a spectrum of racial and ethnic identity . . . a cross-section of people who can claim a number of nationalities, not just that of African descent."

And, as for who can call themselves an Affrilachian Poet or become a member of the restricted group, Mr. Walker says: "Unfortunately, the *brand* of The Affrilachian Poets is taken and refers to this specific community of writers, but if you are a poet who also happens to consider yourself Affrilachian, more power to you! We just ask that you clarify your distinction from *our* brand in any publicity material to avoid confusion. The Affrilachian Poets rarely recruit new members" (emphasis added).

There is a lengthy and rich literary, visual, and musical tradition among Blacks with roots in Appalachia. Ed Cabbell's master's thesis, published a decade before Mr. Walker's term *Affrilachia* entered the lexicon, listed at least two dozen creative literary pieces that are grounded, authentically, in the Black Appalachian landscape. Mr. Cabbell compiled a resource guide for our coedited book, *Blacks in Appalachia*, released in 1985, that included: (a) cultural and service organizations, (b) films and filmstrips, (c) recordings by traditional (old time) Black Appalachian musicians, (d) presentations of the Legend of John Henry, (e) fictional literature (two dozen books, including William N. Harben's 1907 novel *Mam' Linda: A Novel*, about a Black woman in Appalachia), and (f) a summary of sixty-six theses and dissertations focused on the presence of Blacks in Appalachia.

That Mr. Walker did not respect or have knowledge of Mr. Cabbell's work evokes the metaphysical question of what happens to unperceived existences and unobserved worlds. It is an old riddle often called up in my childhood: If a tree falls in the woods, and no one is around to hear it, does it make a sound? If Frank X Walker never heard of mine and Edward J. Cabbell's pre-1990 work on Blacks in Appalachia—let alone that of Dr. Carter G. Woodson, the father of Black history, who wrote "Freedom and Slavery in Appalachian America" in 1916—he should have. His barefaced declarations about his "felt responsibility to make the invisible visible" depended almost entirely on convincing the unknowing that he had come up with something new when, in fact, he launched Affrilachia by obliterating the work of others.

That all said, I give proper credit and polite respect to my brother Mr. Frank X Walker, whom I have known since he came to the University of Kentucky as a freshman almost four decades ago, when I was faculty advisor to the fraternity he joined. But I defy him to convince me that Affrilachia is little more than an amazing trick involving a craftily marketed brand that rests on the most shockingly misleading stereotype of the Appalachian region, which he says he took from *Webster's Dictionary*: "Appalachians are white residents of the mountainous regions of Appalachia." Had he visited Harlan County, Kentucky, even as late as 1991, when he coined the term *Affrilachia*, the *New Oxford American Dictionary* would have one less word.

As both my grandmothers would say, "Bless his heart."

CHAPTER 3

Black Mountain Mantrips and Woman Trips

I STARTED this book with a different title in mind than what is on the cover. When I finished the first draft in 2017, I decided on *Black Mountain Man Trip* as the title.

BLACK—because of the central place of coal or carbon in the space where we lived, as well as the acknowledgment that we were African people, members of a racial group characterized by dark skin color—ebony.

BLACK MOUNTAIN—Kentucky's highest peak, at the foot of which we lived; a highland with very steeply sloped, almost vertical flanks and narrow bottomland, which is nearly always flagged with a creek or a riverbed.

MAN—I wanted my book to speak to the journey I had heard about all of my life from my father and from other Black men I talked with, of what it took for them to become adult male human beings—strong and brave husbands and fathers, protectors, respected, independent adults (not boys!), the family caretakers, people with power and authority, elegant men who'd conducted themselves with courtesy and thoughtfulness, masculine, but also capable of genuine gentleness, civil and well-mannered.

Come on, *man*!
What a nice *man*!
He is a real gentle*man*!
You are the *man*!
Be a *man*!
Be a *mountain man*!

TRIP—an obsessive and often short-lived interest in something.

My God, that was a *trip*!

Don't come 'round here *trippin'* with me! You will get yo' ass whupped!

You be *trippin'*! You crazy, nigga!

MANTRIP—"Earl, Earl, get on up now, honey; you know you can't miss the mantrip."

I heard Mama shout that phrase countless times from the bottom of the stairwell. Her high-pitched yet gently insistent voice ricocheted off the walls early every weekday morning as she called Dad to get up and go to the mine. It was her version of reveille, much like the one drill sergeants use to notify the troops that it is time to wake up, to get up, and to show up for duty.

In the narrow stairwell of our cookie-cutter, company-owned, two-bedroom house, Dad would answer, reliably, "Here I come, honey," as he stirred to his feet in their bedroom, across the three-foot hallway at the top of the stairs that separated theirs from the small bedroom where the five of us—three girls and two boys—slept. It was 1956. I was ten; our oldest sister, Peggy, was seventeen. Marie was fifteen, Irvin was thirteen, and Evelyn was eleven. Speak of stair steps.

As a fertile-minded child, I used to think that our slop jar (a three-gallon portable toilet, called a "chamber pot" by the British), which sat at the top of the stairs, made a different sound depending on how much pee was in it. Even if this were not true scientifically, I do know our slop jar served to magnify Mama's voice the way a coil works inside a loud-speaker. Sounds were always different when they came up our narrow stairway—up everybody's, really, since my friends whose houses were like ours said so. When Mama stood at the bottom of the steps and shouted upward into the narrow, forty-five-degree-angled staircase toward the slop jar and the closed bedroom doors, the tone of her sweet, soft, high-pitched voice changed. I know so because her voice was not the same when the slop jar wasn't there. It stayed outside, behind the house, during the day when the outhouse, thirty feet from the back door, was used. Whatever the origins of my assessment, even as I write the word *mantrip* more than six decades removed, my senses revert back to the unique sound of Mama's voice in the stairwell cavity when the slop jar hadn't been emptied and she called Dad to go to work and I was half-asleep.

The mantrip is a train-like vehicle that carried miners down the sloped rail line into the mine, to the "face" of the coal, at the start of their shift and out again at the end of the workday, which was usually after at least eight, but often after twelve, hours. Mantrips usually take the form of a low, squat train, usually painted industrial yellow, with the riders on metal benches facing each other beneath a netted-like metal screen roof, running on a railway, tethered to an overhead electrical source, operating like a cable car.

By the 1970s, it was neither a far-flung, nor a psychedelic, trip to extend the metaphor of the mantrip as an image or an allegory that characterized the chancy, dangerous, and uncertain work of coal miners. In 1957, all of us waited to exhale for seven hours outside Portal 31 until Daddy was brought out on a stretcher, his left lung punctured, multiple ribs and his left arm broken, crusted blood all over his coal-dust-covered face. When I asked him thirty years later why he went back to work in the mines after escaping death in that roof collapse, he said, "I was forty years old. We had a house full of children that had to be taken care of; mining was all I knew to do. What choice did I have but to go back? I'm thankful that I did—it kept us together as a family."

Our oldest brother, Irvin, was the only one of the seven boys Mama and Daddy raised who took up coal mining to make his living. I was away in graduate school in 1970 when Irvin came back home—from a fast and turbulent post–high school, in-the-streets experience in Newark, New Jersey. He was taken into the mines by Dad. Irvin put it to me and our younger brothers, just as Dad did, but in more vulgar and blunt terms, toughly recommending us to get ourselves prepared for a life that did not involve coal mining.

"Man! This coal mining is a fuckin' trip!"

The mantrip allegory became much more than a figure of speech when it hit me—full force—what our dad meant on those frequent occasions when he would say, in the manner that Alex Haley's old folks spoke of their family's fate to him, "Billy, us Blacks'll be the first ones to go from here!" Mantrip: "Just a little spree, a side trip, a stopover, a little outing!"

Dad said that, matter-of-factly, in one way or another, many, many times, going back to the 1950s, especially as we sat in a johnboat fishing on Cherokee Lake near Bean Station, Tennessee, three hours from home, forty-five miles from Knoxville. That one-hundred-mile trip takes less than two hours presently. Back then, in the days before the Appalachian Regional Commission widened US 119 through Harlan County and cut a tunnel for US 25W to pass under the Cumberland Mountain between Middlesboro and the Cumberland Gap—where Tennessee, Kentucky, and Virginia come together—our fishing trips took three hours at least on a good day. Up through the 1970s, the eighteen-wheelers hauling hogsheads of tobacco were stacked up on the mountain past Cudjoe's Cave, a stop on the Underground Railroad near Harrogate, Tennessee. It was also the course Black migrants had taken a half century earlier when they trekked from central Alabama, up through the piney woods of northeast Alabama, in the shadow of Lookout Mountain and Chattanooga, through Knoxville, and into eastern Kentucky in pursuit of the wages paid by coal mining.

Six decades later, I still return home and look at the silhouette of Big Black Mountain against the eastern sky just behind our homeplace and harken back, clearly and freshly, to how Dad anticipated coal jobs decreasing in real time, crushed under the weight of machines, the way the steam-driven hammer had beaten John Henry down—killed him, with his hammer in his hand—when he worked to build the Big Bend Tunnel for the Chesapeake and Ohio Railroad in West Virginia. Dad had worked in Matewan, West "by God" Virginia, when he was twenty years old—in 1937.

"We're the last generation of Black coal miners, buddy!"

"This job ain't gonna last, boy!"

Alex Haley's family-rooted teachers looked backward at the origins of their family: what happened to them, how they got where they were, and what they had to go through. Dad spoke to where his family would go in our future. He was visibly concerned, troubled in mind, as he squinted, looking into the sun setting, from our front porch, the western wall of Black Mountain as the horizon. He mulled over where his children would go, what we would do after we left his house—the company's house—as we inevitably would have to do if we were to make a living, a career, or profession not then envisioned.

Dad was not looking into some post-coal crystal ball;

instead, he was viewing the matter in real time. In the mid-1960s, central Appalachian coal miners, especially the Black ones, were already leaving the coalfields in droves. "Buddy, I've watched it," he said. "If the Whites were cut off in the same percentage as the Blacks are being cut off this job, they'd not be a soul in this whole damned town."

In the end, he knew his girls would not be miners, and he had always rebuked his sons against following his carbide light into the hole. After all, coal was not blasted and shoveled the way it was when he went into the mines at the beginning of the Great Depression. Coal mining itself was in a booming era in the 1960s, but my father seemed to know, instinctually, and by evidence of the cutoff lists he saw each week, that coal mining itself, overall, was in a depressive and a continuously declining state. Doomed.

In terms that were both prophetic and apocalyptic, Dad would calculate the implications of how more and more coal was being produced with fewer and fewer men. He had seen the kudzu grow and the mountain creep back into spaces where big families like ours used to live. "Just a handful of the Black boys who have graduated from the school in the 1950s have stayed on to work here and raise their families," he said to me when I was a junior in high school, in 1963.

What was once the bounteous flow of cash that the trains moving in and out of the hollow represented became muted, doing so in slow motion. No better storyteller in the world, Dad told me a story—which I remember and have applied to numerous mileposts over the years—to make his point.

> If we are not forward thinking, we will be like the frog that was placed in cool, room-temperature water. It just moves about, but as the heat is turned up slowly, it never notices, and it will slowly cook to death. This water's

> gettin' warm, buddy, and I'm a tellin' you, if it don't last for me a few more years, 'til I can retire, we too will have to jump out of this hollow like everybody else who's been cut off. I shore don't wanna take y'all to no city where we'd have to start over, where we don't have any bearings, don't know our way. Where things are a' goin' is as plain as the nose on yer face.

Dad was completely dead-on about the future of coal, about the future of Black people in coal towns like ours and in nearby southwest Virginia and in southern West Virginia—as far back as a half century ago. Even since Dad died, a little over three decades ago, coal jobs have fallen swiftly—as much as 85 percent by most measures.

In coal-mining areas nationally, there were nearly 140,000 coal miners in 1989, the year Dad died. In 2017, they numbered just over 40,000. The number of Black coal miners in Harlan County can be counted on two hands; the number of Black people living in our home county went from more than 8,500 when I was born—the year after World War II ended—to less than six hundred in 2019. I also considered *The Last Black Appalachians* as a good, appropriate title for this book.

Coal is taxed by the state of Kentucky by the ton, and a portion of that goes back to the counties where it is mined to pay for critical infrastructure such as the building and maintenance of roads and public facilities, water and garbage services, and for public services such as law enforcement, education, and health care. Less coal coming out of the ground means fewer dollars coming back to the coal-producing counties. A big cut of the coal severance tax dollars goes to non-coal-producing counties in Kentucky, like Louisville and Lexington. Between the global market declines in the demand for coal, what are known as the network of "good old boy" financial shenanigans, and the competition from natural gas and renewable energy sources, this doomsday scenario applies to everybody in central Appalachia.

As the numbers of Whites leaving the central Appalachian coalfields over the past three decades have come to resemble the Blacks when they left central and north Alabama just over a century ago, there are fewer tax dollars to be collected in the former coal-producing counties they are vacating. Where is the money to come from in these former coal-producing counties in central Appalachia to pay for services, such as to maintain the water supply infrastructure? Loss of population affects how municipalities come up with dollars to pay expenses, such as maintaining a police force and ensuring fire protection. The counties' fixed costs remain—and escalate—as they did fifty years ago: same roads to keep up, for example.

Where are the reserves, those "rainy-day" dollars, to come from, the money it takes to clean up and repair after the annual spring deluges, which are abetted, in part, by strip-mining along the ridges, which are now bare from clear-cutting the few trees left? Drinkable water is threatened as infrastructure crumbles in once model coal towns like Jenkins, Lynch, and Wheelwright. Even as the catchall remedies, such as eco-tourism, the outdoor economy, and the transition to clean energy, are touted by the politicians, a talk with Black residents exposes—like a strip-mined hillside—a deep skepticism about *their* place in that future.

The future of Blacks in central Appalachia—insofar as their declining numbers in the population goes—has been offset in the past two decades by the upward trend in incarceration rates. The prison industry thrives in central Appalachia. In the last half century, prison building has boomed in the United States from just over 500 to more than 1,600, most of it located in rural areas. In central Appalachia, the newest prisons are sited on land flattened because of mountaintop removal, such as the one in southwest Virginia located in the Lee County Industrial Park. The *Boston Review* published a report in 2018 titled "Building Prisons in Appalachia," which noted, "in over the last three decades, 29 prisons, state and federal, have been built in Appalachia, many of them atop or nearby former mines."

As coal reserves have become virtually exhausted in eastern Kentucky, southwest Virginia, and southern West Virginia, some politicians, local development agencies, and private investors have sought to replace the region's coal-dominated economy with the prison industry—rural, White residents guarding prisoners, the critical mass of whom are Black and poor, most with urban roots. A classic case of this peculiar connection took place in eastern Kentucky, in Letcher County, the home of author and lawyer Harry Caudill, whose important book *Night Comes to the Cumberlands* was the first work to frame the modern-era exploitation of the region's resources and people.

Kentucky's Fifth Congressional District representative Hal Rogers, under the banner "Prisons are innovation," is the chief proponent of this effort. Rogers touted the benefit of prisons, saying of one, "This prison will not be bothered by a recession. It will be there through thick and thin." Rogers's district, which he has represented for more than forty years, has been labeled the worst in the country on "overall well-being."

The incarceration rate is the number of people incarcerated per 100,000 people in that racial/ethnic group. In Kentucky, for example, the incarceration rate in 2015 was 628 for Whites, 625 for Hispanics, 1,023 for American Indian and Alaska Natives, and 2,397 for Blacks. Not only does the number of Blacks in the federal prisons in central Appalachia

(Kentucky, Virginia, and West Virginia) outnumber many times over the total number of Blacks in the populations of the counties where the prisons are located, but also the incarceration rate of Blacks is uniformly a multiple of that of other racial and ethnic groups. One observer described the conundrum as "disposable land and disposable people."

President Lyndon Baines Johnson kicked off the War on Poverty in the same year I graduated high school in Harlan County, Kentucky—1964. Black people in central Appalachia whom I have talked to in the years since were not at the tables in county courthouses because the War on Poverty programs, and the projects of the Appalachian Regional Commission, did not engage them to join the efforts.

Blacks got virtually none of the poverty-related jobs controlled at the magistrate's courts and chambers of county judge executives in central Appalachia, the virtual ground zero of the good old White boys' network. The leadership, boards, and staffs of most of the nonprofit organizations and community development associations that the national foundations endow in the region are as White as the driven snow. Appalshop, the premier media, arts, and education center in the Appalachian region, located in Whitesburg, Kentucky, broke this pattern—at the beginning of its fiftieth year in business—when it named Alexander Gibson its CEO in 2018. Alex, born and raised in the county to the west of where Appalshop is located, is biracial, self-identifies as an African American, and is a Berea College grad and Penn-trained lawyer.

Blacks in Appalachian coal towns remain relatively invisible. Numbers matter politically. Presently, Blacks hold no political offices and are unrecognized, "invisible," for all practical purposes still, as described by Ed Cabbell more than fifty years ago. Ironically, Black people in the central

Appalachian coal towns were regarded as invisible at the very times when their numbers and percentages were much higher than they are today, when they are effectively disappearing from the landscape. No memory stands out more that underscores the declining numbers—the dying out—of Blacks in central Appalachian coal towns than the string of deaths in our family over a twenty-five-year period, starting in the late 1980s, when Dad died.

Naomi Randolph Turner had her beginning (1924) and ending (2001) in Harlan County. Mama stands out as the first and last in our family to call Harlan County home. My three brothers and I were talking with Mama around the breakfast table that occupied the same spot in her small kitchen where we had eaten her meals and talked with her and learned so much about ourselves and our family since she and Daddy moved into House #550, on Second Street in Lynch, Kentucky, in 1940, when she was sixteen. It was 2000, four months past Mama's seventy-sixth birthday. We started off talking about the brother we missed, Irvin, who put almost thirty years in as a coal miner for US Steel and its successor, Arch Minerals. Irv had died—suddenly and certainly unexpectedly—a year earlier.

We spoke, respectfully, as always, about our daddy, who died in 1989, and how he had, over the years, modernized that old house with his own hands. We did a check-off list of his DIY projects, including installing a bathroom, a laundry room, and a patio with a large built-in barbecue pit; installing a metal storage shed where the outhouse used to be seated; fashioning the circular concrete steps off the front porch; and installing an oil furnace and air-conditioning unit in a spacious, ten-foot by forty-foot basement that he dug out, laid a concrete floor in, installed faux paneled walls and recessed shelving for his assortment of tools and fishing equipment, carpeted, furnished tastefully, and made his "man cave." We had one of the few carved out, pizza-slice-shaped stairwells with fifteen banisters in the living room, which Dad had accomplished while installing tongue-and-groove cherry hardwood floors and building walnut cabinets in the kitchen.

Dressed in pink silk pajamas with matching slippers, a white terry-cloth bathrobe, and the headscarf she always wore to bed, Mama added how Dad had made her the envy of her circle of friends when, in 1958, he parked in front of the house a 1957 Ford Country Squire station wagon. My brothers were too young to remember, so I described its robin's-egg blue color, the sophisticated and elegant faux-wood trim, the V-guard front grille, and the wide whitewall tires. The first five of us would pile into our car on some Sundays after church and motor to the home of Mama Turner—the affectionate name we had for Dad's mother—forty miles away over Black Mountain. I remembered to my younger brothers the site of dozens of convicts, mostly Black men in tattered black-and-white prison stripes and with chains on their ankles, who stopped the swing of sledgehammers, wiped their brows, and stared and waved timidly, approvingly, as our family eased by in that beautiful car. They were the state of Virginia's "free laborers" on this section of US Highway 58, this stretch between Appalachia and Coeburn. As we drove by in what always seemed like slow motion, I would glare at the single White man guarding this swarm of Black convicts; he wore dusty all-white Western-style clothes topped off with a white cowboy hat, his outfit trimmed with knee-high black boots that matched the silver-accented breast collar, the bridle, and the saddle on the back of the stately white horse he sat astride, looking menacingly proud. The guard's black holster, the belt ringed with a couple dozen bullets, held a Cimarron .45-caliber revolver with a 7.5″ barrel.

He balanced a double-barrel twelve-gauge shotgun across his lap, all the while shooting a gawk at us through silver-rimmed sunglasses. "That sum'bitch would like to shoot us," Dad would say, not altogether as a joke. I ended the recollection by singing a bar or two of Sam Cooke's famous, though mournful, song, released in 1960, "Chain Gang."

"I'm not surprised you remember that shit," Ma confirmed, sourly, her left hand on her hip, puffing her cigarette, spatula in her right hand, standing back on her legs flatfooted, leaning on her stove just so, as though it was an appendage.

The memory came up of the death of Mama's mama—Granny Ran—who perished in a fire in her coal-camp house fifty yards away from our house in 1996. A verse in the twenty-third Psalm read by our baby brother Jeff before we blessed the food stood out: "Yea, though I walk through the valley of the shadow of death . . ."

Mama was chain-smoking Salem cigarettes and chatting cheerfully that morning while cooking breakfast for us, as she had done in this same space for an uncountable number of times over a period of six decades. A month earlier, I had come home and taken her to the Appalachian Regional Hospital in Harlan, thirty-five miles from Lynch, where we were informed that she had an advanced case of lung cancer. I dared not say a word when she lit a cigarette as soon as we exited the hospital, on the walk from the doctor's office back to the car. I do not remember us talking very much at all during the ride back home. I tried to lighten things up by asking her why she used to eat Argo starch like it was popcorn when we were kids. But she redirected my contrived sense of fun times back at me by saying she ate starch for the same reason I used to eat the red clay that I would dig from the hillside up above the hog pens. We both felt deeply the tectonic shift her cancer diagnosis represented, but we decided not to talk about what we had just heard and felt. The earth was shaking beneath our family tree.

The reason my brothers and I had converged at home from four different directions and hundreds of miles—one from New Orleans—involved a talk we wanted to have with Mama about the disadvantages—the inconveniences for us—of her remaining in our homeplace alone now that she was terminally ill. After all, Lynch was by then an all-but-extinct coal town, and as was the case for most of the widows up and down Second Street who'd given birth to and raised lots of children, none of the ten children Mama had raised were living any closer to "home" than Cincinnati or Winston-Salem, both of which were more than four hours away.

Kudzu now covered the trees in the overgrown yards and crept up the railings alongside the steps to the porches of two houses adjacent to ours. The kudzu looked like a gigantic version of the greenery on the potato sprouts that germinated and grew across the top of Ma's piano. The street was eerily quiet most of the time, day or night, with virtually no cars passing, no kids playing in the street, nobody walking, no neighbors dropping by the house. Before breakfast that morning, we shot .380 and 9 mm pistols and a .22 rifle at cans placed atop sticks in our backyard across a fan-like span of fifty yards. We shot from a distance that was barely ten feet from where Mom was inside cooking. Three decades earlier, those shots would have sprayed dozens of homes where hundreds of people lived whom we knew intimately. In two generations, the tree line of Black Mountain had come within a stone's throw of our backyard. As a boy, I could see hundreds of porch lights at night looking in that direction lighting up the terraces to the tree line, which used to be half a mile up the mountain. That day, now two decades ago, the tree line was less than fifty yards from our back door. Now the tree line is in our backyard. Mama would be quite afraid to live there if she were alive now.

"You can move in with one of us, and we will shuttle you back and forth between all of us—your four boys and our three sisters," I proposed responsibly, now in the role of her oldest son, framing it around the fact that all of us—as she often boasted—were in stable marriages or relationships, had good jobs or professional careers, or, as in the case of Tony and Karl, owned our own businesses. We all had children, some of us had grandchildren, and we lived in what she bragged to her friends were "very, very nice homes" in places as wide-ranging and as diverse as New Orleans, Louisiana; Cincinnati, Ohio; Indianapolis, Indiana; Richmond, Virginia; Roselle, New Jersey; and Winston-Salem, North Carolina—our family's version of the Black Appalachian dispersion. Same as was the case for 98 percent of our schoolmates. In fact, we knew quite well that we were not the first family of siblings that had come home to get Mama.

In the identical way that most of Mama's generation escaped Alabama and came to Harlan County, our generations, while not "pushed out," had to leave the place where we were born and raised. It could be said that we actually migrated out, left to places of our own choosing, and we had a pretty good idea of what it was like where we were going—unlike our mother's generation when they looked backwards. We had come—and gone—quite a long way compared to the generation of Granny and Pops, our grandparents. They told us countless times that they did not have a clue as to where they were going when they came to Harlan County. Granny said, often, "When the train came into Lanch in 1921, the conductor hollered that we had come to the 'end of the line,' the train could go no farther. Instead of me thinking of this as

Rising Star Baptist Church rising above the kudzu, Benham, KY, 2019. William H. Turner Collection.

the end of the line, I thought of it as the end of the world! And if wasn't the end of the world, Lanch sho' wasn't far from it."

My generation, just one removed from tenant farming and sharecropping, could at least make our own life and death choices. In the kitchen that morning, we were there to make the choice as to where our mama would die.

In our individual ways, we all were excellent examples of success to a Black woman born in Harlan County, Kentucky, in 1924, between Machine Shop Hollow and Smoky Row, who had left the Lynch Colored School in the tenth grade after getting married at sixteen.

None of us would experience financial pressures to take care of our mama, as Daddy had reminded us to do from childhood: "When I kick the bucket boys, and y'all's mama gets old or sick, or both, I expect y'all to take care of her. And you bet' not put her in no rest home, neither!" Each of us had promised Daddy, long before this Last Breakfast, that we would do right by Mama.

"I was born in Harlan County," she countered, matter-of-factly. "I ain't never wanted to or ever had to live nowhere else. I have lived here all my life. I met and married your daddy here when I was sixteen, and he never got laid off from the mine, and I was with him 'til he died, for almost fifty years, in this same house. I don't know if I've been a good enough woman to join y'all's daddy in heaven or if I will go to hell; but one thing is for damn sure, wherever I'm goin' after I die, I am going there from *here*—from my home, and your home, here in Harlan County. And don't y'all never sell it. Now, eat your damn breakfast before it gets cold or you piss me off!"

We knew that was that. End of discussion.

Mama lit another cigarette before moseying into her living room, where she slid onto and then scooted the bench to her comfort level at her Wurlitzer piano and began to play and sing her favorite gospel song, "Precious Lord, Take My Hand."

Mama didn't like nor take no mess, unless it was of her making. She died peacefully in her bedroom, the first of our kinfolk to be born in Harlan County and the last to die there, so far.

CHAPTER 4

What's in a Name?

I DO NOT remember anyone from my youth who talked openly about being ashamed of their family name. Not only was the family name an inheritance, an endowment, we also, by accident of birth, inherited our family's reputation for such qualities as the eagerness and commitment to work, to make do and to thrive, to make our personal mark in life. But one sure measure of individuality comes only with the nickname one gets stuck with from childhood.

And while I generally don't live in the past, I gave nicknames straight out of my childhood to my grandsons: I call Hodari Jr. "Junebug," and I call his first cousin "Muletrain," although he is officially named William Lucien, the namesake of my father, me, and his father, William Kenyatta. The nicknames I gave my grandsons, whenever they roll off my tongue, remind me of the delightful taste of some much-beloved slices of bygone days in the place where I was born and lived until I was twenty.

"Junebug" is a common nickname given to boys in Black communities throughout the South and in central and southern Appalachia; at least it used to be, back in the day, as the expression goes. Junebug is derived from "Junior," or more accurately, from "June," which many Juniors are called for short. I have a cousin named for his father, whom we call June. Of course, most know that a junebug—two words to some people—is an enduring sign of blissful summers, especially out in the country, where, as kids, all that was needed for a safe and fun-filled day was a pair of shorts, tough soles on our feet, a creek to wade in, and a junebug tied by its leg with a piece of thread.

That recalls for me countless good and happy and wholesome times in my hometown. The nickname of my oldest grandson, Hodari Jr., brings to mind my pleasant memory of my friend, the late "Junebug" Freeman, otherwise named after his father, James, who lived on the hill behind our house, past two rows of outhouses that lined each side of the alley that separated Second and Third Streets. The pattern of a row of houses on a street and a row of paint-matched outhouses with an attached bin for coal that was used for cooking and heating was replicated up a steep expanse of hillsides that ran more than a half mile west from the Benham line in a curve east along the north side of Black Mountain. From Main Street, where the Lynch Colored Public School was sited, up to Sixth Street, the neighborhoods in what was called "Number 1" were connected by a narrow winding road that twisted and turned and looped, all occupied by Black families—except Main Street, of course. Black people could not and did not live on Main Street.

My Junebug, when he was five, asked, "What's an outhouse, Papa?" When I showed him the photo of ours, I told him about a related cultural feature of outhouses, something my father would say when times would get tough: "It's as rough as a cob, buddy!" I told him "rough as a cob" was a figure of speech I heard from my father a lot; it was his way of relating scenes when times get hard, when people got down on their luck, such as when men were laid off their jobs in the mine and told by the company to vacate their homes abruptly. These families could be seen—and helped—as they packed out their meager belongings, often in the dead of night, sneaking out of town to avoid their creditor—the company store—and moving to some Promised Land like Detroit, where their daddy would hopefully find a new job. "A man's gotta do what a man's gotta do!" Such experiences were the subject matter of blues—and country and bluegrass—music.

He rolled his eyes when I told him "rough as a cob" referred to using a bare, moist—if possible—corncob as a substitute for toilet paper for the cleansing ritual in an outdoor toilet. Since his brow wrinkled when I said the word, I quickly googled "corncob" to show him what the central, cylindrical, woody part of the corn ear, to which the kernels are attached, looked like. At its best, this inventive replacement for toilet paper was always rough; therefore, the expression "rough as a cob," his face and eyes now twinkling, seemed to make a lot of sense. Times got rough a lot of the time. I told him about the optimistic side of things—times were improving when old Sears and Roebuck or Montgomery Ward sales catalogs, or newspapers, showed up in the outhouse. These items also worked like a charm. After asking if that was how the name of Charmin toilet paper was derived, he inquired, "By the way, what's a Sears and Roebuck catalog, Papa?" My Junebug asks a lot of questions, just like I did when I was ten.

"Muletrain" is the name I call my youngest grandson. "Muletrain" applies to those sturdy, very tough, and strong-willed work animals that are hard to match when they're paired with several of their own kind, making for a muletrain when combined as one word.

Mules were also used early on in coal-mining towns to transfer wagon loads of supplies as towns were built, and mules were the virtual engines that lugged carloads of coal from the seam where it had been blasted from the mountain and shoveled onto wagons and then dumped onto the belt lines that took it to the tipples and into what were called hopper cars or gondolas. Early on in mining, those mules lived underground and were cared for usually by a Black man from Alabama who had generations of experience with mules in his very blood.

One of my father's friends, his fellow coal miner and good fishing buddy Mr. Robert Washington, was called "Muletrain." Youngsters called him "Mr. Muletrain," of course. Mr. Muletrain was tall, well over six feet, six inches, and he was what they called "raw-boned strong." Dad often compared Mr. Muletrain's physical might as a hand coal loader to the legendary "Steel Driving Man" John Henry, who, as a steel driver in a race against a steam-powered rock-drilling machine, won only to die in victory "with his hammer in his hand." Some say John Henry died while helping to construct the Big Bend Tunnel in West Virginia in the late 1880s. Those around home I talked with say John Henry died building the Coosa Mountain Tunnel near Leeds, Alabama, twenty miles east of Birmingham, not too far from where Mr. Muletrain—Mr. Washington—lived before he migrated to work in the Lynch mines in 1935.

I hope my Muletrain will be half as strong—both literally and figuratively—as the man whose nickname he bears. I especially hope he is half as nice as Mr. Muletrain. Whenever I lie back and conjure up my earliest and best memories of where I grew up, I think about, first and foremost, the names of people—the Black people—near and dear to me. I have not seen, or more accurately, I have not heard people in either my children's or grandchildren's generations with names and nicknames like those of many, many people near and dear to me in my generation of Black people in Harlan County. I specify Black people because I did not have any significant others who were White people who were near and dear to me in the early part of my life. And vice versa, I would venture to say without fear of being successfully contradicted. The United States modeled the apartheid that South Africa perfected. Racial segregation in Harlan County was not my choice; but it was what it was.

"Fats" is what my grandfather Edward James Randolph, whom we called "Shootdaddy," called our grandmother, Mama's mama, whose given name was Minnie Lee Mabry Randolph. Most of the kids and many of the adults called her Miss Ran, but our family and close friends called her "Granny," and she called our grandfather, depending on her mood, "Shoot" or "E. J."

They nicknamed our mother, Naomi, "Punkin," a shortened form of *pumpkin*. I will stop here with the quotation marks around names because that implies a kind of artificiality, as though these names are said as the person uttering them is holding their hands up, arms apart, and pulling down on their first two fingers as if to say "so-and-so quote, unquote." Pops called our oldest sister, whose real name was Barbara Ruth, Jim, and our next oldest sister, Marie, he called Rusty Ree. The rest of us shortened Pops's pet name for Marie simply to Ree.

Shootdaddy always called me Billbo. I will not go into the seed of the hundreds of other nicknames people went by in our town, but it is important for me to explain why my grandfather, Pops, called me Billbo, since this book is written, partially, with my grandchildren in mind.

For a reason he never explained, Pops knew a lot about Theodore G. Bilbo of Mississippi. Mr. Bilbo, a Democrat, served as the Magnolia State's governor for two terms and as a US senator between 1935 and 1947. Bilbo was described by historians as a "staunch segregationist," a term that always mystified me because *staunch* meant faithful, loyal, steadfast, dependable, and reliable. Staunch segregationist was applied to most White politicians—governors and members of Congress in the South in those days—when Blacks could not vote. Bilbo had counterparts throughout the South called the Dixiecrats. Clearly, during my youth, most of the voting White public, those who were not "staunchly" segregationist, and therefore racist, could be described as being "wavering segregationists," uncertain and indecisive, yet still segregationists and white supremacists.

"That sum'bitch talked a lot of shit," Pops, born in Brunswick, Georgia, in 1896, said to me when I asked him why he attached me to the name of Mississippi's notoriously racist governor Bilbo.

"Until I come up here from Georgia into the mines in the early 1920s, where I started working side-by-side with White men, I had seed some awful and nasty thangs done by crackers," Pops said to me when I was ten, while twiddling his thumbs. When I told this story to my grandchildren, I had to stop and explain that twiddling, a lost art, involved interlocking the fingers and rotating the thumbs in succession. Twiddling is what one does while just killing time or waiting idly for something to happen. I remember the conversation clearly because it was around the time Emmett Till, a fourteen-year-old Black boy, was killed in Mississippi for allegedly whistling at a White woman.

Pops said he'd "run away" from the Deep South, Georgia, but like most Black people who migrated to Kentucky's coalfields in the first two decades of the 1900s, my grandfather had no trust for most White people, especially those who were supposed to uphold the law, not to mention those who were charged to sustain the direction of some moral compass so that White people would be civil. Pops described to me how he witnessed a lynching of a teenage boyhood friend of his while hiding himself in nearby bushes. He recognized one of the leaders of the hanging, one of the town's most well-known White men, a civic leader and deacon in the largest White Baptist church in town, whose grass he helped his uncle to cut.

Pops said he left Mississippi and went to live with relatives in Georgia, and he also stopped going to church after witnessing the hanging. I understood why I never saw Pops in a church in Lynch or anywhere else. Had he been a formally educated man, he would have put forward an explanation of how racism and slavery and racist oppression were interwoven with Christianity; but, in his dialect, he explained clearly to me why he "didn't cotton too much for church, or any of that sorta bullshit": "If slave masters and the rest of them crackers wuz Christians lak they claimed they wuz, I can't 'magine how they mighta' treated us colored peoples if they hadn't a' been Christians."

When my grandfather was "funeralized," as burial rites were called by the Black elders, in 1981, at Mount Sinai Baptist Church in Lynch, he was eighty years old, and that was the first and last time I ever saw him inside a church. I was thirty-five.

Pops never got past three formal grades of schooling, but the lack of any significant educational credentials did not keep him from retaining an everlasting memory of Mississippi governor Bilbo's rabble-rousing, racist speechmaking. "Learn how to talk and speak like you got some sense," he counseled us constantly, revealing that he'd learned that Bilbo was "nothing but a piss po' cracker" but with enough education so that most of the poor White folk all over the South started following his teachings: "Piss po' crackers wuz taught that colored peoples wuz they enemies!"

Pops said he nicknamed me Billbo because he wanted me

to "make something of yo'sel' and fight against crackers like Bilbo." Simple. Billbo is what just about everybody, everybody Black, called me at home in Lynch, even to this day. My nickname, Billbo, had counterparts: there was an older man, one of Mom's classmates, who was called Bimbo. Another, only slighter older than me, my sister Ree's classmate, is still called BoBill.

"That's got to be somebody from home," I muttered to myself a few years ago, in a Walmart, when from across the bank of cashiers someone yelled "Billbo!" It was Willie Marie Smith, who grew up across the street from us in Lynch and was now living in Houston like me. I never met any woman named Willie Marie except in Harlan County, Kentucky. She was named in honor of her maternal grandfather whom everybody, including my father, called Mr. Will. He lived across the street from us.

Oddly enough, my other siblings Peggy, Evelyn, Tony, Karl, and Jeff did not have nicknames, at least ones commonly recognized. On the other hand, Irvin Rudolph, "the oldest boy," as he always reminded the rest of us, was by all measures and opinions the most colorful person in our family, maybe in the whole town and in the entire area within a hundred miles. Irvin had various nicknames, depending on who was calling on him and in which of his many circles. I have heard him called everything from "Pig" to "Pimp." A twist on a once-popular marketing campaign for Sara Lee bakery products marked our oldest brother's life: "Everybody doesn't like something, but nobody doesn't like Irvin Turner."

We shared our duplex with the Brown family. Mr. Brown, a massive, very dark-skinned man, was bear-sized but very quiet; he was appropriately called Big Brown. His wife, the exact opposite of Mr. Brown in skin complexion, with a much-freckled face, was known as Miss Mae Cee. The oldest girl in

George Massey and Irvin Turner, US Steel employees, Lynch mines, 1991. William H. Turner Collection.

the family, Audrey, did not have a nickname, but her brothers did. The oldest brother William was always called Pal, and the other, James Kenneth, was better known as Pokey. This second sister in the Brown family, who still occupies the homeplace, is named Linuell Phinea; but she is known, first and foremost, by her nickname—Nanny. The baby sister in the Brown family was baptized Kennetha, but she is still called Pete. Pal, Nanny, Pokey, and a girl named Pete.

Pete is known presently as "First Lady Miss Pete" by the congregants of Faith Chapel, a megachurch pastored by her husband, Pastor Mike Moore. Both are Berea College graduates. Faith Chapel is located just outside Birmingham, not insignificantly in Ensley, the place many Blacks who migrated early on to Harlan County called home. They do not do it—give names—like that in families anymore.

Directly behind our outhouse, across the alley, and up eighteen wooden steps lived the Green family. Virtually every one of them had a nickname: Oop, Booger, Head Logan, Honey, Mutt, Wank, Booneyman, and Ugly Buddy.

Across our narrow side yard, where our back and front doors faced, lived the Amos family—a dozen of them—headed by another massive man, but unlike our neighbor Mr. Brown, Mr. Jack Amos was a gregarious and very outgoing man whose signature was the way he smacked and popped his ever-present Doublemint chewing gum. He made it sound the way some people could snap their fingers, only louder. He had a trademark very loud laugh, about which my dad would lightheartedly say, "That damn Jack squalls like a wildcat." Mr. Jack, as kids called him, was best known as Chewing Gum Jack, or, more fully, we called him by his complete, proper nickname, Yakety-yack, Chewing Gum Jack. "Yakety Yak" was a rock and roll song made popular by the Coasters in 1958; its lyric tag, "Yakety Yak, don't talk back," was attached onto Mr. Chewing Gum Jack.

I was present in 1987 during an interview with Mr. Jack that I arranged with Bob Hill, a reporter for the Louisville *Courier-Journal* who christened the veteran coal miner, in his report titled "Black Home in Appalachia," "a big, beefy man." When asked about his salary over the years, Mr. Jack answered, "When I came here in 1935, I was paid $1.80 per hour and when I retired in 1980, I made $76 a day." Mr. Jack and his wife, whom we called Miss Eula Mae, also an Alabama native, raised eleven children.

Mr. Jack's namesake and oldest son was not sacked with his dad's nickname, but his mom and siblings and everybody else called him either June or Jack Junior. I learned that they had brothers named John and LeRoy when I was a grown man. It never occurred to me to ask what the "real names"

Author's next-door neighbor Jack Amos and grandson, 1988. William H. Turner Collection.

were of my buddies whom we all called Meatball and Hudepohl. Mr. Jack was an exceptionally good catcher for the local minor league Negro Baseball League team—the Lynch Grays—and he was a passionate fan of the game. His backyard, less than ten feet from our back door, was the gathering place for his baseball-loving cronies, and on summer weekend afternoons in the fifties and sixties, they would play checkers and dominoes and listen to radio broadcasts of Cincinnati Redlegs games called by Waite Hoyt and Joe Nuxhall.

The sound of Mr. Jack's Doublemint gum snapped along in harmony with the rhythm and cadence and volume of a pileated woodpecker on a hollow tree while the loud banter of his sidekicks blended perfectly with the loudness of the sounds made by dozens of us kids moving about, out in the street, as we ducked in and out to let the regular procession of cars pass. On payday weekends, they would drink bottles of Hudepohl beer—the sponsor of Redlegs' games. Nobody called the team the Reds. The Pool Room—Harlan County's equivalent to the famous Apollo Theater in Harlem, New York, a city many of the kids in the street would move to in the sixties and seventies—was at the bottom of the Second Street hill, a stone's throw from the Lynch Colored School and the ballpark. The Pool Room was also the meeting place for our community's self-help organizations: chapters of the Prince Hall Freemasons, the Knights of Pythias, the Improved Benevolent and Protective Order of Elks of the World, the Order of the Eastern Star, and the Grand Court Order of Calanthe.

These self-help and benevolent "secret society" groups were responsible for the annual celebration of Independence—or Emancipation—Day, known popularly as the Eighth of August. How festive this day was in my youth, throughout the coal towns, along the ridges and in the hollows, and among the Black communities of eastern Kentucky. The Black people would be moving all about all day long, fires for cookouts in virtually every yard. The ballpark across from the Lynch Colored School would be like an ant colony, the schoolhouse doors were open, the teachers the official day marshals. The Masonic lodges and local chapters of the Improved Benevolent and Protective Order of Elks of the World (the exalted ruler often present) and the Eastern Star groups—all dressed up with colorful sash bandoliers across their shoulders and with all manner of stick-on emblems, badges, and purple accessories—would march up and down Y Street and Second Street. It was reminiscent of a Marcus Garvey–led parade in Harlem in the mid-1920s. The pride was tangible; the sense of an independent and dignified community was profound.

For Daddy, the coal mine was out of mind on the Eighth of August, an official United Mine Workers of America holiday. A framed copy of the title page of the speech called "What to the Slave Is the Fourth of July?" by Frederick Douglass, given on July 5, 1852, hung beneath a portrait of Douglass that decked the main hallway of our school. I always wondered what courageous and thoughtful person put it there, not to mention if the White people who visited our school took notice of it. The school janitor, Mr. "Chief" Cross, who said he was "ill-lit-trate," often talked of the clever, creative, and subversive ways the school staff worked against the racist system. Later, in literature class, Mrs. Knight taught us about the Trojan War. It all made sense later.

Three of the men who were almost always in the Amoses' yard, usually playing dominoes or checkers when the Redlegs were on the radio, were nicknamed Red. One was James "Red" Almond, who had a son named after him, another June. The other was O. D. "Red" Moore, pronounced "Mo'", as in Red Mo', but pronounced as one word. I never learned what O. D. stood for in Mr. Red Moore's name. And two biracial men would stop by the broadcasts often: one, a coal miner named "Buster" Jones, and the other—one of the three local numbers runners—was called Big "Red" Robert and was also among the best pool hustlers in the area. At the time, in the mid-fifties, the word *biracial* was not in my vocabulary. *Real light-skinned*, or *half-White*, but not biracial. Black women with Mr. Buster's and Red Robert's hue were called "high yellahs." "Yellah," not yellow.

Oh, back to June as a nickname. Jack Junior was not, by a long shot, the only June in town. The oldest son in the Hall family—who lived across Second Street from us and the Amoses—was also called June. Their dad, James Henry Hall Sr., was known widely as Tuff—Mr. Tuff to us minors.

Out of respect for his durability on the football field, Mr. Hall's full nickname was Tuff Titty.

Those are just the nicknames of some people in my immediate surroundings—next door and across the street. Many, in fact most, colored people in my hometown had some very colorful nicknames, as was the case in towns just like it for miles around. In his southwest Virginia hometown, our dad was called Peanut; his brother, Uncle Robert, because of the elongated shape of his skull, was nicknamed Railhead. Uncle Roy was called Sandy but not for any biological quirk. Our grandfather was named Alexander, Sandy for short.

So prevalent were nicknames that I wrote a short story of an imaginary conversation and situation involving the handles of just a few people I knew personally:

> At some time in the past, in Harlan County, Kentucky, a fellow branded with the name Birdbrain, who had a cousin named Tweedy Bird, was talking to a boy simply called Bird, who had the Guts to slap Mooneye, which, naturally, gave him a Bigeye, which teed-off Radio, who, along with Little Toe and his big brother Big Toe, sometimes called Toe Joe, began to scuffle with Dog Head and Head Logan.
>
> Among the spectators were Scrap Iron, Goose Grease, Sugar Titt, and Tuff Titty. Tight Eyes came along with Wank and Boo and Boo-Boo and Boobie and Three Knots and Headquarters and Knots. Next thing you know, Nub started playing the dozens with Meatball who was laying down the story of the signifying monkey in the pool room with Tater Pie, Teacake, Buckdust, Buttermilk, Bo Diddley and Pap Peeples, not to be confused with Pap Owens, or his big brother Pee Wee. Pee Wee and Pap.
>
> Tootsie Roll and Tooney were Rowdy and Pops and Pop and Bo-bill and Bimbo and Mobile were looking with

romantic eyes at Mutt and Nanny who were on the dance floor, doing the funky chicken. Mr. Carbide, in the corner slurping a Coke filled with peanuts, just grinned, toothless, his face glowing.

Pokey got pissed and called Brother, also known as Pal, and their sister, a girl nicknamed Pete. Next thing you know, Junebug was there with his little brothers, Tank and Head. Punkin was playing piano while Chewing-gum Jack and Red Dog and Fluffo were posing for a picture for Smokie Pipe, the local photographer, while Manchie and his big brother Smoky were arguing with Florida Kid and Ugly Buddy, both of whom were shooting craps while Uncle Buck, Buck, Chief, Monk, Turk, Booney Man, and Ship Wreck were fiddling over a scratched shot, but Sonny, who had two quarters on a side bet in this game of Keeley, sipped on a cold bottle of Hudepohl.

Teeny Bit was dancing, doing a boogie twirl called "the slop" with Seaboat and his son Schuchie, along with Leachie and his brother Biscuit: all at the same time. Miss Gussie and Mr. Red Mo' put their older brothers Blue and Bibby out for smoking rabbit tobacco, so they all went walking with Mr. Muletrain, Mr. Big Timer, and Soldier Boy, accompanied by Mr. Bonnie Blue, Snake, Jake, Pig, Crip, Neutlum, Ree, Pee Roy, Deek, Double J, and Kokomo.

Zeno and Narso slept through the whole thing while Peanut and Peanut Man said the whole situation was a bit Coo-coo, as did Big Molly, who told Chalk to stop writing on the wall.

I wrote this short story for my English class when I was a senior at Lynch East Main High School in 1964. The year before, 1963, was the last year of Lynch Colored Public

School, where my four older siblings and I attended, as did our mother. It was in the second tense week of classes. I wrote this essay after the teacher, the first White teacher any of us Black kids had ever contended with, called the roll. A formal roll call was rarely, if ever, done by the teachers at our colored school. We, the colored students, were quite amazed and shocked and stunned to hear some of our friends' real names.

At the Lynch Colored Public School, the teachers knew all their students by sight—and by their nicknames. There was no need to waste valuable class time calling out everybody's name. So much for getting to know our friends' real names—and leaving behind our nicknames—at the White school.

Closer to home, literally inside our family, there was a dramatic rub on the matter of names. Three of my grandchildren have what my mother always referred to as "funny African names." The way Mama expressed displeasure with our grandchildren's names was totally inconsistent with her web of girlfriends, many of whom also had colorful, flamboyant, and lyrical nicknames. Some of our community's womenfolk were expressions of a unique sort of whimsical rhythm because of the middle name Mae. There was Annie Mae, Audrey Mae, Bessie Mae, Bertie Mae, Beulah Mae, Carrie Mae, Dorothy Mae, Ella Mae, Eula Mae, Fannie Mae, Gertie Mae, Hattie Mae, Jessie Mae, Julia Mae, Katie Mae, Lula Mae, Mattie Mae, Nanny Mae, Rosa Mae, Sally Mae, Vera Mae, Vertie Mae, and, of course, Miss Willie Mae. There were also mellow and honeyed-sounding names like Billie Sue, Katie Sue, Lula Belle, Betty Sue, Betty Jean, Mary Lou, Carrie Lou, Mary Sue, and Betty Lou.

In our family, there were Dad's sisters, Annie Ruth, Mary Elizabeth, and Clara Bow, and my first cousins, Rebecca Susan, better known as Becky Sue, and her sisters Polly Ann and Emma Jean. Dad's brother John Henry, as far as I am concerned, had the most famous name in the Turner family. Uncle John Henry (two words) spent time on a railroad line—like John Henry, the "Steel Driving Man," after whom he was named—with a maintenance crew in southwest Virginia in the early 1930s, working as a gandy dancer. Across the South, prior to the advent of automated equipment to service railroad lines, most of the railroad line building and maintenance crews were African Americans. The tag *gandy dancer* originated from the name of the Chicago-based Gandy Manufacturing Company, where most track-lining tools were invented and constructed.

"They worked our asses off; mainly Black men and boys like me!" Uncle John Henry told me the first time I met him, when I was fifteen, in 1961. He recounted how some gandy dancers moved the heavy steel railroad tracks with crowbars while others put heavy crossties in place while still others hammered the eight-inch spikes that held the track to the crosstie—all done while a "caller" sang a chant, a track song. The rhyming cadence, along with the dance-like movements of the crew, "kept everybody uplifted," he said. "Our way to make it through the days of this slave-like work!" Uncle John Henry taught us several gandy dancer chants, such as "Linin' Track."

This leads me back to the name game in our family. You see, my mother did not take to, to put it lightly, the names Vivian and I gave our children: Kisha, whose full name is Kisha Tawala Turner, and our sons William Kenyatta, always called "Jomo," and Hodari Love. Love is Vivian's maiden name. Such Africanized names were extremely popular during the late 1960s among young Blacks—like us as newlyweds in 1969—who were then firmly embedded in the Black Power and Black is Beautiful movements and many other associated political activities.

We took Kisha to Lynch when she was just over three months old during the Christmas holidays of 1971. We had driven from Baton Rouge, Louisiana, where I was teaching at Southern University, at the time the largest of the public historically Black colleges and universities. Mama smiled and tutted in that incredibly special and approving way that only grandmothers can and do as she cuddled Kisha, her second grandchild, for that first time.

"What's her name again?" Mama asked, in a tone of voice that was clearly mocking, while she drew in the smoke from her ever-present cigarette. All eight of her children and four grandchildren were present. We were sprawled all over the crowded fifteen-by-twenty-five-foot living room of the same house where we grew up. The room used to be fifteen feet by fifteen feet until Dad extended and enclosed what used to be our front porch, making it part of the living room. I still miss the three-person cypress wood swing that occupied our front porch, suspended from the ceiling by galvanized metal chains.

That Christmas Eve, my twenty-fifth consecutive such celebration gathering with our family, the stockings were hung behind the Warm Morning stove—with care, of course—and everything was all decked out for the holidays in our nine-hundred-square-foot home. The fifteen of us would be together through New Year's Day.

Vivian and I knew already where Mama was going with her interrogative, cross-examining-like line of questioning—and implied critical analysis—of Kisha's name. After all, Mama Punkin was well known for being abrasively direct. On her piano, she often played the Thelonious Monk composition "Straight, No Chaser." Later, after Mama died, we would say that a sibling was having "a Punkin moment" when one of us said or did something that was abnormal or peculiar.

Without building up to her point by saying anything along the lines of "with all due respect," Ma asserted, "I'm just gon' tell y'all straight up, I don't like this funny African name y'all gave this baby!" as she sauntered into her kitchen, her control center, with Kisha hip-hung and in the bend of her elbow. The way she carried Kisha was very much an African cultural retention, I thought to myself, but dared not say it.

She started off revving her vocal engines, burning rubber: "Bill done changed a lot since he left and went to college and come back here with all this Black mess, always talking that 'Black Power shit.'" We all just moved into a collective "That's Mama" mode. As I followed her, I looked again at the photo of Florence Fields—whom I dated in college—that Mom kept on her piano, right next to the wedding photo of me and Vivian. Not only is that Mama, but this is Mama's house.

Mama's caustic reaction to Kisha's name never really changed, and it was essentially the same when we introduced her and the rest of the family, three Christmases later, to our second child, a son we named William Kenyatta, who we call Jomo. We named him in honor of my father and the Right Honorable Mzee Jomo Kenyatta, the first Black president of independent Kenya, in East Africa.

Beep. Beep. Bang. Bang. Ungawa. Black Power! I had chanted that in person with SNCC devotees Willie Ricks and Stokely Carmichael.

During the Christmas holidays of 1979, by which time my parents had as many grandchildren as they had children—eight—Hodari, then a bit more than a month old, our third and last child, was the focus grandchild in Mama's house. Now it was his name that was the center of Mama's "funny name" disquiet. We danced around it a bit, but I interrupted her before she could get into second gear after starting her rant, "Now what kind of damn name is Hodari? Hope y'all can stand somebody nicknaming him 'Ho'!"

Last straw!

"Mama," I started off, standing up and walking toward her, speaking first with a reserved tone of voice and a glare, then said, "Now look here, Ma, I'm not about to disrespect you, but I am sick and tired of you disrespecting our decisions as to the choices we made for our children's names, so I need to tell you a thing or two right now!"

Dad scooted up onto the walnut kitchen counter he had built by his own hands, between the refrigerator and the sink where he always sat when we gathered around the kitchen table, cupping his swill of Jack Daniels. He looked at me quickly with a devious beam of approval. The room got so quiet that our brother Irvin later said you could hear a gnat piss on a cotton ball. The exchange between me and Mama was not without hard edges because she would often say that I was "just like your daggone daddy; you think you know every damn thing." I was proudest when she would say that about me.

"Times have changed!" I exclaimed.

I sounded off to Mama about how Vivian and I had thought long and hard and had prayerfully and deliberately chosen African names for our children. She stood, hand on hip, listening to me near her cooking stove, dressed in her ever-present apron and headscarf, the spent smoke swirling ceilingward from her lit Viceroy cigarette that was perched in an ashtray nearby. The buzz in the ten-by-fifteen-foot kitchen, the size of which you couldn't whip a cat in, as Dad would say, was intense. Sisters Peggy, Marie Antoinette—otherwise known as Rusty Ree, or just Ree—and Evelyn Earnestine, who scowled and might slap or slug any of us who had the courage to call her by her hated nickname Piggy, all sat stoically, partially glad to see someone finally confront Mama, since they could tell that Mama had not become up in arms, so to say, about the confrontation.

There were as many separate conversations and chit-chats going on as there were cups of liquor or beer bottles to lips and hands reaching to grab items from the smorgasbord Mama had placed on the table. Brothers Irvin Rudolph, Mark Anthony—always called Tony—Karl Darnell, and Jeffery Gene were, well, shooting the shit, but simultaneously spurring me to take Mama on.

"Ma, just think about it, how can you—of all people—say our children have 'funny names'? What about three of yours that you named Marie Antoinette, Irvin Rudolph, and Mark Anthony?" I asked this rhetorical question with intentional contempt, as I went around the table tapping each on the head. Dad changed his look a bit, furrowed his brow, and focused his eyeballs as though he had not thought about the names of three of his children, at least not in any analytical way. Only me and our sister Barbara Ruth (whom we called Peggy) bore family names. I had Dad's first name, and Ruth was the name of Dad's oldest sister. Mama's oldest sister was named Peggy.

I shifted this generational divide into third gear.

"At least our children's names are based in Black peoples' stories in African history and culture!" I voiced the word *African* with reverberation.

I wondered aloud just what Mama might really know about Marie Antoinette eating cake and getting beheaded. I went so far as to offer Mama twenty-five dollars if she could give me the dates of the French Revolution—within a century.

"Irvin Rudolph—did you really give this boy this 'funny' name because you learned a key or two of Irvin Berlin's piano magic?"

"So why not Marcus Antonius, the authentic Italian name, rather than Mark Anthony," I asked scornfully, but playfully. "It's a wonder you didn't name this one Karl Julius Caesar!"

Time stood still until I finished my dramatic monologue by saying that Black people were no longer "gay darkies."

" 'Tis summer, the darkies are gay," I sang from the official state song, "My Old Kentucky Home."

"When will Black Americans stop stepping in every cultural track that White folks lay for us?" I asked with Malcolm X–like exaggeration, while treading across the kitchen floor tiles in a zig-zag string. I was hugging and dancing with Ma, doing steps from popular dances known as the Jerk and the Fly.

Pokey, our duplex neighbors' son, also home for the holidays from his job at General Motors in Detroit, walked in our back door, not having knocked. Irvin's classmate, red-eyed and tipsy, asked, "What y'all talkin' so much shit so loud 'bout 'round here?" Marie and Irvin and Tony were high-fiving me at the time. Everybody was "all lit up like a Christmas tree," in keeping with the lyrics from the song "Merry Christmas, Baby," which bluesman Charles Brown was then crooning on the stereo. Daddy was stress-free and happy.

My point was taken—if not well—by Mama. The discussion of names of the children in my family never came up again. Well, it did come up again, in February 2001, just over two decades after that uniquely countrified, contentious, but contented Christmas gathering.

No music.

No bourbon.

No Scotch.

No beer.

No cigarettes.

No bullshitting around.

We were gathering around Mama's bed, her deathbed.

She had made it to the spot from which she had always said she would depart to meet her maker. She had been diagnosed with lung cancer a year earlier, in 2000, the year Irvin died. Dad had passed on a dozen years earlier. It was rougher than a cob, buddy!

Hodari and his wife Lillian had come to the homeplace in Lynch with the rest of the family. Our vehicles, with license plates from Louisiana, New Jersey, North Carolina, Ohio, and Virginia, lined up in front of the Amoses' and the Browns' houses on both sides of ours. Four generations of us were now in the old homeplace—a space now deeply rooted into our bloodlines, our hearts, and our memories. But from the looks we gave each other as we glanced at each other's faces and then to Mama's dimming, glazed-over, graying eyes, and with the whir of the oxygen tank having replaced the music, there was a profound and unambiguous feeling that we—as a family—were coming to a time of that final and conclusive intersection between the past and the future. The piano keyboard, with the ivory worn off several keys, was closed, showing a film of dust. Mama could not play her piano any longer nor keep it sparkling and shiny. It was a sign of the times—her end-times.

Kisha was thirty, Jomo, twenty-six, and Hodari—the new father—was twenty-two. We all were standing around Mama's bed, now raised at the knee fold, when Lillian laid their four-month-old baby on Mama's fragile rib cage. Time went on hold, and everybody's movements seemed to be suspended as Mama put her broomstick-sized arms under the baby, lifted her up to her face level, and asked, at the same time, "What kind of funny-ass African name did y'all give this pretty little thang?"

We giggled and laughed and cried, all together, in the same moment.

"It's not an African name this time, Grandma," Hodari said, humbly.

"Africa *is* her name. Africa Turner."

Mama died a month later.

A coal miner's daughter.

A coal miner's wife.

In late 2020, Karl's son Justin and his wife, Kiyana—both Stanford grads living in Los Angeles—whose first daughter is named Amara, named her sister, Zuri, which means "Beautiful" and is of Swahili, East African, origin.

I call Africa "Punkin" sometimes.

CHAPTER 5

Black Folk Done Lost Their Stuff

BILL WITHERS, a coal miner's son from Slab Fork, West Virginia, near Beckley, was one of the twentieth century's most prolific songwriters and singers. My favorite Withers traditional song was "Grandma's Hands." The ballad "Lean on Me" was a close second because both compositions were spot-on remembrances of the life force and energy of our maternal grandmother, Minnie Lee Mabry Miller Randolph. Over the years, as I watched the dream of Dr. Martin Luther King Jr. turn into a nightmare, I would often lean on the woman we called Granny Ran for answers to my questions about our family, about life's ups and downs and dilemmas, race matters, and other subjects—"stuff" that she often indicated were the sources for "worration."

Minnie Lee Mabry Miller Randolph lived most of her 102 years at the foot of Black Mountain in the same company house, 181 First Street, in Lynch, Kentucky. She died in that house in a fire started by a cigarette she left burning in an ashtray she kept inside an often-seen feature in coal-camp homes, a starched circular figure that had arches and loops with intricate patterns, an ornamental mat made of cotton thread that was called, alternatively, a crocheted doiley, doily, or doyley. Often the doily was used as a place mat for a lamp. Granny was lying on the plastic-covered sofa where she often watched television or napped. Although she smoked at 102, she was fit as a fiddle! I do not ever remember her visiting a doctor or being hospitalized. She delivered our mother and our two aunts with the help of a midwife in their two-bedroom house along Smoky Row—behind the coke ovens, where only Black people lived—in Benham, in the area known as Machine Shop Hollow.

Our granny was certainly not the only old Black woman who knew a lot about the medicinal marvels of sassafras tea, cone (corn) liquor, cornpone, and asphidity bags that she would hang around your neck to clear congested lungs. Granny would chug me with a tablespoon of castor oil for anything from a cold to colon cleansing. No doubt a carryover from her upbringing on a farm outside Macon, Georgia, she produced pot likker from boiled collard and turnip greens seasoned with smokehouse pork long before Whole Foods affirmed that the concoction had all of the essential vitamins and minerals, including iron and vitamins C and K. Granny did not work roots like an experienced hoodoo practitioner, but she could tell you a thing or two about mojo bags and what blessed and protected a home and the right way to install a horseshoe above the front door. She never lost certain traditional connections, and she made sure we were exposed to them.

It was Granny who had firsthand knowledge and personal experiences—and, like our dad, she led me to know and value Black history, especially biography—about people who looked like and were generally treated like us. I lived under the guiding hands of Granny from the time I was two until I was six. Even though she had but two formal grades of

Minnie Lee Mabry Randolph, "Granny Ran," author's maternal grandmother. Dwight Lewis Collection. Used with permission.

schooling, quite often she would cry out—in order to assert the authenticity of her business shrewdness and her pride for her general ability to grasp most things, especially to "know Whitey"—"I went to Paine College, fool!"

Paine College, where Granny managed to study by hook or by crook from 1900 to 1903, was, like most private historically Black colleges and universities, founded by the Black Church, in this case, the Colored Methodist Episcopal Church, in 1880, fifteen years prior to her birth in Augusta, Georgia, "to train Negro teachers and preachers so that they might in turn appropriately address the educational and spiritual needs of the people newly freed from the evils of slavery." Granny left grade school because her hands were required in the cotton fields with her siblings, working from "can't see to can't see" as she put it straightforwardly, "looking up the south end of a north-bound mule." Sharecropping was the life and work of her family until, as she put it, "I went 'long with my cousins to Kentucky in 1919, where I got married to that preacher, Rev. O. L. Miller, the year I got c'here."

Granny, until the end of her life, liked to recall, in the most colorful of terms, the specifics of her times in the Roaring Twenties, when she was in her thirties. When our mother was born in 1924, Granny and her first husband, Rev. O. L. Miller, lived in a ramshackle three-room dwelling behind the coke ovens in Benham, the International Harvester Company–built coal town just downstream from Lynch, on Looney Creek, to the west.

Shortly after Mama was born, the Miller family moved to Lynch, which was then christened the "Cadillac of Coal Towns" by *Coal Age Magazine*, where the "World's Largest Coal Tipple" operated. Lynch was thriving, noisy, and prosperous, "with colored people everywhere," as Granny often called to mind. Within a decade after the Lynch Colored School opened in 1923, two female teachers who took jobs at the school boarded with Granny. Those same teachers taught our mother as well as me and my four older siblings—until the school "fell victim to integration," an expression commonly heard from alumni.

Granny was a classic teller of tales and an extremely popular bootlegger, one who delighted in placing before her guests a bottle of beer, a glass of homebrew, or a shot of bourbon or moonshine on her plastic red-and-white-checkered kitchen tablecloth. Up through my preteen years, I listened to her talk to people about Marcus Garvey, Sojourner Truth, Harriet Tubman, Ida B. Wells, Bessie Smith, Ma Rainey, and, of course, Booker T. Washington. I remember clearly Granny telling me and a couple of my friends when we were seventeen in 1963, on the day they announced that the Lynch Colored School would be merged into the Lynch White school, that she would love for us to go to "that March on Washington" to "be with all those beautiful people and to see and hear that good-talkin' and good lookin' young preacher, that fresh Dr. Martin Luther King Jr. fellow," who was from her home state of Georgia.

She muttered something about how "backwards and behind we are here in this place," adding "probably ain't no coloreds from 'round here going to the March on Washington, the company would run them off if they did!" Granny kept copies of *Jet* and *Ebony* magazines and the *Louisville Defender* and *Pittsburgh Courier*—Black newspapers—around her house, all sent weekly by her oldest daughter, our Aunt Peggy, who, after graduating from the Lynch Colored School, studied at West Virginia State College in Institute and went on to work for, and retire from, Bell Telephone in Newark, New Jersey.

Over the years, as a teacher and freelance journalist, I benefited immeasurably and immensely from the opinions of my Granny Ran on everything from how to get along with my wife to the impact of racial integration, changes in Black culture, and the prospects, psyches, and souls of Black folk. She was like my own personal version of the famous African American folklorist Zora Neale Hurston. I accompanied Granny every year until I was in college on trips to a house she bought in New Jersey with moonshine money. We traveled from Bristol, Virginia, to Penn Station in Newark—by way of Union Station in Washington, DC, and the Thirtieth Street Station in Philadelphia—aboard the Silver Meteor, operated by the Pennsylvania Railroad Company. My desire to travel started when we would arrive at the colored-only section of the train station in Bristol, Virginia, just north of the Tennessee state line. Today, ironically, the address of the station is 101 Martin Luther King Jr. Boulevard.

It was at Granny Ran's knee that I was first taught to have a bright smile and to practice compassion and kindness. When I hugged her and told her on the occasion of receiving my doctorate from Notre Dame University that I got all my good habits at her knee, she quipped, "Yeah, and you got your bad habits from some other joint!"

Granny, like most Black Southerners of her generation, such as Zora Neale Hurston, most often talked in clichés and proverbs, and she had a saying for just about any situation. Granny was neither burdened by the etiquette of political correctness nor was she ever long and drawn out with her opinions on things in life. It was as though she had already thought through anything that anybody might ask her. She always cut straight to the chase, often saying, "The only thing in the middle of the road is white lines and dead possums!"

Granny knew a lot about a lot of stuff. First, a primer on the word *stuff.*

The word *stuff*, in the South of the United States at least, refers to a wide range of things—material and nonmaterial—that are commonly encountered in life. Of course, as a word with generic reference points, *stuff* is so powerful culturally that, depending on how the word is used, it can be both subtle and subconscious and also right to the point in terms of everyday reality.

Stuff, as a figure of speech, is multilayered—and complicated—and it can be used in sentences and statements ranging from the imperative to the declarative, which is its most common usage. *Stuff* is also used when something is being questioned, or for an exclamation or for exclamatory functions. The word *stuff* is used so widely, by Southerners anyway, that it does not require the use of quotation marks around it, as when the speaker is being cynical, mocking, or sarcastic.

Finally, *stuff* can be found in command sentences. I did not think about it at the time, six or more decades ago, but I learned this stuff in my ninth-grade English class at the Lynch Colored School. The word can be employed as any of the eight parts of speech: as a noun, verb, adjective, adverb, pronoun, preposition, conjunction, or interjection.

"What's that stuff?"
"That's some good stuff!"
"That stuff is horrible."
"That stuff ain't no good for you."
"Grab your stuff, let's get out of here."
"Somebody's moved my stuff."
"Get your paws off my stuff."
"She can sho' 'nuff strut her stuff."
"That no-good sonofabitch really talks a lot of stuff."
"That mechanic really knows his stuff."
"You better leave that stuff alone."
"Don't mess with that stuff, I done tol' you!"
"I tol' you not to mess with that stuff. Now look what you done gone and did!"
"He got the stuff beat out of him."
"He had some stuff on that ball."
"He's lost his stuff."
"I don't think about stuff like that anymore."
"I don't believe in that stuff."
"I have too much stuff to do."
"Girlfriend, you need to get your stuff together!"
"Stuff happens, y'know, just when you least expect it to."
"You can take this job and stuff it."
"Who told you that stuff?"
"I can't believe you eat that stuff."

Siblings and close friends, especially boys, have their most intense and acrimonious fisticuffs when one takes the other's stuff. Mothers, otherwise like white-on-rice with their daughters, start eyeballing them when the young lady begins to find use of her mother's stuff. My wife might raise an eyebrow when I move some money from one account to another—to cover the unexpected cost of a new fishing rod or accessory for my boat—but her dandruff really gets up when I move some of her stuff around in our bedroom, or in the master bathroom, or even under the kitchen sink.

My wife always knows where the most insignificant stuff is in our house. My mother-in-law, a hoarder if there ever was one, kept a house that was crammed full of stuff in every room. But I learned real quickly to keep my opinion of her love for her considerable collection of odds and ends—her stuff—to myself; after all, it was her stuff, not mine.

How often did my granny, and countless others, issue a correction to us kids by simply saying, "Y'all cut that stuff out, and I mean now!" One clear sentence, no stuff! There were lots of women like our granny in the community, some called "Big Mama," but all of whom had the tendency to smother their grandchildren with love flowing from their grandiose, diva-like personalities. Most of them would always greet you with a warm embrace and a big, wet kiss on the cheek, some leaving a drivel of snuff juice.

In the years since the death of Dr. Martin Luther King Jr. in 1968, and up to the time of Granny's death on November 9, 1996, while I was honing my skills as a budding journalist, my grandmother and I talked at least twice a week. Toward the end of her life, when I would ask her opinion on this or that to explain what was going on in America in the lives of Black people, she would often begin, for example, as she did about the confirmation hearings of Clarence Thomas to the Supreme Court (1991) or the O. J. Simpson murder case (1995), by saying, "Black folk done lost they stuff!"

What is the *stuff* referred to by this Black coal-camp centenarian, you might ask?

For Harriet Tubman, *stuff* was the track on which the Underground Railroad lay.

For W. E. B. Du Bois, *stuff* was the "Souls of Black folk."

For Aretha Franklin, the Queen of Soul, *stuff* was spelled "R-E-S-P-E-C-T."

For James Brown, *stuff* was the heart of the matter, the genetic foundation of "Soul."

For Booker T. Washington, *stuff* brought us "up from slavery."

For Alex Haley, *stuff* was the ground in which our "Roots" were sewn.

For Mahalia Jackson, *stuff* helped one to "move on up a little higher."

For Dr. Martin Luther King Jr., *stuff* was the substance of "dreams."

For B. B. King, *stuff* was why "everybody wanted know why I sing the blues."

For Granny's meaning, *stuff* referred to attitudes, beliefs, customs, dances, jokes, information, moods, legends, opinions, prejudices, soft skills, superstitions, techniques, traditions, and values, most of which were embedded in witty sayings and coded language. Granny *stuff* was peppered with insight and unpretentious commentary.

The accounts of things Granny gave me as a child; the way she described experiences; the stories about our people, especially in our family; fairy tales; anecdotes; fabrications; outright lies; old wives' tales; remedies for bee stings; how to place a strip from a brown paper bag between my upper lip and gum to stop a nosebleed; jokes—all that became my *stuff*.

It formed my essential value system, my attitudes, and the very language I use to describe what I saw, what I said, what I came to believe, and what I do. All this became, ultimately, my philosophy toward life and the basis for my personal and social actions, my fate, and my destiny.

Without a doubt, all of us get our stuff from somewhere. One is not born knowing *the stuff*. Dr. Martin Luther King Jr. wrote and spoke extensively about where he got his stuff. His entire family was deeply steeped in the stuff of the Southern Black Baptist Church. That is where he got his stuff. He refined it at the knee of Dr. Benjamin Mays at Morehouse College and at Boston College and in the streets of America. He had his stuff long before he emerged on the world stage.

When my grandmother would say, "Black folk done lost they stuff," was she stressing that it was lost because it was not trendy enough, or "White" enough? Granny hinted that the loss of this Black stuff was the rhyme and reason why so many Blacks—in the twenty-year period after Dr. King's death—appeared to seethe in anger, despair, depression, discontent, emptiness, hopelessness, and lack of enthusiasm towards life itself.

"Lift Every Voice and Sing"—called "the Negro National Anthem" at the Lynch Colored School—was written as a poem by James Weldon Johnson in 1900 and set to music by his brother John Rosamond Johnson in 1905. There is a stanza that speaks to Black people straying from the places where they met God when they partake too liberally of the trappings "of the flesh."

Where are those places? They are the places where we discovered *the stuff*. Then, we got drunk, smashed up and tanked up, with the stuff of the world. Losing or misplacing or ignoring this Black stuff, as far as Granny was concerned, was revealed in the lives of those Black people who seem to be forever searching for something to connect the past with the present and the uncertain future. The stuff is what bridges a people from one generation to the next, the stuff that gives perspective from one generation to the next, cultural stuff that provides the fluid for the transmission of values from grandmother to grandchildren. Granny was right: we, as a people, lost that stuff along the way over the past two generations.

For the loss of their stuff, many Blacks daze themselves with alcohol and drugs and all that stuff on television—and, more recently, into that deep White hole called social media. Could she have meant that Blacks—while in the process of being like every other group in America—threw away their old-fashioned stuff, as though they have cleaned out their cultural closets, threw it all away because Gran'ma and Gran'pa had died and the old, outdated stuff was no longer needed?

Granny's stuff became unfashionable.

Granny's stuff became obsolete.

Granny's stuff became old school.

Granny's stuff became useless.

Granny's stuff, the traditions she consciously sought to pass on to us, became behind the times, too conservative, too moderate, too temperate, too restrained, and much too conformist for an age where everybody was encouraged to be an individualist and "do your own thing." Even though they were sharecroppers when Granny entered the world in 1895, she and her siblings were raised to move away from conditions of dominance and degradation. At bottom, the philosophy of Booker T. Washington promoted self-reliance and freedom from Blacks' total dependence upon White financial, and other social, institutions. That is the essence of the stuff that Granny talked and tried to live, and it ran against the dominant theme of Blacks' assimilation into mainstream American White society and political culture.

Granny called phony those Black people who ranted about *them* taking over *our* stuff when it was the very stuff that Black people had discarded for the latest fad. Then that Black stuff showed up in the popular culture landscape and on performance stages, packaged as though it was something new, something novel, when, in truth, it had simply been adopted, co-opted, adapted, and repurposed, usually by a White artist. Granny recalled to me what she thought as we watched Elvis Presley on the Ed Sullivan Show in 1956: "That colored girl Big Mama Thornton ain't never gon' see her Hound Dog no mo'."

I believe to the very marrow of my bones that the problems many in America's Black communities agonize over are but the consequences that resulted from the disappearance of some real important Black stuff. Granny gave countless examples of the Black stuff that had been pilfered or taken from Black people, as though they were not looking or paying attention to what was happening. She talked more often of "splibs givin' they stuff away"; especially those who, in self-mockery, scoffed at the simplicities of the ancestors. In the 1960s, the term *splib*—which combines the word *spade*, another word for Black, and the label *liberal*—came into usage, paradoxically among Black Power activists to describe African Americans who, deep inside, wanted to fight segregation but didn't want to rock the boat. Malcolm X called such people "house negroes," as contrasted to those he called "field negroes," the majority on plantations—those who worked in the fields and lived in the worst conditions, who wore the barest threads, ate the worst food, and received the nastiest treatment from the master. Granny would put most coal-camp Blacks into the category of field negroes. Field negroes typically hated their masters, or at the very least, they did not trust their owners or bosses or those placed above them simply as a function of tradition, custom, or law.

How abandoned Granny must have felt when—in response to her sage advice—some young whippersnapper would assert, "Shucks, I ain't gon' never do that stuff, Miss Ran!" Some of Granny's stuff is no more than a coping mechanism—going along to get along until you could go on. Many Blacks lost their jobs—or their lives—not knowing when and how to apply those tools.

Her stuff was optimistic, the message being that there was much, much more to life than idleness and foolishness. Granny spent lots of time with people—especially young women—who sought her opinions on some of their most intimate stuff. She kept many a soul from doing some crazy stuff. "That's the stuff you gotta watch, child!" she would warn them, artfully but openly.

Granny was a Keeper of the Stuff, those elusive and abstract yet extremely critical things that one generation must always transfer to the next if they are to survive, let alone thrive.

We are poorer for the loss of pure, unassimilated Black Southern Stuff. Stuff like helping Granny can stuff from a garden that you dug and planted and tended yourself while she was just behind you, talking softly, instructing. We miss the family reunions at her church and the stuff she shared about, such as how to teach the kids "the right stuff."

Now all we hear is kids in the mountains "doing senseless stuff," "being on stuff," or "messin' with that stuff," "stuffin' a gun," and "a lot of killing each other and stuff."

Mountain Black people should find and reclaim and praise their stuff. According to Granny, all people have their special stuff.

The Jews have their stuff.

The Kurds have their stuff.

The Mexicans have their stuff.

The Indians—from New Delhi—have their stuff.

The Sikhs have their stuff.

America's Indigenous people still have some of their stuff.

The Irish have their stuff.

The Japanese Americans have their stuff.

The Scandinavians have their stuff.

The French—the Creoles and Cajuns—have their stuff.

The Italians have their stuff.

The Egyptians have their stuff.

The Syrians have their stuff.

The Jamaicans—and the people from throughout the Caribbean—have their stuff.

The Ghanaians—and the people from throughout the African continent—have their stuff.

Granny's stuff had a lot of meaning. It was made of hopefulness in hard times, of patience when others were in a hurry, and it spoke of not settling for the immediate feel-good; her stuff spoke of sense and sensibility when all around you are being fools. She transmitted the stuff of self-reliance and self-sufficiency: "Boy! Ain't nobody gon' never give you shit, 'cause don't nobody owe you shit!" She might add, "But, somebody will take your stuff, or you just might lose it!" That is, if you do not preserve and improve upon and pass on to your children those ways and means that carried the generations that came before you.

The 1968 documentary *Black History: Lost, Strayed, or Stolen* still stands as a groundbreaking and inspirational analysis of the transference of stuff from one generation to the next, even though the film's executive producer, actor Bill Cosby, "America's Dad," was disgraced by a scandal late in his career in 2018.

I think of Granny every time I hear the old West African saying that Alex Haley often injected into his speeches:

"When an old person dies, it is like the burning of a library." It is more than paradoxical that the disposal of Alex Haley's material possessions is a case in point of some above-average stuff being lost, strayed, or stolen.

In early fall 1992, the estate of Alex Haley was put up for sale to the highest bidder. I accepted an invitation from Mr. George Haley, Alex's brother, to the private "tendering of offerings," as it was called, which was held two days before what seemed to me like a rummage sale on the Haley Farm and in a warehouse owned by the University of Tennessee in Knoxville. On the Haley Farm, the sale was arranged on dozens of six-by-three-foot tables that were placed around the lake, which from a distance looked like raised tombstones or mausoleums. Smaller display tables lined the fifty-foot walkway out onto the pergola where items for sale were in trays and boxes, arranged like items at a fancy farmer's market.

The autographed copy of the book *Blacks in Appalachia*, which I coedited with Edward J. Cabbell and had given to Alex as a gift, was on a table, marked five dollars. I bought it. A pair of brown, brogue-style Johnson & Murphy shoes we gave him one Christmas went for twenty-five dollars. The matching black pair of the same-styled shoes we gave him were on his feet, to be seen through his glass-covered coffin at the funeral held eighteen months earlier.

I published an appeal in the *Los Angeles Times*, September 28, 1992:

> The plight of our fellow citizens in Florida and Louisiana faced with Hurricane Andrew provides an excellent analogy for what is now brewing in East Tennessee, the results of which will scatter hither and yon yet other precious landmarks of this fragile world: Alex Haley's estate.
>
> The untimely death of Mr. Haley in February of this

year (African American History Month) devastated me. During the last dozen years, he had become a surrogate father to me and a source of professional inspiration. We became fast friends when he moved from Los Angeles to the foothills of East Tennessee—the locus of my interests on the social history of black people in Appalachia.

During this time, I became captivated not only by the pristine setting where he carved out the Haley Farm and Retreat, but I was also smitten more by the message of his life: *"Find the Good and Praise It."*

I sat under the canopy of his spirit countless times and came to know a man, who having transcended race in spiritual terms, was simply loving, caring, giving and humble: a man whose impact on others was measured not only by the classical writings that mark his place in history, but by his quality of spirit. He clearly "cared less" about material possessions, although he had what many of us could never buy!

That the Haley estate is now poised to "deal with the tangible legacy that Alex left, including the farm and most of Alex's other possessions" devastates me more than his death. While I don't care to know the internality of things (why was Alex broke?), I am overwhelmed by my powerlessness to interrupt or obstruct the privatization of his manuscripts, papers, memorabilia, collections, awards and other contributions to the material culture of America and the world.

Among the manuscripts to be auctioned are four sections of text that did not make it into the "Autobiography of Malcolm X," letters shared between Haley and others who've made a difference in our collective cultural lives: from Malcolm X to George Lincoln Rockwell.

Soon, Haley's "tangible" possessions will be the property of anonymous high bidders, who then will have in their parlors what will become little more than objects of idle ownership and brag.

"Oh that? That's the derby worn by Chicken George in 'Roots'!" The same thing happened to Omoro and Binta Kinte's son, Kunta. "Wonderful, isn't it dahlin! We acquired Haley's Pulitzer Prize at the auction . . . a most unique steal! Columbia University tells us that it has no recollection of a Pulitzer Prize ever being sold!"

"And that . . . well, our lawyer is negotiating a film script based on Alex Haley's letters to 20 students whose education he sponsored . . . it's a great story!"

Alex Haley enriched and endeared himself to a generation of Americans. His love of family (the family of humankind) is both the tangible and intangible legacy being let for bid this week.

It is my hope that some of the people associated with Alex's work ("Roots" and "The Autobiography of Malcolm X")—entertainers, writers, producers, wealthy individuals, corporations or universities—would intercede and preserve Haley's works intact so that there will be free and open access to that which he gave so freely: the significance and uniqueness of the human soul and its aspirations.

Such cultural products belong in the National Afro-American Museum, National Archives, or the Smithsonian Institution. Alex Haley was an American institution. We all should want that for Alex Haley and for ourselves. Hurricane Auction Alex is one we can prevent.

Granny left the world saying that many Blacks, especially the ones who should be at the head of the line to lead the conversations and devise ways to restore dignity and a sense of rootedness to Black people and to generate new stuff, are the very ones who are "full of stuff!"

I wonder if a century in the mountains where coal used to be produced was enough time for Black peoples' distinctive mountain stuff to jell, to solidify, and to preserve their legacies. If not, Granny's stuff was in the Greatest Black Generation, the last ones before the stuff got cleared out. My life has spanned three generations of Black stuff becoming extinct.

Among the most noteworthy in the Greatest Black Generation, a Keeper of the Stuff on a world scale, was the founder of Johnson Publications of Chicago—the parent company of *Jet* and *Ebony* magazines—John Johnson. Much of the cultural stuff of Black America was lost in 2015, when in the hopes of raising $40 million, Mr. Johnson's heirs put up for sale the photographic archives of *Jet* and *Ebony* that contained more than five million of the most iconic images of African American life and culture. That the venerable Black-owned firm monetized these valuable cultural assets reminds me of a saying I first heard from my Georgia farm-raised grandfather, who told me, "Billbo, don't ever eat your seed corn." Seed saving, also called "brown bagging," is the reproductive practice used from year to year by traditional farmers and serious-minded gardeners to preserve the inherent genetic pureness of crops.

The seeding of my mindful journey to know as much as I could about African American life and culture started when I was ten years old in the form of a photo in *Jet* magazine. It was September 1955 when Pops handed me the issue of *Jet* magazine, the one with the cover photo and story about Chicago teen Emmett Till, who was brutally murdered in Money, Mississippi, for allegedly whistling at a White woman. For me, and millions of others, young Till's horrifically disfigured head became the hallmark image of the world that Black Americans in my generation would see and live—and try to change—for a long time to come. I am sure that murder of the young Till refreshed Pops's memory of a hanging he witnessed in Georgia in 1906.

To really grasp how much *Jet* and *Ebony* influenced me as a small-town Black boy growing up in the fifties and sixties, you have to appreciate how carefully Mr. John Johnson—who, with his wife, Eunice, founded a publishing company in 1942—controlled the message of his magazines. In every issue, always, *Jet* and *Ebony* pressed the positive angle of any story, even to the point of being criticized by mainstream media of being little more than feel-good channels for Black Americans.

At the darkest times in segregated America, I could read any issue of *Jet* or *Ebony* and feel content that Blacks—that I—could still excel in any human endeavor. Good times, cheer, and optimism filled the pages; profiles in the progress of the race and of individuals left me with a monthly dose of optimism concerning what lay ahead for me beyond the isolations of the mountains. Even the advertisements were framed by rose-colored prisms. These signature Johnson publications—in addition to another, *Negro*, later renamed *Black World*—were to the civil rights movement what Facebook, Snapchat, Instagram, and Twitter are to contemporary social movements.

Over the years, I put my faith in *Jet* and *Ebony* to inform me of things that I was taught intelligent Black Americans cared, or should care, about, always delivered with superb photographs framed inside an editorial perspective directed to meet the needs of Blacks who were bombarded and besieged by the dehumanizing effects of racism. *Ebony* and *Jet* were the correctives, the balm in Gilead, soothing positive reinforcements. In my youth, I would deliberately look for these periodicals as essential fixtures on coffee tables in the homes of forward-thinking Black people.

I did so the same way my grandfather would judge the readiness of a watermelon when he would thump it with his middle finger, listening for just the right sound, the echo of ripeness. *Jet* and *Ebony*—for most Blacks born between World War I and the passage of the Voting Rights Act in 1965—were to the growth of Black social consciousness, political awareness, and progress what rain and sunshine were to a healthy farm. A Black-owned barbershop without frayed, aged copies of *Jet* and *Ebony* was a sign of an imitation Black barbershop.

All that changed at the beginning of the twenty-first century. Johnson Publishing Company sold an equity stake in the company to JPMorgan Chase. Similarly, Time Inc. bought 49 percent of *Essence* magazine in 2000 and absorbed the rest in 2005. Viacom Inc. purchased Black Entertainment Television (BET) a few years ago for $2.3 billion. But by that time, BET's owners had exchanged the *E* to stand for *Entertainment* rather than *Education*. That signaled an especially important difference in emphasis, in programming.

It is to a point where the words *a Black perspective* and *American media* can't fit in the same sentence. Ebony-hued diehards like me meet for coffee at McDonald's and reflect among ourselves about the good old days. Farm-raised folk like my grandfather, those who advised, "Don't eat your seed corn!" are spinning in their grave sites, at least in the ones that have yet to fall victim to development, growth, gentrification, and what is generally referred to as progress. Change is not the same as progress.

Ebony and *Jet* were like cultural heritage seeds that came through Black hands and minds in America for seventy years. We ate some of the corn, and we kept some seeds, kernels of legacy and tradition, to plant for the next generation to reap. Now the seed corn is being consumed. Our grandchildren will have nothing to put in the ground. The farms—the cultural grounds on which we stand—will be lost. Blacks will be poorer for this cultural loss, soon broke altogether—all for the sake of money. Granny and Pops stop spinning!

It's one thing to mourn the loss of lifeways and find myself having my hair cut by a White female in a place called Supercuts, but it's an entirely different level of loss to witness the demise of a mountain. Black Mountain was not just a backdrop, a piece of scenery, but it was something, something material that I saw the first thing when I walked out onto the porch each morning. I heard its sounds, the echoes of life, from a babbling brook called Looney Creek to the chirping of robins and crickets and the loud shrill of cicadas on hot summer nights and doves in the morning. In fact, the mountain was a vital part of our stuff, the physical stuff of our environment, and its majesty and dominance were as natural to us as skyscrapers were to city dwellers. Imagine the ruin, the loss, if the New York City skyline was crushed and routed.

In 1990, while headed to speak for Black History Month at the University of Virginia at Wise, driving from Lynch, I stood on a ridge at the top of Black Mountain, on the Virginia side, and looked out onto how this ancient and biologically rich mountain, the land itself and the headwaters of streams, had been destroyed by the most caustic form of extracting coal: mountaintop removal (MTR). Another great loss.

I had, since the 1980s, joined members of a citizens' group known as Kentuckians for the Commonwealth (KFTC) to oppose MTR, where coal companies use heavyweight explosives to blow away the mountain ridges to get to the seams of coal below. They then dump the dirt and rubble, what the coal companies call "overburden," into adjacent valleys. MTR became a full-blown bang-up on the Virginia side of Black Mountain in the late 1980s. The ridges just over the mountain from my hometown, like Inman, Virginia, and in around the town of Appalachia, were devastated, as were stretches of mountainside all along US 58, the route between the town of Appalachia and our dad's homeland in Coeburn.

Some were claiming that MTR was one of the ways that would "bring coal back." But on that January morning, I sat in my truck at the top of Black Mountain and wrote about what could never be brought back—the mountain itself. It was a most appropriate time to apply phrases from Dr. Martin Luther King Jr.'s "I Have a Dream" speech to what is, for most, an invisible place—Black Mountain, Kentucky's highest peak, which lords over the heart and soul of our hometown.

> I salute Kentuckians for the Commonwealth as they protest the strip-mining of Black Mountain. I have a dream that their creative and nonviolent dissent will go down in history as a successful demonstration against this most environmentally destructive and morally reprehensible form of mining, one that profits few, yet denies many life, liberty, and the pursuit of happiness. Profits trump morals in America.
>
> I have a dream that their petitions will stop the progress of the blasting and the growling of machines that have already torn asunder—forever—the Virginia side of this ancient fortification, which is but a fly rock's throw from the town of Appalachia. Flying rocks are to mountaintop removal what melting glaciers are to global warming.
>
> I have a dream that the protests against strip-mining above Lynch and its sister city, Benham, will be heard—from every mountainside—by the Environmental

Protection Agency and that a momentous decree will be issued that will save the mountain. It has long been treasured and awed by people who worked underneath it and who now languish in a place that sent the profits to Pittsburgh, the headquarters of US Steel, the company that owned Lynch for almost a century, starting in 1917, before deserting it and stripping it of its proud legacy as one of America's model underground coal-mining towns.

The mountains are high in Harlan County, and they separate its residents—many of them suffering in poverty—from those who have the power to put a stop to the shameful and unhealthy conditions that strip-mining Black Mountain brings.

I have a dream that Black Mountain will become like the National Mall was in 1963 when Dr. Martin Luther King Jr. spoke there, that the mountain will become a sacred and hallowed spot where demonstrations against the inexpressibly horrific images left by strip-mining will be sent out around the world.

It would be fatal for the nation to overlook the urgency of preventing the strip-mining of Kentucky's highest peak. In the process of meeting our energy needs, we must not be guilty of wrongful deeds.

Let us not seek to quench our thirst for light and heat—and the fortunes of a few—by tearing down the mountain. Our destiny is inextricably tied up with the fate of the flora and fauna on the hillsides and the creatures that live in Looney Creek, the fountainhead of which springs from the gut of Black Mountain, into the Cumberland River and on to the Ohio River near Paducah, Kentucky, beyond to the Mighty Mississippi River, to the Gulf of Mexico. We all live downstream.

We have seen enough of what strip-mining does; examples of its nightmarish results are abundant throughout eastern Kentucky, southwest Virginia, and southern West Virginia. Countless once-lush green valleys are now filled with rock debris while once-exalted peaks and prominent inclines are little more than bumpy, rough, rutted, and uneven molehills made low, the crooked creeks buried beneath what was revealed, majestically, 450 million years ago, its life-affirming magnificence awesome and inspiring, the ecotourist's dream.

I have a dream that one day, when my four grandchildren visit the mountain I hiked in my youth, they too will be able to jump across nature's own stones of hope and tiptoe in the creeks of our ancestors' pride and not be repulsed by the appalling sight of mountains of despair, the evidence of the greed of man.

I dream that they will roam and wander the relatively unsullied hills around my hometown beneath which their relatives lived and worked and died and are buried.

From no mountainside should the hammers of strip-mining ring.

From every mountainside, let scenic views reign. Let waters of hope and scenes of economic justice flow like a mighty stream, from Jellico Mountain in Tennessee to Coal Mountain in West Virginia.

And when this happens, when the piercing sounds of strip-mining are hushed, may the people in every village and every hamlet and every town, in every extraction zone—places like Lynch and Benham—join hands and sing together the words of a new mountain hymn, "Our mountain is free of strip-mining! Free at last! Free at last! Thank God Almighty, our mountains are free—of strip-mining—at last!"

I have never kept count of the number of lectures, speeches, formal and informal focus groups, and presentations I have given over the past forty-five years about Blacks in Appalachia, but I am sure it's in the high hundreds. I have been privileged to speak in places and spaces as varied as the Militant Pillar and Ground of the Truth Church of God—pastored by Elder Willie Lamb and located in Tom Biggs Hollow in McRoberts, Letcher County, Kentucky—to Yale University, in a classroom named after world-class African American photographer, musician, writer, and film director Gordon Parks, when I was hosted there in February 2019 by Sterling Professor of Sociology Dr. Elijah Anderson.

Of all such keynote addresses, orations, and talks I have given on the broad subject of this book, the most memorable talk I ever gave was at a gathering of the Eastern Kentucky Social Club, a confederation of Black coal miners and migrants from eastern Kentucky coal towns. There is more about this alliance later in the book, but this 1991 gathering in Atlanta was special. I stood before twelve hundred or so people, many of them literally among my longest-known and closest friends, in the downtown Marriott ballroom. I wanted to emphasize to them, by way of analogies and metaphors about mountains, what it meant for us, on the one hand, to lose our places on the mountain but to keep the mountains in our memories on the other.

The gathered throng was in a festive mood, and as the main speaker, I got this great introduction from the local chapter's president, Sergeant Garfield Gist, a career army veteran ten years my senior. A pool shark—one of my skills—could not have asked for the balls to line up more invitingly after Sarge set the table. I decided to take them on an allegorical journey through our common roots on Black Mountain, opening in my best Black Southern Baptist preacher voice: "When God asked me where I wanted to be born, he presented me with a list of mountains."

I started that way because I knew that, despite the party-like atmosphere, most of the attendees, at least the older ones, were quite grounded spiritually and religiously. I knew too that most of them were Baptists. Mount Sinai Baptist Church in Lynch was always the largest Black church in the mountains of eastern Kentucky. Members of the venerable old house of worship, past and present—in some cases, four generations of the same family—were present.

"Mount Sinai," I told them, as inspirationally as I could, "was also known as Mount Horeb or Gabal Musa, a mountain in the Sinai Peninsula of Egypt that is considered a holy site by all three of the Abrahamic religions—Christianity, Judaism, and Islam."

"Go back and reread the book of Exodus," I expanded, heading into the middle of this current and common sermon that I knew many of them had heard many times over. I threw in a little "dry bones in the valley." A deacon from Mount Sinai, my lifelong friend and coal miner George Massey, was now standing, screaming like a wildcat, as Dad would say, bellowing, "Go 'head, boy!"

"Look at other books in the Holy Bible, or in the Qur'an or writings in the Torah, any teachings of the Jewish, Christian, and Islamic traditions, and you will see that the biblical Mount Sinai was the place where Moses received the Ten Commandments."

I found myself, almost reflexively, pushing my audience, my people, to see themselves as Old Testament people. I was intent on anchoring my thoughts in the symbolic meanings of mountains. After all, we were all mountain folks, woodsmen. My father, certainly the first environmentalist I ever met, was no analytical psychologist, but he knew and told me many things about how the lush forests that surrounded us represented mystery, the unknown, the unexplored, and that mountains—our landscape—were places, unlike cities, where life—animal and plant—thrived. My objective in this speech was to style all that mystery in a way to make it come alive in less than thirty minutes. After all, these people were gathered for merriment—chatting, eating, dancing, and drinking.

"Mount Horeb," I told them, "another name for Mount Sinai, you learned about that place in Sunday school," was the peak on which Moses had been given the Ten Commandments by God. The Mountain of God. I told the crowd within the first five minutes of the speech that I had respectfully declined God's invitation for me to be born on any of these sacred mountains, not even near Ramallah, another Mountain of God.

"No, no, not here," I chanted rhythmically, like I was Howard Thurman or Gardner C. Taylor, in response to each place God said I could be born and raised—at my choice. My preacher tone of voice now ticked off the names and locations and elevations of some of the most familiar mountains around the world. I pulled the audience into visualizing me, us, swaddled in God's arms as he transported us above the summits of Mount Everest in Nepal, the highest point in the world, to Argentina's Aconcagua. Then, as though we were being beamed up by Scotty of *Star Trek* fame, we whizzed above Denali in Alaska and over the length and breadth of Kilimanjaro in Tanzania and back in a flash, looking down upon the dry stretches of Ojos del Salado in Chile, knowing full well that most of those now giving me the "Amen" cheers did not have the slightest clue as to where any of these places were. Not to matter, we, together, were in the moment, in that zone. It was enchanting, spiritual.

"No, no, not here," I repetitively said as I talked to God

while rubbing in liberally the principles of rhetoric I had learned in the Lynch Colored School, transforming myself—fully focused—from public speaker to homilist, to preacher. I knew from experience with a crowd like this that "God talk" always worked.

After pulling them into the now plain image of God taking me over Mount Everest, Aconcagua, Denali, Kilimanjaro, and Ojos del Salado, some of the places I could have chosen to be born and live, I whisked the room over Black Mountain in eastern Kentucky.

"Here, Lord, right here! I see my people. Leave me here."

"This," I said, now sweating and prancing, "is where I know I belong. My people are here!" The reaction was astounding and stupendous. I summarized much of what follows in this book in that speech to include how people consigned by fate to live in mountain regions—no matter where in the world their mountain is located—have common life practices and cultures, which are defined in large part by conflicts and paradoxes. I waxed a bit about how mountain people everywhere face community and financial freeze-outs, especially if it is an extraction zone, the lifeblood of which are valuable resources that rest in the veins of mountains, as coal does.

"Don't be fooled, don't flip the plot," I chanted and warned, speaking in the past tense. That isolated place and the people there—us—have been defined as backwards and out of the mainstream. I explained how we were tied to a global economy and how—in less than a century—we had become expendable objects, that the mountain itself was disposable in pursuit of capital markets for what brought our foreparents there—coal.

I ended by starting a song, inviting those who knew it—and, of course, many of the old heads did—to do a singalong to "Rough Side of the Mountain," written by Rev. C. F.

Barnes. My kith and kin and kind had walked the words of this hymn. They had come this far by faith. Though the decline of what had been the homeplace for almost a century was at hand, and the realization of that fate quite depressing, the vitality in the room was extraordinary, the reaction warm and energetic. I had just been blessed with the best use of my breath in my life.

The experience, however, was not a spontaneous one, not by a long shot. If for me this was my trial sermon, I believe the congregation would have voted overwhelmingly to license me. On the other hand, I heard the calling many years prior, but, unlike my hero James Baldwin, I chose not to answer it. I never lost touch with some things I heard in coal-camp churches.

It occurred to me when I was twenty-four, just four years removed from lifelong membership and regular attendance at First Missionary Baptist Church in my hometown, that Deacon Joseph Belton had memorized a Southern Black Baptist version of the Presbyterian *Book of Common Worship*. My familiarity with the Presbyterian *Book of Common Worship* came about when I got married to Vivian in Westminster Presbyterian Chapel in her hometown, Concord, North Carolina. Concord was also a company town, a cotton mill township twenty miles northeast of Charlotte where the wealth was built by planters through the cultivation and refining of cotton; the work was done by enslaved African Americans, including her grandparents.

During the course of my youth, having served as a junior deacon from the age of eleven through the age of twenty, I heard a prayer that, when rendered by Deacon Belton, had exactly the same narrative, the same rhythm, and the same tone every time he petitioned the Lord at First Baptist Church. Some rendition of Brother Belton's rhythmic and humble words could be heard every Sunday morning in the Black Baptist churches of central Appalachian coal towns, whether it was Town Mountain Baptist in Hazard, Mount Moriah Baptist in Middlesboro, Rising Star Baptist in Benham, or, among others, Macedonia Baptist on Sanctified Hill in Cumberland, Kentucky.

Deacon Belton's enunciations and pronunciations are looked upon by some as being unschooled, ignorant, primitive, antiquated, and old-world, but I am sure that God heard him just the same. I know I did. It was awe inspiring, and it struck the fear of God in me and often brought me to tears! Same prayer. Every Sunday. Same recitation. Same poetry.

I still get goose pimples when some old-school Black Baptist, while praying in the style of Brother Belton, asks God to "Bless des peoples and dis ch'uch!" *Church*, in the dialect and colloquial speech of many of the older folk who were born and raised in Alabama, was pronounced as though it rhymed with *touch*, which is spiritual and transcendent in and of itself. Sam Cooke, perhaps the greatest of gospel singers, from Clarksville, Mississippi, sang of a broken woman who just wanted to "touch the hem of his garment." To get touched in ch'uch on the mo'ning (mourning) bench was especially sanctified. "Touch Me, Lord Jesus, with Thy Hands of Mercy" was a much-loved hymn that our mama, the pianist, could solid play.

This prayer was followed by a program that climaxed in a sermon that was oftentimes delivered with an acrobatic flamboyance. The preacher—whether Rev. M. L. Gabriel or Rev. J. C. Middlebrooks—would sometimes jump off the raised pulpit onto the floor some eight feet away and two feet below, just 'a sweating. The amens and yeses—call and response—roared, and the approving clapping and shouting synchronized with the preacher's bouncing and swiveling with the rhymes and timeworn free verse he cited. Invariably, another deacon or sister in the choir would line-out a hymn, a form of a cappella hymnody in which a soloist gives each line of a tune as it is to be sung followed by a comeback of the lyrics from everybody present.

As a junior deacon at First Baptist, where our father served as trustee, from the time I was in the eighth grade through my sophomore year in college, I could not help but to commit Deacon Belton's prayer to memory—almost verbatim—because he said it almost exactly the same way every Sunday. I heard it quite often, and I considered it a living visit from the Black Southern voices raised by Paul Laurence Dunbar, the first influential Black poet in the United States, whose parents, not insignificantly, were born enslaved in Lexington, Kentucky. Dunbar's portrait donned the hall of our school because he was internationally acclaimed for the way he incorporated into his verses what has been called Negro dialect, African American English, Black English, Ebonics, nonstandard Negro English, and Black talk. Deacon Belton's voice—and that of many of the Black elders—could be read in Dunbar's works, such as *Majors and Minors* (1895) and *Lyrics of Lowly Life* (1896), which were published around the time Deacon Belton was born. His prayers and appeals went pretty much word for word as follows:

> Almighty and all wise Gawd, our heavenly Father, 'tis once more and again that a few of yo' humble survants are gathered to call upon yo' Holiest name. First, giving honor to God who rules over us and to the Holy Trinity: the Father, the Son, and the Holy Ghost.
>
> We bows at yo' footstool, Holy Masta, thankin' you fo' watchin' ober us whilst we slept 'n slumbered last night, and stirrin' us wid yo' gentle hand ob Mercy, early dis

mo'nin'. We thanks you so generously Lawd, for not letting the bed we slept in last night be aw'va cooling bode and the covering that warmed us not be aw'va winding sheet. We's so glad you still are giving us a potion' of healf 'n stren'th 'n habing us wake up early this mo'ning still clothed in aw'va right mines. Thro' yo' strong arms of 'tection 'round 'bout us dis mo'ning, Lawd, and bind us in lub and unity. Bill us up where we's tow down 'n streng'en us where we weak, Heb'ly Father. Now Lawd, you knows where we was at las' night, you knows aw'va hearts. You knows aw'va comins and aw'va goins. Father God, dis mornin', 'member the man das gon' stan in de Holy Ground and brang de word to us, his flock. Stand by him and his fambly dis mo'ning Gawd and take him deep down in the treasures of yo' Word.

And Lawd, when dis yo' humble servant done did all he can do, I axe you to ah'foud me a home in yo' kingdom. Please, Masta, keep us a prayin' chu'ch till that day when every day will be Sunday and the sorrows of dis old wurld will be no mo'.

Dese blessins and all others we axe in Thy Son Jesus's Holy name. Ah'mane!

I got frightened sometimes as a young boy when otherwise easygoing old women, "stricken by the Holy Ghost," would spring from their seats with a force that ejected them straight up from the pew, stiff as a board, possessed by the Spirit, their arms flailing and flashing, dresses lifted so that their thighs and corsets showed. Frequently, some worshippers would do the Happy Dance—an act of praise, a spontaneous hip-hop, a rhythmic jitterbug-like movement that took the possessed one into the aisles, often ending when the dancer, sometimes

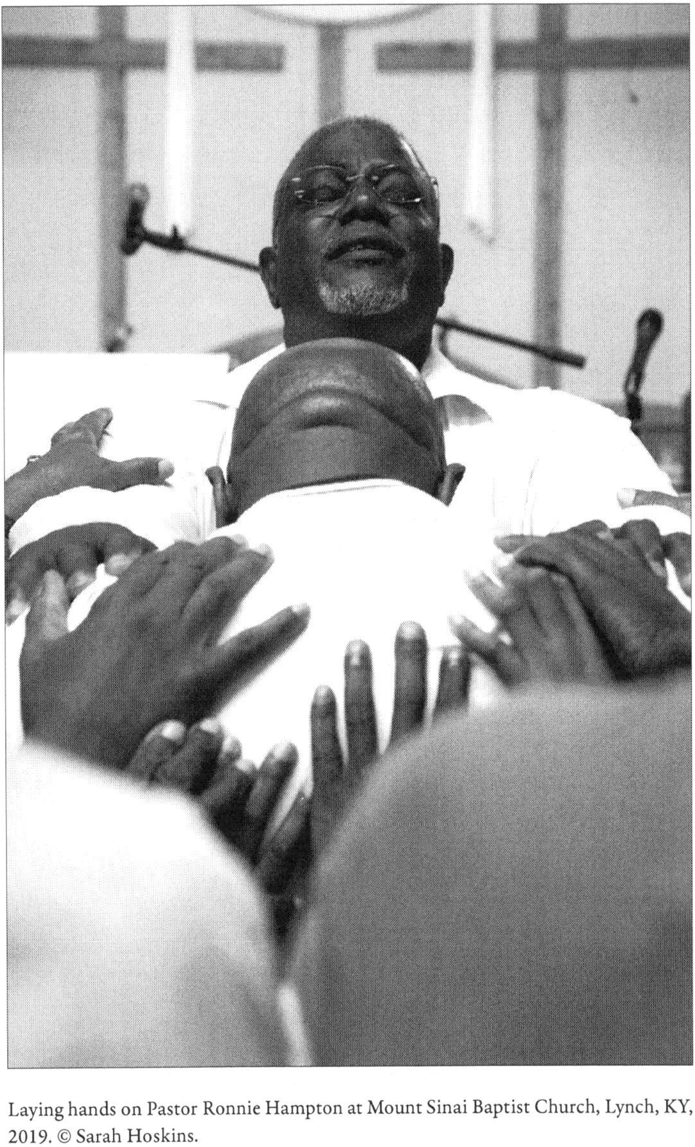

Laying hands on Pastor Ronnie Hampton at Mount Sinai Baptist Church, Lynch, KY, 2019. © Sarah Hoskins.

having pranced around the whole church, simply tired out and collapsed into a huff on a pew, often rolling on the floor.

Another deacon, Dad's fishing buddy Mr. Eddie Stevenson of Mount Sinai Baptist Church, summoned several of Brother Belton's same phrasings in his prayers most of the time, but he added elements about God as a mother to the motherless and a father to the fatherless. In Mr. Eddie's diction, commonly used by the men of my grandfather's generation, God, pronounced "Gawd," was a doctor in the sickroom—not in a hospital. People of my grandparents' generation often suffered through their pain and sickness—and died—in their homes, surrounded by family. The wake was also held in the home. Last rites. Last rights.

Mr. Stevenson uttered his supplications with the blessed assurance that the Lord, or "de Lawd," was also the best lawyer, just in case one found oneself in a Harlan County courtroom, commonly pronounced "coat room."

Renditions, interpretations, remakes, and retentions of these old deacons' prayers can still be heard in Black Baptist churches in Appalachian coal towns. Fewer and fewer souls hear them, just as there are fewer and fewer Friday night fish fries or songs blaring from Wurlitzer jukeboxes in nightclubs and bars—what were called juke joints—from which many churchgoers on Sunday had emerged only hours earlier. There was Big Knox's Café in Big Stone Gap, Virginia, and Big Mollie's Place in Cumberland, and The Hall, in Georgetown, the colored section of Harlan, the county seat.

The joy and the despair these songs and prayers exemplified probably still oozes up in Hazard's "Nigger Bottom," or a stone's throw from "Niggerhead Rock" just outside Pennington Gap, Virginia. Pennington Gap constituted what my father—who was born and raised in the next county—called "a hard row to hoe" for Black people. For those uninitiated

Referred to by locals as "Niggerhead Rock," this formation near Pennington Gap, VA, now known as "Old Stone Face," has a railroad tunnel running through the neck. Appalachian African-American Cultural Center, Pennington Gap, Va. Collection.

in countrified phrases, the Appalachian conversational expression "hard row to hoe" refers to a particularly difficult or problematic task, situation, or set of circumstances to contend with or confront. Legal structures in Pennington Gap—and throughout the Appalachian South—kept Black people in their place; the place where Black people were restricted to live in the town is *still* called "Buck Town." If I must write out the word for which *buck* was simply a code,

I need to start this book over again. Of course, a *buck* is the male of some horned animals, like a deer, or it's a dollar, "one buck," or it's the article placed as a reminder before a player whose turn it is to deal at poker. But, most certainly in Pennington Gap, I would assume that it is acceptable to capitalize *Buck* because it is framed as a proper noun, a place-name. But who knows? Praying for the offenders, the old saints could be heard saying, quite often, with an air of resignation, "Lord, have mercy Jesus," which came off as one long, multisyllabic word.

Beyond doubt, the power of faith in God and the role of the church to enrich the human spirit—called spirituality here—gave a type of nourishment to Black coal-town people the same way support timbers kept Black Mountain off our fathers as they toiled beneath it.

The church—whether Baptist like mine, Old Regular, or Primitive Baptist, Colored Methodist Episcopal, African Methodist Episcopal Zion, or Pentecostal, also known as Holiness—was the station of security in the world of Black mountain people where all else was in flux—either boom or bust, always heading toward bust. Songs and prayers were the avenues to solutions to any of the problems and uncertainties that were part of the daily fabric of life in coal towns.

It was from the old Black women, primarily, from whom I constantly heard references to the ways of being and keeping in touch with "the Spirit." I can close my eyes whenever I want and still hear Mrs. Helen Cameron, an Anniston, Alabama, native—and the wife of a miner-preacher, Rev. Willie Cameron—who lived just across the street from our house, singing "Every Time I Feel the Spirit."

Spirituals invited us to move as close as possible emotionally to the very source of all existence: God. There was no other way to truly develop the power to endure and the inner strength and will it took to survive, to traverse the social landscape of central Appalachia, which was highly racialized, even as the White people sang the same songs to the same God. Distinguished scholar of Black religion James T. Cone made reference to the lyrics from "Every Time I Feel the Spirit" in his 1972 book, *The Spirituals and the Blues*: "The mountains may be high and the valleys low, but 'my Lord spoke' and 'out of his mouth came fire and smoke.'"

Little was standoffish or restrained in the services of these coal-town churches, with their all-Black congregations, no matter what denomination; they were small and intimate and immensely powerful representations of Black mountain identity and culture. The Spirit overwhelms one upon entry to these spaces. Baptisms and funerals are big deals. Of late, of course, there are virtually no baby christenings, and funerals far outnumber weddings. The consolidation or merging of the small congregations is still out of the question. Often, for the past three decades, most of the preachers who serve the Black flocks in the interior of central Appalachia reside in moderate-sized towns or cities outside the small coal towns, somewhere on the periphery. In a recent survey, I found preachers in five churches between Cumberland and Harlan who resided in Knoxville, two doing so for twenty-six and thirty-two years respectively.

I did not know it at the time of course, but I now firmly believe that the old Black men and women, while praying in the church about "the many dangers, toils, and snares," were inviting God to protect us. They had apprehensions and fears born out of many concrete experiences, not the least of which were the frequent misfortunes involved in mining: a severed finger here, an eye blown out there, a smashed foot, a broken leg or arm, or the constant vexation that came from not knowing when one's own name would be posted on the cutoff list that was posted at the lamp house, where miners checked in and out near the entrance to the bathhouse.

"We come this far by faith, leaning on the Lord, trusting in His Holy Word. He never failed me yet!" That song kept many a soul sane. The lyrics of certain Negro spirituals and gospels became folk sayings heard commonly in these talks/prayers. They were a type of defense mechanism used to widen the zone of safety between confidence and faith, on the one hand, and doubt and fear on the other.

The despair of the present and the hope for the future were united psychologically and mystically. Through this, most of us were imbued with a positive consciousness and empowered to live the present while hoping for the best in the future, something better. Religious life among the people was really something that could be *seen* and *felt*. There was a spiritual for that too: "My God Is Real!" Where Kentucky, Virginia, and West Virginia come together, physical survival was connected to spirituality. The colored section of Cumberland, Kentucky, was not called Sanctified Hill for nothing!

Black people in coal towns were not only separated and isolated from mainstream America, but they were pushed further toward the margins because their White neighbors were also scorned by mainstream society. Only God, as an all-powerful and protective force and ally, could provide joy and hope under those circumstances.

Being spiritually grounded made God infinitely more powerful than the company. Spirituality—the search for meaning in life—provided people with an enthusiasm for life that emanated from a place that was not influenced by what the company did or did not do for or to them. Despite living somewhat unnoticed, a strong individual faith, a sense of community, and a collective spirituality moved Black people toward unity for survival. They knew that, despite their isolation, they were part of the larger, universal, human experience. It gave them a positive disposition toward themselves and a dogged determination to overcome life's challenges. The essential quality of Black spirituality in Appalachian coal towns is no different than the religious view that permeates the general philosophy of most poor and working-class people about their experiences.

The central thread that binds the ethos among the community of believers in Black mountain communities is the belief that God is whole, the supreme commander, and he is the basis of, and power over, all life. Life for Blacks in the mountains did not always allow for an optimistic social gospel that supported the belief that hard work would always bring a sure reward. The religious and spiritual creed among mountain people, Black and White, therefore, is more realistic than it is idealistic. My mountain hometown was full of good people, and most of us pulled for each other. We had genuine, caring relationships, and we helped each other. *Helped* was noticeably pronounced "hoped" by many in my grandmother's generation, and we trusted each other. In the purest sense, giving courage and hopefulness to believers is one of the functions of religion.

A variant of a repeated theme in this book is that life for Blacks in the coal towns ain't been no crystal stair, or that it's been a hard row to hoe, or that it's been full hard times. Few of the old people who raised me ever spoke in abstract or philosophical terms; their answers to questions about destiny were noticeably short, very direct, and deeply grounded in their personal realities and their immovable faith in God. The quality of life and the opportunities for social mobility were, for Blacks in the coal towns, a chorus from a popular

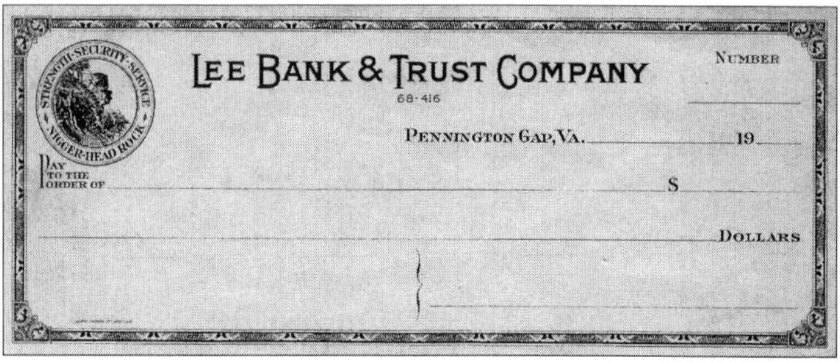
STRENGTH · SECURITY · SERVICE
NIGGER-HEAD ROCK
LEE BANK & TRUST COMPANY
68-416
NUMBER
PENNINGTON GAP, VA. ____ 19__
PAY TO THE ORDER OF ____ $ ____
____ DOLLARS

Checks issued by Lee County Bank showing "Niggerhead Rock" on logo. Appalachian African-American Cultural Center, Pennington Gap, Va. Collection.

gospel: "Going up the rough side of the mountain." But, from that climb to the mountaintop—and perhaps because of it—a style of existence emerged that enabled and empowered these people to carry through in spite of the isolation—and even amid both the indirect and glaringly bad face of racism.

Faith and religion were the breastplates these Black Appalachians put on to buffer themselves from the impacts of long-term isolation, manipulation, and, yes, exploitation. Old Testament canon helped them to maintain their self-esteem against attacks to their sense of human dignity. Mental and emotional balances were maintained by the spiritualism—the *stuff*—that sheltered them against the storms of life, without which their souls and spirits would surely have been ravished.

Dr. Martin Luther King Jr. had Black coal-town people in mind when he said, "I have been to the mountaintop, and I have seen the Promised Land." The Blacks in central Appalachian coal towns have—starting a half century ago—now largely moved out or died out; either way, they have been virtually wiped out from the region. Most knew intuitively

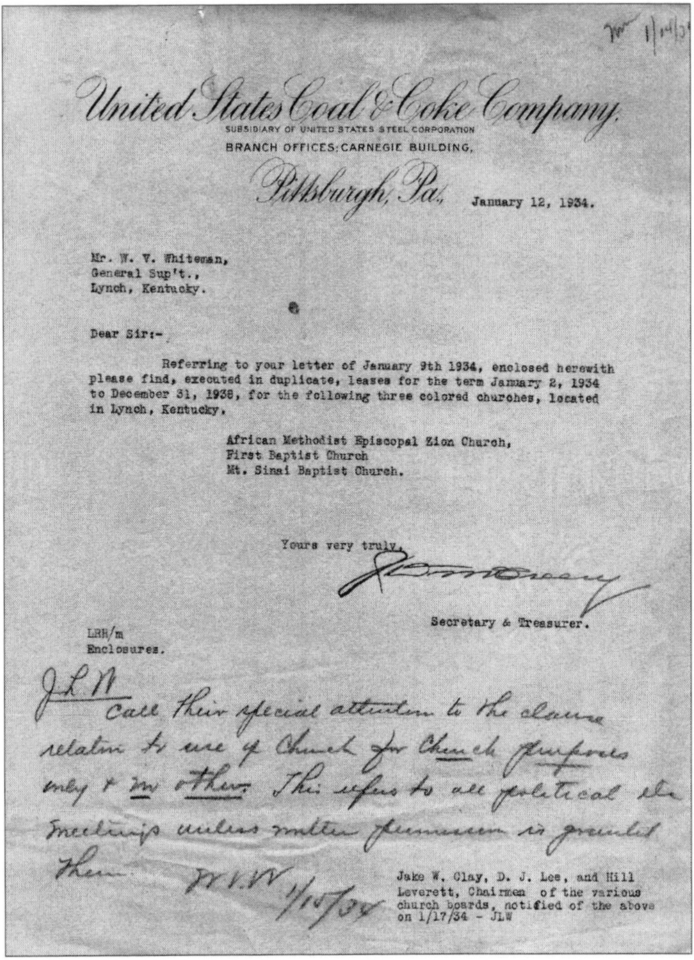

W 1/14/34

United States Coal & Coke Company.
SUBSIDIARY OF UNITED STATES STEEL CORPORATION
BRANCH OFFICES: CARNEGIE BUILDING.
Pittsburgh, Pa. January 12, 1934.

Mr. W. V. Whiteman,
General Sup't.,
Lynch, Kentucky.

Dear Sir:-

Referring to your letter of January 9th 1934, enclosed herewith please find, executed in duplicate, leases for the term January 2, 1934 to December 31, 1938, for the following three colored churches, located in Lynch, Kentucky.

African Methodist Episcopal Zion Church,
First Baptist Church
Mt. Sinai Baptist Church.

Yours very truly,

[signature]

Secretary & Treasurer.

LRH/m
Enclosures.

JLW
Call their special attention to the clause relating to use of Church for Church purposes only & no other. This refers to all political [illegible] meetings unless written permission is granted them. WVW 1/15/34

Jake W. Clay, D. J. Lee, and Hill Leverett, Chairmen of the various church boards, notified of the above on 1/17/34 - JLW

Letter from Pittsburgh-based US Steel officials warning Black church officials of "non-political" activities. William H. Turner Collection.

that their sojourn from central Alabama to the mountains of central Appalachia was just to work for a spell—a short trip—and from there they gained the strength it took to live on "the rough side of the mountain" so that the next generation would be able to see alternative Promised Lands, somewhere just beyond, wherever that might turn out to be.

CHAPTER 6

The Common Narrative of Black Appalachian Coal-Camp Families

ON JULY 20, 1946, our dad emerged from Portal 31 of the United States Steel Mine Works in Lynch, from beneath Big Black Mountain. He recounted the day to me.

As he lumbered along toward the bathhouse—again worn out from another twelve-hour shift—one of his best fishing buddies, who was heading into the mine, Mr. Dan Deadwyler, whom Dad always called Rap-Hair, relayed to Dad, "Punkin done give you another mouth to feed, another boy!"

After a shower in the colored section of the bathhouse, Dad walked up the hill from the bathhouse, past the post office, and into the "big store," the enormous, three-leveled, company-owned shopping-mall-under-one-roof that dominated the business district of Lynch. He would pick up a little something—"a box of candy, I think it was," he said—to take to the company-owned hospital, Notre Dame, where Mom had given birth to their fifth child in just over seven years. A bit over a quarter century later, the two of them came to Notre Dame University to see me receive a doctoral degree, handed to me by Father Theodore Hesburgh. Dad reminded me of that turn of fate, in real time, in South Bend in 1976.

Daddy was thirty years old when I was born. By then he had been a coal miner for sixteen years. He told my mama to name me after himself and his youngest brother, Hobert Hampton Turner, a World War II casualty killed in Italy a year and a half before I was born on February 10, 1945.

Our uncle Hobert joined the US Army Air Corps in Richmond, Virginia, in 1942. He died while a member of Company A, 317th Engineering Battalion—a Buffalo Soldier. His Ninety-Second Infantry Division was the only African American infantry division to see combat in Europe during World War II as part of the US Fifth Army fighting in the Italian campaign from 1944 to the war's end.

The Ninety-Second Infantry Division was formed on November 29, 1917, as the single Negro combat division organized by the US Army in a segregated military. The entire enlisted personnel of the Ninety-Second Division was made up exclusively of African Americans, then called Coloreds or Negroes, and both terms were sometimes not capitalized. The staff and field officers, the officers of the supply units, quartermaster corps, engineer corps, and artillery units, were all White.

When Dad's father died in 1929, leaving a wife and ten children, Dad quit school, at twelve, and began loading coal in a mine along Tom's Creek near his home in Coeburn, Virginia. He roamed about the region, from pit to dog hole, nomadlike, toiling in the mines in such places as Grundy, Virginia, and Matewan, West Virginia, the last of the dog-hole mines he worked until he heard about better wages and working conditions in Harlan County, Kentucky. He hitchhiked to Harlan County with everything he had "in one of those plaid soft-back suitcases." It was 1938.

Married when they were sixteen and twenty-two respectively, Punkin and Earl Turner became parents five times—to three girls and two boys—between 1939 and 1946. Later, between 1952 and 1958, they had three more boys. "Y'all's mama had a baby every nine months and thirty minutes" was the family wisecrack line told almost as frequently as the one that accounted for the fact that most families in our town had lots of children, all tightly clustered together. Dad quipped that the clamor of coal trains—whistles blaring and metal clanging as steel wheels moved over steel tracks—made people wake up early each morning, at a time when "it was too late to go back to sleep and too early to get out of bed."

Most of the mothers of my neighbors and friends had a "heap" of children, a heap defined as five or more offspring. In comparing notes with friends who also lived in two-bedroom houses occupied by at least seven people, many of their mothers, like ours, did not read the books that warned of the adverse effects that screaming and threatening and cursing had on the emotional growth and development of their children. This is not a blanket indictment: I carried a certain envy of some kids who also lived in crowded two-bedroom houses whose mothers did not hurl disheartening tirades at the little ones.

"She's a coal-camp woman, born and raised right here in Benham, boy, and you gotta understand how that upbringing made her a bit testy and bitter." Dad said that Mama "didn't really mean no harm with all that cussin' and fussin'." Plus, "She had five of you crumb snatchers in seven years, and I can imagine what that did to her sense of being calm—four kids in diapers at one time, starting at sixteen years old, done quit school, still in a coal camp. Yer mama is just a' bluffin' when she cusses. She just don't know no other way to stay in control of a noisy situation. Just mind what she says and do what she tells you, no matter how she says it." My first lesson on stress management. Good then that there was no Dr. Phil around or else I could lay my tendency to say a choice word or two myself on the reason that I sometimes imitate my mother. Just the opposite of taking personal responsibility for my own badly behaving ways.

Lynch and Benham were situated at the easternmost tapered points in a very narrow, funnel-like valley that opened out on its western flank and walled in by Big Black Mountain, which rose up on the northern and southern sides of the Looney Creek basin like two cusped hands. The town, its inhabitants, its mine-related buildings, and the houses all held close to the steep hillsides and flat spots nearest to the creek.

I can still hear quite clearly in my memories the intense noise and hustle-bustle. I can even see the night-lights of the coal camp where I lived for my first twenty years. It was a vibrant, very lively, and loud manufacturing space with an unbroken hubbub as the change-of-shift whistle blew every eight hours like an area-wide alarm clock. The mile-long line of railroad cars made a motorized clang-clang-clang rumbling sound—a chugging sound on top of screeching whistles as the brakes of the trains hissed. There was what sounded like an electrical transformer hum, all day and all night. A literal "buzz." A cloud of grime spewed from the diesel locomotives that routinely deposited an oily film on the windows and curtains and walls in the houses, on the cars on the streets, and on the clothes our mamas hung on the line to dry.

Coal dust was also in everybody's lungs—especially workers like Dad and Grandpa. Men—coal miners—spat a lot. I am sure it was saliva mixed with coal dust and Brown Mule or Red Man chewing tobacco. Dad did not chew tobacco. Instead, he was a Lucky Strike smoker who justified his nightly shot of moonshine or bourbon as though it was quite natural and necessary, a restorative potion that scrubbed his throat like a decontaminant mouthwash.

The trains that came and went twenty-four seven sounded loudest at night due to the way the mountain's elevations refracted the sound, depending on the temperature gradients. When empty—when they were returning from the coal-washing plant in Corbin, ninety miles away, through Harlan and Pineville—the coal cars, also called gondolas and hoppers, sounded distinctively different by rhythm, reverberation, and tone than when they were loaded with coal.

The diesel locomotives blew their horns in the typical one short, one long blasts that ricocheted and vibrated from each side of the mountains—up the hollow to the east towards Virginia, where the sound bounced off Big Black Mountain's highest point, which itself was effectively a 4,500-foot-high refracting wall. The sound of the whistles and screeching of the locomotives would come rolling, undulating, reverberating, and roiling back down the valley, repeating itself like the roar of a giant, mythical, sphinxlike lion that was sitting majestically atop the mountain.

The train stopped at the world's largest coal tipple in Lynch; its *clickety-clack-clickety-clack* sound came to a screeching halt when it made its stop, followed by a wave of *bump-bump-bump* sounds as the high-sided steel gondolas stretched back a mile or more past Benham. The tipple complex was the heart and lungs and guts of the physical infrastructure that gave and sustained life in Lynch.

Dad took me several times as a boy so I would know what went on at the tipple because he and the White man who ran the operation were good friends. Otherwise, being caught inside the tipple's perimeter was treated as though you had trespassed onto the grounds of Fort Knox. Black diamonds were sorted out here, boy—off limits!

The tipple complex was a massive sorting machine that organized the coal into various sizes when the cars dumped their contents from their bottoms into a hopper that came across Main Street, fifteen stories up from Portal 31 on a conveyor belt called an apron feeder. All sorts of shakers and screens and sifters sorted the coal into different sizes. It was then loaded onto cars based on whether it was going to be used for commercial purposes, such as at the Gary, Indiana, steel mills, or used up domestically, such as the type of coal we burned in our home stove for cooking or in the fire grates and stoves that provided heat. Coal, like people, was separated and classified according to its type and use: it was either called block, egg, nut, or stoker.

By the time Dad died in 1987, my parents had raised—legally adopted—two of my nephews who had been born in New Jersey, where my two oldest sisters, Peggy and Marie, had moved to find work after high school in 1958 and 1960 respectively. "We took 'em in after our girls broke up with their husbands. Boys have to be raised by a man!" Dad declared. No questions asked. That was that. Two more brothers. Not old enough to understand, both Richard, Peggy's son, and Frederick, the son of Marie, referred to our mother as "Ma" and called their mothers by their first names—as though they were siblings. Not uncommon among Black families in our neck of the woods.

A typical Black coal-mining family, our parents stayed married a year short of a half century and raised ten children. There was nothing exceptional nor remarkable about our Black Mountain family. Like most single miners, when Dad arrived in Lynch, he lived in a boardinghouse, a family home that was authorized by the company to rent rooms to single miners. He shared a room with three other men; there were only two beds available because they worked different

Girls walking by US Steel coal tipple in Lynch en route to school, 1950. William H. Turner Collection.

shifts. On weekends, they swapped between who would sleep on the floor. The lady of the house in the family he boarded with for almost a year supplied two meals a day and laundry service—a twenty-five-dollars-a-month package. Granny ran such an enterprise in which she and our grandfather also sold bootleg liquor, an add-on to his coal miner's stingy income. On weekends, young miners—Dad included—rubbed shoulders and bent elbows at Granny's while listening to her teenage daughter perform ragtime, jazz, blues, and gospel on the upright Wurlitzer piano that she was taught to play by one of the first teachers at Lynch Colored School, one of Grannie's boarders, Mable Hardison Parker Smith.

My father was self-aware of his "mountain-ness," considering himself distinct from and different from the Whites whom he'd known all his life, some of whom he sometimes called "everyday peckerwoods." *Peckerwood* was, no doubt, a racial slur used by Blacks in reference to the really poor Whites, the ones who didn't live in the coal camps but lived instead in the isolated hollows, the genuine hillbillies who carry perhaps the most onerous epithet: "poor White trash." I also heard the older Blacks refer to some White people as *hoogies*, pronounced "who-gees." *Cracker* was an insider word in the community too, and later, in the sixties, the wickedly mean word *honkey* could be heard. *Peckerwood* was about the foulest I ever heard from my father, although he never preceded it with a profane adjective.

I often wondered if Dad was the only Black man around who knew the rhymes and verses—and sang—"Your Cheatin' Heart" and Tennessee Ernie Ford's "Hey, Good Lookin'." Truth is, Dad's was a southwest Virginia dialect rather than a central Alabama one, like most of his Black contemporaries. Our friends always said that Dad "sounded White," which was natural for him; after all, like his mother and grandmother, he grew up in a Black version of Loretta Lynn's Butcher Holler! For years now, linguists have recognized Ebonics, or what is called African American Vernacular English. Dad employed a variant on Ebonics that is peculiar to the southern Appalachians. Call it Y'allbonics!

He put *h* on the word *it*, such as in "Hit don't matter to me, Buddy!" He pronounced the *i* in the words *night*, *right*, and *fight* with the hint of a hard *a* tossed in, so they would come out as "naight," "raight," and "faight." *Ice* and *rice* rhymed, but Dad peppered both with the tone of the word *eye* so that *ice* sounded like "eye-ce." Same with *nice*, which came out as "nyce." Dad referred to someone whom he considered not too bright as "ig'nert," usually qualified with the finisher "as hell." And to hear his pronunciation, you would think that a blaze on the hillside was the place from which the three wise men in the Bible came: "afar." *Wire* came out as "war," and the fire tower on top of Black Mountain rolled out of his mouth as "far tar." His truck sometimes needed "tars." Whenever I acted disgracefully or shamefully, Dad would say, "You got the crud, don't you, boy?" Of course, *crud* was also the Appalachian-assigned word for a sinus infection or a wet cold.

Of course, like any self-respecting central Appalachian native, Dad pronounced the word *Appalachia* with a short *a* sound and with *latch* as the third syllable. Appalachia, as in, "He threw an apple at cha!" He never referred to himself or anyone else as an Appalachian, but we knew we were close to his hometown when we went through the town of Appalachia, Virginia.

Sometimes he would compare himself—locate himself—in a different place as compared to other African American miners who had migrated to eastern Kentucky from Alabama, a place he considered depressed and bereft of even the slightest scintilla of civility, especially when it came to the treatment of Black people. He maintained that the lifeways, the customs, and especially what he considered the unpolished manner of speech exhibited by many of the Blacks with Alabama roots reflected on their being raised in the Heart of Dixie. On the other hand, he would talk, with a warped sense of smug, about how in his native land—Virginia—the Black people exhibited a relatively heightened level of good manners. I never knew the basis of the comparison.

"I always thought Virginia was better to Negroes, at least, better than Alabama," he would say. But then he would add, almost in the same breath, "Shit, then again, all of us ended up in the same damn place, working like a damn slave for nothing, never to get ahead. Didn't really matter where you were from. Like they say, when you're layin' face down in a creek, it don't matter how deep the water is."

My father also often and proudly boasted of our family's ties to Nat Turner, which were unsubstantiated; but he banked the validity of his claim to being related to the man who led the most well-known Virginia slave rebellion on the fact that his own father was named Samuel Alexander Turner, which was also the first name of the man who owned Nat, who systematically butchered White civilians in the 1831 uprising. I've yet to research that element of our family history, but I know that Dad really believed the tie existed. He once expressed how self-contradictory I was to have a close, personal tie to Alex Haley and yet I "never did a study" of my own family roots. I am still working on it.

Lynch, Kentucky—like many settlements in eastern Kentucky that were developed by coal companies in the early twentieth century—was named after the president of the company that owned the town. Thomas Lynch was the president of US Steel and Coke Company in 1917.

As a prying youngster, I often asked my grandmother why the Black people in her generation pronounced Lynch as "Lanch." Then, after her countless scowls at me whenever I asked the question or tried to pry an answer out of her, she said one day that I would figure it out when I got older. Sure enough, when I got older, at the time I heard some men talking about "what they did to that Emmett Till boy," it hit me. "Worse than ah' lynching," one whispered dolefully.

Imagine: Black people so sensitive to mob-executed violence that they chose, subconsciously maybe, to change the way they uttered the word *Lynch*, not to matter that it was the president of US Steel after whom the town was named. To say *lynch* so that it rhymed with *inch*, at a conscious level, called to mind the memory of Black men being tortured, sometimes because some White woman said she was unhappy with something she claimed a Black man said or did, or didn't say or do, to her. Out of respect to these elders, I have pronounced the name of my hometown as "Lanch," and I take the time to explain why.

CHAPTER 7

Blacks Moving between Central Alabama and Central Appalachia

JUST AS my young grandchildren who live in the Houston, Texas, area never talk about their conscious awareness of growing up at ground zero of the goings-on of the petrochemical industry, neither did I, as a boy, realize that I lived in a town that was a corporate fiefdom, that US Steel, in its heyday from the late 1930s through the 1970s, dominated the economy the way Walmart, Google, Facebook, and Amazon do today. I knew—but I never knew why—there were no other sources of employment than the US Steel–owned coal mines. I now have a comparative reference point to how things were in my hometown when the company suddenly shuttered the mines, shut down the physical plant around the town center, sold all the houses, and pulled up stakes; things came to a grinding halt. The comparison rolled up to me when the COVID pandemic came down like a lead curtain in the spring of 2020.

The sinister side of US Steel was always fresh in the mind of Mr. Benjamin Long—also known by his nickname, Ben

"Short" Long—the longtime "rack man" at the Pool Room, which was five houses down the same side of Second where our family lived for sixty years. He invited me into his circle, as his assistant, with my dad's accord, when I was ten. When the outcome of a game of eight ball being played was about to happen, I would exclaim, "Rack man, come and get the Black man!" I got to be surprisingly good at pool but by no means in the same league as those whom Mr. Ben would say "could solid shoot!" But, by age fifteen, when I could hold my own with the best of them, Mr. Ben would often bet on my game and give me part of our winnings. When there wasn't much going on, he and I would just sit and talk, sometimes for hours on end, along with his buddy Mr. August Miles, the superintendent of the Sunday school at our church, who lived three houses down from us. I listened to these old men courteously, respectfully, and with reflective, reverential intent.

Mr. Ben's father worked in a mine in the late 1880s near Hueytown, Alabama, a few miles southwest of Birmingham, where Mr. Ben was born in 1895. Mr. Ben came to Lynch to work for US Steel in 1920.

Like my grandparents—and my father, to the extent that he acquired only three years of formal schooling—Mr. Ben was poorly educated: he neither read nor wrote nor counted with ease or fluency. But, also like my grandparents and my father, Mr. Ben was nobody's fool. He understood perfectly and could articulate in clear terms how the system worked that got him into the coal mines. He told me how his father did not choose mining, but that mining chose him.

> Back in them days, you gotta remember my grandparents were born slaves, and my daddy was on a sharecropping farm back then, the 1880s and 1890s. My mama told me how my daddy got rounded up with a bunch of other

> colored boys one day when I was a baby, maybe four or five years old, and they wuz all sent off to jail, locked up. Said they wuz idle and panhandling. He served his time, more than two years, working in a coal mine—for nothing, no money. It was what they called convict labor. My daddy worked for US Steel before I did. I knowed about them before I come up here with the man who worked for them, he'd come down there and talked us into coming up here, brought eighteen of us up here in a big truck bed along with a bunch of watermelons and vegetables he sold to the Black peoples already here.

Mr. Ben's stories described the lives and the deaths of thousands of Black men who worked in mines that were owned by US Steel in Alabama at the turn of the twentieth century. Untold numbers of them perished in the custody of the state, housed in horrific conditions in convict coal camps in Alabama. It is easy to frame Mr. Ben inside a book Dad gave me to read when I was fourteen. I still have the book, sixty years later, now tattered and torn and yellowed: Langston Hughes's 1933 *The Ways of White Folks*. Black coal miners like Mr. Ben and Mr. August embodied Hughes's character Cora, who knew "something about the teeth in the trap of economic circumstance."

The Southern states might have lost the Civil War, but during Reconstruction, they passed a series of interconnected laws that locked Blacks into a system of dependence that was not much different than slavery. These laws, commonly known as Black Codes, became the basis for what is known as the "Jim Crow" way of life. Put in place as early as 1865, immediately following the abolition of slavery, the Black Codes enforced segregation that specified when, where, and how Black people could work and for how much. Jail terms were given out for the smallest trumped-up charges, and, of course, unable to pay the fees, Blacks were sentenced into forced-labor-camp arrangements, sometimes back on the very same plantations where they had been born or to lumber companies or to coal-mining operations. An all-American gulag system. What we refer to currently as the mass incarceration of Blacks—the prison-industrial complex—had its origins in Alabama and other Southern states more than a century ago.

In 2008, Douglas A. Blackmon published *Slavery by Another Name*, which thoroughly sketched the use of Black forced labor by the US Steel Corporation in Alabama at the turn of the twentieth century. The well-received book won the Pulitzer Prize for General Nonfiction in 2009 and was adapted as a documentary film for PBS, also titled *Slavery by Another Name*.

In effect, by the time Black people—and their native White and immigrant compatriots—were getting settled in Lynch, US Steel had been in the lead of structuring an economy that transitioned agricultural slavery into its industrial equivalent. The use of convicts as laborers in their coal mines was nothing less than the Middle Passage between the two systems. The first Middle Passage is well recorded—in Haley's book of family memory *Roots*, for example. Gorée Island, off the coast of Dakar, Senegal, is known for its role in the Atlantic slave trade between 1536 until 1848, when slavery was abolished in Senegal. In this second Middle Passage, the passage from agricultural to industrial-labor peonage, thousands of young Black men were arrested—calculatingly and systematically—given extremely long sentences, and then leased by the state and municipalities to coal companies who put them into the heart of their coal mines in the innermost Heart of Dixie: underground.

Between Jefferson County, Alabama (Birmingham), and

Harlan County, Kentucky (Lynch), US Steel amassed great wealth. *Black Coal Miners in America: Race, Class, and Community Conflict, 1780–1980*, by history professor Ronald Lewis of West Virginia University and published in 1987, details the use of Black convict labor in Alabama coal mines during Reconstruction. Lewis gave a picture of the practice as though it was as tortuous a slice of US history as slavery itself.

As late as 2011, Mark Melvin, an inmate at the Kilby Correctional Facility in Montgomery County, Alabama, was banned from reading Blackmon's book *Slavery by Another Name* by the Alabama Department of Corrections. The authorities believed inmates might be incited to violence if they read the book. This is the same Alabama prison that housed the Scottsboro Boys, the nine African American youth who were arrested and sentenced to death for the rape of two White women in 1931 in this community in the Alabama piney woods. Over the years, I talked to several Black men in Harlan County about their personal ties to these wrongly convicted youth and how the incident influenced their migration, their escape, to Harlan County. After all, for a young Black man in the 1930s, a coal job in the backwoods of Kentucky, a place that he'd never heard of, offered an unheard-of level of economic and social security compared to being in the piney woods of north Alabama. But there was a deep, dark price to pay for going into a coal-mining job at this time, an out-and-out dilemma: damned if you do and damned if you don't.

If the production of coal at the turn of the twentieth century could be compared to the role of computerized technologies in the current age, Lynch could be said to be the level base of the Silicon Valley. Indeed, what Bill Gates is to the Information Age is what John D. Rockefeller, Andrew Carnegie, and J. P. Morgan—coal barons all—were to the Industrial Age, when King Coal held sway at the top of the industrial food chain. Silicon, the most abundant element next to oxygen in the earth's crust, is a by-product of coal mining, the major precipitant of black lung disease, which most coal miners have after less than five years in the mines. Silvery silicon particles are constantly inhaled by coal miners, causing scarring in their lung tissue, which turns black as the condition worsens. Coal miners spit a lot of dark phlegm.

An estimated nine hundred, mainly African American, tunnel workers died of acute silicosis, a lung disorder caused by prolonged inhalation of silica dust, after working on a tunnel project in Fayette County, West Virginia, in the early 1930s. Their deaths at Hawk's Nest, near Gauley Bridge, marked one of the worst industrial "accidents" in US history. Hundreds of these workers, who had been recruited from Alabama to the Gauley Bridge tunnel work, migrated deeper into the Pocahontas coalfields of southern West Virginia to work as miners after the disaster at Hawk's Nest. A critical mass of them went to Gary, Keystone, and Welch, all in McDowell County.

Like all the coal towns in central Appalachia, Lynch literally sprang up in the second decade of the 1900s from within the nothingness of the backcountry where only virgin woodlands had existed less than two decades before.

US Steel first hewed from these mountains a temporary work camp. Then they completed spur lines to connect the mining camp to the main railroad lines—the Louisville and Nashville Railroad, for example. With the right-of-way issues solved, the company followed with railcars filled with carts and buggies, straps and buckles, all the fittings for work mules, and the equipment, provisions, wagons, machinery, and tools necessary to fashion the entire town, which included a massive sawmill facility used to tailor the locally harvested

Lynch under construction, 1918. Southeast Community College Appalachian Collection, Cumberland, KY.

lumber to build more than a thousand houses. The designation *coal camp* derived from these temporary encampments, which is all they really were. The label *coal camp* stuck, with all its implied meanings, undertones, and color. Our house was in Camp 1 in Lynch, which had six camps overall.

From the time the mines were ready for excavating coal, labor recruiters for the mining companies met ships loaded with European migrants at Ellis Island in New York and transported them straight to Pennsylvania's coalfields and on over the Alleghenies into West Virginia, Virginia, and Kentucky. Other mining-camp recruiters fanned throughout the upper South, where they found easy entrée to the Black sharecroppers, farmhands, and experienced miners, both free and convicts. Our mother's parents were out in the fields of central Georgia in 1918. Most of our neighbors' families were brought in from central Alabama. Central Appalachia waited for them with open arms and proceeded to fill their powerful bronze hands with picks and shovels.

The bituminous coal that these people unearthed—first with picks and shovels—fed the fiery ovens that produced coke, which was necessary for making iron and steel. Coal was the primary resource that fed the Industrial Revolution. Later, the metals needed for military armaments in World Wars I and II were fabricated using coal. Job opportunities in the coal mines of central Appalachia rose and fell with global economic and political developments, especially military stockpiles and wars.

Legions of people with the same backgrounds as my grandparents escaped from sharecropping—and sometimes from Alabama coal camps where they were leased to coal companies from the state's prisons—to eastern Kentucky to work in places with names like Ages, Arjay, Benham, Black Joe, Black Mountain, Black Star, Bon Jellico, Caywood, Corbin, Coxton, Cumberland, East Bernstadt, Evarts, Fleming-Neon, Fourmile, Harlan, Hazard, Highsplint, Hulen, Jenkins, Kenvir, Kitts, Lenarue, Lily, London, Lynch, Manchester, Middlesboro, McRoberts, Pineville, Redfox, Verda, Vicco, Williamsburg, and Wheelwright. In Harlan County alone, fifty-four coal camps opened and closed during the great coal boom: the Harlan Renaissance.

Most coal camps in eastern Kentucky, southwest Virginia, and southern West Virginia were hurriedly built. Most were intentionally temporary in nature, as the objective of the small companies was to get in, get as much as they could as cheaply as they could, and get out. On to the next place, the next hollow—high profits from short-term investments. In these relatively small, family-owned enterprises, the investments made by the business operators for workers' housing, health care, and educational and recreational needs were minimal at best.

On the other hand, there were coal camps like Lynch, Benham, Jenkins, and Wheelwright in eastern Kentucky, which were known as "captive mines," meaning that these plants were owned by large outside corporations that used the coal mined for their own production purposes—to make steel—rather than selling it on the open market. There were also substantial corporate-owned company towns in southwest Virginia, such as Appalachia, Big Stone Gap, Clinchco, Dante, Norton, and Stonega. But it was southern West Virginia—the Pocahontas coalfields, from one place to another like Bluefield, Beckley, Gary, Keystone, Man, Matewan, and Welch, the really *big* operations—to which the greatest numbers of Blacks migrated. They came from the uplands of South Carolina, but more came from central Alabama.

Of these coal camps, the most highly capitalized locations were Lynch, Kentucky, and Gary, West Virginia, both owned by US Steel, one of the first billion-dollar companies in the United States, headquartered in Pittsburgh, Pennsylvania. Lynch was the family name of the president of US Steel. Over the years, the coal operations in Lynch and Gary became part of the behemoth money machine of J. P. Morgan's company, which later acquired Marathon Oil. US Steel is known today as USX on the US stock exchange.

J. P. Morgan's planners divided the then-uninhabited place they called Lynch into six numbered sections. Our four-room, two-story, and two-family duplex house was among the one thousand or so residential structures built in what was called Number 1. There were four boardinghouses constructed for single men. Lynch had three theaters; the big company store, with its three branch locations; a three-story, full-service hospital; and a bank and post office building—all in the part of town called Number 5.

At the big store, miners could buy a car from the company's garage and have it serviced at the company gas station. The children went to one of two schools (one for the Whites, one for the Blacks), with a well-kept baseball and football field, near to the Lynch Colored School. There were two bowling alleys; several dance halls; ice cream parlors; a fire station; an electrical generation plant; a company office complex; a very large bathhouse divided for Black and White miners; and finally, the well-designed, elegant, and stylish company-owned 133-room hotel, which White businessmen visiting Lynch stayed in. Most of the service staff at the Lynch Hotel were Black.

Thomas Kelemen wrote his master's thesis in 1972 for the sociology department at the University of Kentucky on the development of Lynch. He condensed the evolution of the place—from 1917 to 1930—from a stark wilderness to the planet's biggest coal-producing center: "Lynch could lay little claim to being an ideal community, but it could make a strong case in the 1920s for being the greatest coal camp in the world. Lynch not only had the largest coal tipple in the world, but it was also—for a time between 1930 and 1945—the largest coal camp in the world."

In Lynch and in Gary, West Virginia, US Steel invested heavily in permanent structures—many still standing—made of cut stone, brick, or concrete.

The company put its reputation at stake, and consequently, according to Kelemen, "there was competition for good employees, the architecture was more ornate, the housing more substantial, and commercial buildings included an abundance of recreational facilities."

By the time I was born, Lynch had a population of just under twelve thousand people, representing thirty-eight nationalities. Almost a third of the people in town were Black. While growing up, except when I read something or saw some pictures in *Life* magazine—or went somewhere outside Lynch, which was quite infrequent—I thought that most children were growing up in a town just like ours! Black Mountain was high and all-enveloping, and I could only imagine what was beyond it. That we were but little cogs in a global economic wheel of fortune never occurred to me. I am sure my dad, an ardent trade unionist, had an abiding sense of class consciousness for a working man, but I know too that he was a practical person, so he never framed things in those terms. He had a good, logical grasp of where we were in the larger scheme of things.

I never heard Dad or any other mindful men and women refer to our situation as "welfare capitalism," but most of the adults were aware enough to know that our surroundings in Lynch—in contrast to nearby towns that were not "model"—were designed by US Steel not only to keep their workers happy and assure the steady production of coal but also to prevent or forestall unionization for as long as possible. A generation before President Roosevelt's New Deal, coal companies like US Steel and International Harvester put in place complex codes and social programs and collective bargaining agreements that were designed to instill a sense of security in their workers. This industrial paternalism extended to the company "taking care of" its employees in the broadest sense of protectiveness, even to the point of being overly solicitous and condescending. US Steel—in an annual arrangement with the United Mine Workers of America, the union to which Lynch miners belonged—would bring together families, outside its big store, to pass out baskets of nuts, fruit, and candy at Christmas time.

US Steel in Lynch and International Harvester in Benham built, staffed, and maintained state-of-the-art health-care facilities. I was born in the hospital owned and run by US Steel in Lynch. It certainly was not dubbed socialized medicine, but it was indeed free health care for all—all who worked for the company. Employment by the company was permanent, until it was not.

CHAPTER 8

Close-Knit Central Appalachian Coal-Camp Black Communities

LIVING IN LYNCH through my twentieth year left mainly pleasant memories for me and for most of my peers, as many have told me over the years. For the past fifty years, I have attended forty of the reunions held by the Eastern Kentucky Social Club—a confederation of Blacks born and raised mainly in Harlan County who migrated mainly to the Midwest and the north central states starting in the mid-1940s.

I wrote the afterword to *African American Miners and Migrants: The Eastern Kentucky Social Club*, a book by Thomas Wagner and Phillip Obermiller. This first-rate work contains and summarizes interviews with dozens of Black people from the area, all affirming a deep attachment to their mountain roots. Reassembling in my mind the place, its people, and the signal events of our collective existence over the past half century is easy because the arrangements and substance of life were simple—and very, very, very routine and predictable.

Men waiting at Lynch Colored School for start of Masonic lodge meeting, 1951. Photo by Robert "Smokypipe" Rutherford. William H. Turner Collection.

Routine is a very meaningful word because life in company-owned coal towns was, by design, highly structured and orderly. Such towns were the prototypes of socially engineered, or planned, communities. The firmness about order—sameness and kept schedules and patterns—started with each workday.

It was not like so-and-so went to work here, in that direction, on that road, and so-and-so went there, in that direction. In Lynch, everybody, all the Black men except the schoolteachers and preachers, did the same line of work that supported virtually every family. They all generally went to the same place, traveling along the singular route—the main street through town, Main Street. For the most part, among Blacks, our mothers were homemakers. Not only were there no places—industrial plants or manufacturing facilities or businesses—where Black women could find work, but they had enough to do at home. I stuck my foot completely down my throat in an interview with the lady who lived across the street from us, Miss Annie Mae Hall, who, just like our mother, had eight children, when I worded the question, "You have never held a full-time job, have you, Miss Annie Mae?" With a hands-on-hips air of genuine seriousness, she snorted her reply: "Billbo, if you don't think raising this many chur'en and taking care of my husband wasn't a full-time job, you ain't as smart as I thought you were!"

The most well-known Black person in the United States when my grandparents arrived in Lynch was Booker T. Washington, even though he had died five years earlier, in 1915. Booker T. Washington's father worked in the salt mines near Malden, West Virginia, in the Charleston metro area. As a teenager just at the end of the Civil War, Booker T. became the live-in houseboy and servant in the home of the richest and most prominent White family in Malden, the Ruffners. Ironic that Washington's autobiography, published in 1901, from Tuskegee, Alabama, where many of these migrants came from, was titled *Up from Slavery*. Indeed, Blacks in Appalachian coal camps in 1915 were just that: up—just a tad—from slavery.

As strange as it might sound, as far I could tell, nobody's daddy in Lynch and Benham didn't work! The right to live in Lynch, in any of the residences—and that was everywhere—depended upon the man being employed by the coal company, US Steel. In coal towns, the right to live there, and the right to work there, evolved unevenly. Working in the mine—for the company or its associated businesses, such as the company store—was not simply a way to make a living; there was no other choice of employment, at least for the Black people, except teaching or preaching, although there were a half dozen or so involved in health-care work. There were Blacks who worked as orderlies in the hotel and as the help in the Whites-only country club. However, the teachers and preachers also worked at the mercy of the company. After all, the company owned and operated the schools, and the company built churches and approved—or disapproved—who the congregation selected as the pastor. Some Black women worked in the homes of the company's Whites-only management class, most of whom lived in a section of town high up on a hill that was called, fittingly, "Silk Stocking Row."

Daily styles and courses of action, and practically all connections and relationships between people, took place in the backdrop of this highly structured setting. To be sure, there was a place for everything and a place for everyone. Personal and social discipline and uniformity were virtually ordained, monitored, and controlled by the company. While growing up in this place where virtually all elements of our lives were designed and controlled by the company, I saw virtually no men who were idle or unemployed, because once they were "cut off" from their jobs, men and their families were compelled to get out of town.

My life—and the lives of all the Black people I knew at home—was bound inside a web of matched lifestyles and similar expectations and goals. We were anchored and fixed, so to speak, in a finite place, in both space and time. It seemed that everybody knew where everybody else was or was supposed to be, what they were doing or were supposed to be doing when, and who else would likely be at the same place, at the same time, doing the same thing.

The same shape and pattern of 99 percent of the dwellings also accounted for the sense of order and sameness in Lynch. There were slight differences in the exterior color of the houses, but the type of house everyone lived in did not vary appreciably. The other 1 percent was made up of the bosses' relatively massive residences. Otherwise, most of the houses were pretty much the same—a kitchen, a living room, two bedrooms upstairs, a screened porch with a swing suspended from the ceiling, and yards that were roughly equal size. The houses were set closely together, in neat rows, equidistant from the narrow streets where cars were parked on one side, making for traffic jams on certain days.

"A man can't fart around here unless somebody is there to hear it and smell it," Dad used to say, not always jokingly. We—like most families—lived in a duplex. Our stairwell was in the exact mirrored spot as our conjoined neighbors', the Browns. Our mothers often started communications with a knock on the wall followed by planting her ear onto the cardboard, paper-thin wall and talking, as in, *knock-knock*, "Hey Mae Cee, I need some sugar; Billy will be right around there." That very same simple way of communicating between neighbors continued after we got a telephone in 1960, which for the first two years was a party line.

Through the wall, any verbal communication louder than normal family arguments and the dressing-down of the children—and especially the occasional boom-and-bang sounds which signified a fight—could be heard, clear as a bell. We could always count on either Mr. Brown or his wife—Mom's best friend for life, Miss Mae Cee—to come around on those infrequent occasions when things got out of hand between Dad and Mom. Likewise, our parents went around to mediate on the Brown side of the house when the sounds of flared tempers seeped through the walls. Thin walls made for good, strong, loving, and caring neighbors.

Work in the coal mines, during the boom cycles, was regular and regularizing, and, quite frankly, it was coercing. Truth told, the viewpoints and ways of being that most of us developed, the way we behaved, our personal habits, and the customs we came to appreciate—our very inclinations—were related to the fact that the community, in its totality, had been intentionally designed and managed. Much later, in my first sociology class in college, I learned about social engineering.

By cultural design and historical retention, there was something else that restrained the children's ignoble impulses and whims: there was always somebody, some neighbor in a darkened window or somewhere, who always saw everything. It was commonly practiced among such good neighbors who looked out for each other to inform one another of what their children were doing; and if it was troublesome, that snooping neighbor exercised their right to chastise and even discipline the offender right there in the street in front of everybody. Immediately afterward, the adult "correction officer" would go directly to the parents of the now-put-right child and tell them what happened and what they did about it. Usually what they did to discipline the child, depending on the severity of the infraction, was doubled by the parents. It took a village to raise—and sometimes to raze—a child.

Was coal-camp life like being in prison? I did not think so, but I did know that things could have been much worse. Early on, the only road that led into Lynch was gated, monitored by company security guards. But still, my grandparents and parents often said things that indicated to me that they were doing much better financially than their parents and grandparents had done, such as how our grandfather said often that

Lynch was where he got his "first real paying job." Until he came to work for US Steel in 1921, he worked on his father's sharecropper plot.

I also knew that there were people in places—over the mountain, somewhere—who lived "better" than the way we lived. We knew that there were people who had better things, like better houses, better cars, and who probably ate better food and went to better schools than we did, but our folks never told us that those people, White or Black, in those better situations were better *than* we were.

"The cow must graze where it is tied," Dad would often say, telling me in various ways that I would get to greener pastures, that life would get better, and that the best thing to do was to do my very best with what we had in the present and the future would take care of itself. All that said, at the end of every day of my young life, for the most part, I went to bed with a feeling of comfort, safety, and security. I had the immeasurable benefit of knowing that we had a stable family, as did most of my contemporaries, neighbors, and close friends. One thing that stands out—above all other memories about life in this coal town—was the virtual sanctity of family life. I do not remember any married couple in our network going through what is known commonly today as a legal divorce. For better or for worse, or because they had no alternatives, they stuck it out.

The strong stress on family togetherness—which could be seen and felt deeply—was a carryover from the rural Southern tradition of my grandparents' generation. But coal-camp couples also stayed married, despite many difficulties and problems, because maintaining the family unit was in the best interests of everybody—the topmost reason being the loss of access to credit at the company store and the loss of a place to live if the couple divorced.

Reece Mabry, a coal miner and the author's maternal great uncle, and his family at home in Beckley, WV, 1954. William H. Turner Collection.

Blood relatives surrounded me, but to a much lesser extent than was true for a lot of the kids I grew up with whose families were from Alabama. Our Uncle Robert—Dad's brother—and his family lived nearby, a mile or so away in Camp 5, at the top of Gobbler's Knob. Mama's parents lived but a stone's throw away. Hardly a month passed that Dad did not take me along when he drove to Coeburn, Virginia, to visit his mother and his brother, Uncle Roy, a master carpenter and brick mason—the one who, along with his wife, Aunt Mae, raised thirteen kids. Uncle Roy left coal mining after an explosion caused the loss of his right eye as a teenager in the same mine he took Dad to work in when he was thirteen.

I remember the many sets of brothers and sisters and cousins in my father's generation who'd come to eastern Kentucky from a fan-shaped district of Alabama that stretched from Birmingham northwest to Florence, Muscle Shoals, and Athens and northeast to Anniston, Scottsboro, Fort Payne, and Gadsden. How often I heard their memories of Eutaw, Butler, Selma, Opelika, Phenix City, and Leeds: the Hearts of Dixie. The US Census recorded 210 colored people in Harlan County in 1880, but by 1920, their numbers increased to nearly four thousand. In the next three decades—by 1950—there were almost forty thousand Blacks living within a seventy-five-mile radius of Harlan County, and six in ten of them listed Alabama as their state of birth. It's called chain migration nowadays, but these Black nomads from the same region of Alabama often sent back for their brothers, uncles, and cousins, who readily came to take one of the many miners' jobs that were readily available. Within a generation, from 1920 to 1940, hundreds of Blacks, intergenerational families, many from the same town or region in central Alabama, called some space in eastern Kentucky home; in our case, that was Lynch, which became the place where the largest number of them congregated.

Membership records from churches and stacks of obituaries I have collected over the past four decades show a high number of families in which two brothers married two sisters, which made them related in plural ways. The children of such unions were called "double cousins."

Up through the mid-1950s, Lynch was a very compact and densely populated place, its overall number of residents consisting of many groups of these companion, blood-related families with common geographical roots in central Alabama. Family, neighborhood, and other social networks overlapped. Kinship and fellowship and membership in the same organizations and clubs—and especially churches—made it easy for people to observe and interact with each other frequently and intimately. Love was not just a word. Extended families stretched from one end of the town—the county—to the other.

Reports—better known as chinwag and gossip—about what other people did, however personal or intimate, were quickly and efficiently recounted and conveyed. Modern social media platforms like Instagram and Snapchat could well have been modeled after the word-of-mouth portals in Appalachian coal camps. Like the circuitry in a digital gadget, or the channels in a television or on a radio dial, the Black community was alive with the exchanges of information, and, depending on the reliability of the source, it might be accurate and spot-on, or it might be deceitful, untruthful, just a flat-out lie. It was hard for a person or a family to be isolated. Everybody knew everybody, and everybody knew everybody else's business. Everything and everybody were linked in some way or another. While the town was literally gated, and the police kept tabs on all movement and supposedly prohibited activities such as bootlegging and gambling and plenteous other earthly stuff that went on just beneath the surface of civility, Lynch was an all-American town.

Social class distinctions were of little consequence, and social spacing was not possible for all practical purposes. For most Black mountain people that I knew in the 1950s and 1960s, being poor was a state of mind. It had to be hard to keep the small houses—so full of children—from not reflecting their scarcities outwardly, but most people I knew managed very well. A family's reputation was built on what they did with what little they had. Cleanliness and neatness and orderliness differentiated families. It was not uncommon to see just anybody's mama sweeping a barren yard with a broom, often made of hedges, a shrub tied to a long stick. Being dirt poor had nothing to do with being nasty and filthy and trifling. Clearly, you could clean dirt. The morning ritual of emptying the family slop jar in the outhouse was a routine way of greeting the neighbors.

We got a television when I was sixteen, in 1962, and Dad put a bathroom in the house the next year. It was not strange to see aluminum foil or a clothes hanger on the top of previously owned black-and-white television sets, which were often turned on and off, and the channel was changed, with wire pliers. Nor did anybody realize how deprived they were because the children were well scrubbed, often two at a time, every Saturday night in a galvanized tub next to a potbellied stove in the kitchen. I am practically certain that everybody's mama in our network kept their couch covered in plastic and their children covered in Vaseline petroleum jelly.

We went barefoot a lot in the summer, and a favorite winter's evening game before the first five of us went to bed—in the same room—was to stand next to the open fireplace, let the butts of our pajamas get hot, then run to sit on the bed. Preheat to 250 and go to bed. Sometimes, on those cold, windy nights, Mama and Daddy would stand together in the doorway to our ten-by-fifteen-foot bedroom and watch us romp and scamper from the coal-burning fireplace to the beds—three girls in the queen-sized bed against one wall, two boys in the other, a single rollaway bed, each with his feet in the other's face. Brothers and sisters. I learned in those years how to listen to women and to respect them.

Coal-town life and culture had a consistent "make do" refrain. We developed great measures of inner strength and pride, which, I am convinced, made later challenges—faced in the cities to which we migrated—trivial and petty by comparison. If you can make it here, you can make it anywhere.

Admittedly then, even if it was illusory, there was a genuine sense of comfort and security. There were wide-open spaces, including in peoples' minds, where you could always be with someone with whom you could be at ease, whom you could love, and who loved and protected you. Most of the kids I knew, like me, did not leave Harlan County for any length of time, even during the two weeks our fathers got a vacation from the mines, which shut down the week before and after the Fourth of July. We took school-sponsored trips every spring, sometimes to the Cincinnati Zoo, but regularly and repeatedly, we went to Cumberland Falls or Dr. Thomas Walker State Park—both near Corbin, Kentucky, a notorious sundown town, legendary for a 1919 incident when all the Black families (at least 250 people) were railroaded out of town, literally.

A *Father Knows Best*–style family vacation to Myrtle or Panama Beach was something for Whites only, those who could afford such extravagances. As far as I knew, none of the Black families could afford such luxuries as a vacation on the beach. The nearest beaches were hundreds of miles away, in South Carolina or Florida, and besides the cost associated with going to such distant places, we were barred from most beaches anyway. When *Jet* magazine ran a story on the *Green Book*, that fabled guide used by Black interstate travelers during the days of segregation, I remember glossing right over it because its contents did not apply to us.

When we left home any longer than a few days—to visit relatives, in our case—we went to New Jersey. It wasn't until after graduating from high school, when I traveled out of the region, for example, that I came to realize that the things the Black people in New Jersey owned or what they accomplished were not of any great measure above what we had and what we did back in the mountains. It was all relative! Fact is I dropped my jealousy of my city cousins' lifestyles when it became apparent that they too never left their immediate environs; in their cases, not even to go into midtown New York City, thirty minutes by bus or train. Their living spaces were just as narrow and as confining, relatively speaking, as ours were.

My city cousins who lived near 125th Street and Amsterdam Avenue could not take me from central Harlem to the Empire State Building. They rarely chanced to go far from their noisy and crowded city blocks, as I did in my frequent and sometimes solitary venturing for miles into the deepest parts of Black Mountain. I was less afraid of bears or rattlesnakes or copperheads than they were of drug addicts or would-be muggers out in the streets in front of their twelve-story apartment building. In those visits to where our granny had used her profits as a Harlan County bootlegger to buy a house in Roselle, New Jersey, in 1952, I had to be told not to talk to people I did not already know, and I was instructed not to smile. What an awkward way to live, I thought. How could you ever get to know people here when you are taught to treat most of them as perpetually dangerous strangers?

Back home, at least, everybody knew everybody, especially the "crazy niggers" as well as those poor, ignorant, and degraded Whites whom my father sometimes called "redneck peckerwoods." I do not use these labels lightly nor use them as expressions of insult. They are, or were, logical groupings that people carried around in their heads. The history behind the word *redneck* is traced to striking coal miners who tied red bandannas around their necks during the march on Blair Mountain in West Virginia. In the early 1900s, coal miners were fighting for the right to organize and to stop the practice of using mine guards. They also wanted an alternative to shopping at coal-company stores and being paid in scrip instead of money. In the early 1900s, miners led a series of strikes in southern West Virginia leading up to the climactic march on Blair Mountain in 1921 where they distinguished themselves with red bandannas tied around their necks. Black miners wore these red bandannas too. How the red bandanna, once a symbol of courage and interracial working-class solidarity, became a distasteful label I will never know, even though I asked continuously.

At Christmastime, we got lots of store-bought toys, invariably from the company store. The boys got play guns, "cap busters," and cowboy outfits, complete with fringed chaps. Older boys, preteens, got BB guns. On Christmas Day, when I was twelve, in 1958, Dad gave me my first real gun, a twenty-gauge 26″ single-barrel Stevens shotgun. Our three sisters and most of the girls in the neighborhood got "girl stuff": dolls, play kitchen sets, and play dishes. We usually got two pairs of shoes in a year—one for school and one pair that were called "Sunday shoes." I would get a pair of black-and-white (Converse) or red-and-white (PF Flyers) shoes, which we called "tennis shoes," for summer wear, although we never played tennis. Often, we would go barefooted, especially when wading in the creek to catch minnows to sell. The surest way to speed up the wear and tear on gym shoes was to get them wet in the creek or the river.

Easter was indeed a time of renewal because everybody seemed to get new stuff. Lazy summer days and early evenings were spent picking blackberries, fishing in Looney Creek, sometimes hoboing a train—cane poles and bait buckets in tow—and traveling twenty miles or more to the Clover and Poor Forks of the Cumberland River near Harlan. We would catch the same train back home; it would be running faster then because its gondolas were empty returning to Lynch—the end of the line—from its run to the coal-cleaning plant in Corbin.

US Steel also owned the West Virginia town named Gary, but, in addition, the massive corporation also had possession of the huge steelworks in Gary, Indiana, which it founded in 1906 as the home for its new plant. US Steel's "works" in both Indiana and West Virginia were named for lawyer Elbert Henry Gary, the founding chairman of the US Steel Corporation. Lynch-mined coal supplied the Gary Works of Indiana, and, not surprisingly, many Blacks, when they were laid off from the Lynch mines in the 1950s, migrated to Gary. Same employer. US Steel's Birmingham Works—six hundred miles to the south, straight as the crow flew—was like a bookend from Gary, Indiana.

US Steel not only owned the store that its workers were literally required to patronize—using company-printed money called scrip—but the company also owned the church houses—Baptist, Catholic, and Methodist—which it rented out to its workers so that they could reverently seek salvation and everlasting and eternal life.

In a 1934 memo sent to Mr. W. V. Whitman, the general superintendent of the Lynch plant, about the leases to the "three colored churches—African Methodist Episcopal Zion, First Baptist, and Mt. Sinai Baptist"—the Pittsburgh-based US Steel secretary and treasurer reminded Mr. Whitman, noted in pencil on the bottom of the letter, that he should "call their special attention to the clause relative to use of the Church for church purposes *only* and no *other*. This refers to all political meetings unless permission is granted them."

Also jotted in pencil on the bottom of the correspondence was an instruction that Messrs. Jake Clay, D. J. Lee, and Hill Leverett, the chairmen of the boards of these colored churches respectively, had been notified of the stipulation that the leases forbade political activities in the churches: "church purposes *only* and no *other*."

"Company Towns," a poem by thrice Pulitzer Prize winner Carl Sandburg, captured the way by which companies like United States Steel exerted total control over the lives of their employees. In Lynch, United States Steel set out centralized plans that regulated the development and behavior of the residents—from the provision of employment, housing, and educational, recreational, and health-care facilities to shopping centers and neighborhood stores, buildings for worship, and graveyards. The company took care of everything, including social arrangements that created the conditions for a sense of belonging.

The company sponsored Black and White baseball teams and Little League baseball for boys. Preteen boys invariably got involved in the church-sponsored Boy Scout troop and stayed in it through high school. Every community had a "juke joint," a community meeting place where high school kids would socialize on weekends.

There were bootleg houses on every street in the Black neighborhoods of Lynch. In the forties, fifties, and sixties, the official, legal nightclub frequented by Black people—under the auspices of the Veterans of Foreign Wars—was called, appropriately, "The VFW" or "The Vet's Club." In fact, there were two VFWs: the one to which Blacks regularly set out and the one patronized solely by Whites. Both were in Cumberland, one directly across the street from the other. After all, military units were segregated until after World War II.

At the VFW Club, the adults gathered and drank alcohol and danced and raised the roof, while in a back smoke-filled room, some men gathered to gamble, either rolling dice ("shooting craps") or playing card games like Georgia Skin or poker. Chicken. Fish. Chitlins. Pig's feet. Potato salad. Greens. Pop. Cold Beer. Thirty-eight-caliber Smith & Wesson snub-nosed pistols. Switchblades and straight razors with ebony

Tony Foster and fellow coal-mining friends bending the elbow at a weekend party, Lynch, KY, 1953. Photo by Robert "Smokypipe" Rutherford. William H. Turner Collection.

handles. Fog-like clouds of cigarette smoke floating against a low ceiling.

After hours. All night. Friday and Saturday. A live rhythm and blues band, like the Scat Cats from Kingsport, Tennessee. One could count on the Wurlitzer jukebox blaring 45 rpm records, three plays for a quarter. Sweat. Couples grinding, touching, and then "pulling a creep," which meant they would go out of the club, apparently to catch some fresh air. When they came back in, everyone would pretend that they did not look refreshed. Bluesman Little Milton immortalized our VFW in his hit song "Annie Mae's Café." Back in those days you could find one in every coal town. Not anymore.

CHAPTER 9

On Trash-Talking and Signifying along Looney Creek

AN EVER-PRESENT measure of the intimacy and chumminess of residents in the Black coal-camp communities of my youth was the ritual of exchanging boasts or insults, signifying, jaw-jacking, or merely shooting the bull. Two words carried the most emotional explosiveness—*Black* and *nigga*.

Off-putting comments about people with dark skin—like Dad and Mom and her mother and me—were not tolerated in our house. The old saying "the blacker the berry, the sweeter the juice" entered my awareness when I was a young boy, less than six. The expression was always used in response to a taunting or insulting remark directed to dark-skinned Black people, especially highly melanized Black girls, since *sweeter* had a feminine ring. It was a comeback that removed the sting of her being called, for example, a "Black bitch" or, as was hurled towards dark Black boys, "a Black-ass nigga!" You can't taunt the bull and not expect to be gored.

It was in that process of becoming human—particularly where human and race come together—that I came to understand the differences between people that were attributed to race. It was in that space that I was taught about the word *nigga*.

I understand—I get it—when those who read this section start wringing their hands and gnashing their teeth because of the distinctively negative history of this word. But before I was out of middle school, I was clear on the way certain words shaped the beliefs about race in the United States. I knew what my grandpa meant when he would say, quite often and quite loudly to me, "You my nigga if you don't get no bigga." The lighthearted phrase meant I was valued by someone who loved me, and based on his education and folksy ways, that was probably the best way that he knew to tell me so, in shorthand. He would not say it often, just at the appropriate time, and he would always smile and have a certain twinkle in his eye when he said it, usually when I had fetched something for him or said or did something nice without being told.

He had also heard that expression in his youth. The reference also informed me of what he expected of me—never to outgrow my britches in relation to him. It told me where I stood with him and what was required of me—to always respect and honor him. It never occurred to me that my grandfather—and other older Black men who used that phrase, in that context—was stigmatizing, marginalizing, or bringing shame on me. It was also around this time in my life—middle school—that I began to hear, regularly, the expectation from my teachers, my parents, and grandparents that I was expected to be a "credit," and not a disgrace to my race. Acting disgracefully meant acting "like a nigga."

When I was ten, I got my first real sense of how we too, Blacks, had internalized the normal use of the word *nigger*. It was during the annual tradition when the local chapter of the United Mine Workers of America handed out brown paper bags filled with Christmas treats to children lined up with their parents to receive peppermint candy, fruit, and nuts. In the hubbub of this much anticipated and joyous occasion, the boy in front of me and my daddy, when handed his bag, opened and examined its contents and asked the White man who'd handed him his bag, "Mister, can I please have some more of those nigger toes for my sisters?" Daddy clutched my hand firmly, pulled me to the side, leaned over, looked me dead in the eyes, and said to me, "Don't you ever let me hear you say that, boy!" He did not have to explain to me what he meant. Like everybody else, at home, among ourselves, we too called Brazil nuts "nigger toes." Situational ethics. Comic Chris Rock captured the distinction in a 1996 special when he sniped about Blacks behaving negatively: "Black people can be out having a good time, and then along comes a bunch of niggas!"

Cultures change. Language changes. Language changes culture, and vice versa.

I think all the kids "got it"—this word *nigga*—and they got it quick. We got what it meant, depending on who used it, in what context, and how and where it was used. I rarely heard it used by Blacks in a sinister way, not with the harsh, racist impact as when it was directed by a White to a Black person. But I never heard the word used in that menacing, racist way when I was young because the Whites who took the liberty to venture into Black spaces regularly had sense enough not to cross that line.

On the other hand, I always got a little nervous, expecting trouble—a fight, possibly bloodshed—when the word *nigga* was used in a feverish and overexcited way, such as when one Black person called another a "Black-ass nigga!" That expression—especially when it was preceded by one of the participants using a phrase that ordered the other to have sex with themselves—almost invariably triggered a physical fight. Those were far beyond just fighting words! It was clear to me, even as a child, that the weakness for some people to be so fight-ready was based in being contained and restricted in so many intangible ways—wound up, as it were, spring-loaded and predisposed to fight at the drop of a hat. I never thought out then that such psychological tendencies had their basis, at least in part, in racial oppression and subordination. Aggressive behavior then, for some souls, became the likely—and expected—response to even the most trivial insult or act of disrespect, whether real or imagined.

Most often, however, when I heard the word *nigga* when I was a child, it was used another way. First, it was not used frequently, but when it was used, the word came off in a casual and pleasant way, as a term of attachment, caring, fondness, liking, and warmth—as in "You my nigga!" Nothing bad was thought of it. Another expression, "You're my ace boon coon," was one Black man's way to inform another, in the sense of a salute, that he trusted him, that they were good, loyal, and reliable friends. With its use, the racial epithet *coon*, which was often used by Whites to disparage Blacks, was turned into an affirmation of friendship, rather than a piercing insult.

Personal respect always meant a lot in Black coal towns. Work was the primary channel through which a person, a man in those days, was recognized and valued. Since, by design and order, every man worked in the same place, a man's character, and therefore, his disposition—and not the nature of his job—was the key mark of the person, as a man.

Some Black men were known for having the temperament that described a "bad nigga." In slavery times, a "bad nigger," the way Whites pronounced the word, for example, was the Black man who simply did not go along with the

East Benham High PTA, 1953. *Left to right*: Evans, Callaway, (Unidentified), Ellison (teacher), Johnson. Southeast Community College Appalachian Collection, Cumberland, KY.

system and was openly prepared—emotionally and physically—to accept the consequences of his rebelliousness, which included beatings or death, when intimidation did not work. Haley's character from *Roots* Kunta Kinte defied authority and took lashings and constantly looked for opportunities to escape the status of slave. At the Lynch Colored School, Mr. Easterly, the history and math teacher, taught us, in effect, that Black people like Toussaint Louverture of Haiti and Harriet Tubman, Frederick Douglass, Sojourner Truth, and Nat Turner were "bad niggas."

When I was growing up, while learning and acquiring the choices of racial—and human—identity, I learned another description of a "bad nigga": a Black man who was quarrelsome, disagreeable, and simply obnoxious. In Black coal towns, there were men in the community who were bad, known by all to be ill-tempered, humorless, and "a bit tetched in the head," which made the man display the hostility associated with a scoundrel, a crook, or a rogue. Later, while reading *Another Country* by James Baldwin, where he analyzed his abusive stepfather, I understood better how the economic system under which we lived arrested the development of some Black men, creating what Baldwin called "stunted authoritarian masculinity." Like Baldwin, I saw many Black men who "could not bend, could only be broken." Thankfully, there were many more bent men in our community, men who lived the same existence, worked the same backbreaking mining jobs, and had large families to take care of—just the same as the broken ones—who knew when to bend and who demonstrated, at the same time, that they could never be broken.

The wife and children of such bad niggas was another matter. The word *abusive* is relatively new. In the jargon of the elders, such a man was "mean to his wife and chur'en." The families of men who beat their wives, or those who were known to fly hot at the drop of a hat, or worse, those who had actually killed someone, were embraced by the community in a comforting, pitying, sympathetic, and understanding sort of way. Whoever said "the child shall suffer the sins of the father" did not visit too many coal towns. Most people kept a certain distance from bad niggas because they were unpredictable and dangerous. But some just "went for bad," playacting to be a bad nigga to keep authentically bad niggas at bay. The wannabes were known for "selling wolf tickets"—they were little more than harmless shit-talkers. A shit-talker had "wind in his jaws," or was "just a bag of wind," and for sure was "a nigga that wasn't half as bad as he wanted people to think he was!" When such a person got on the last nerve of someone who wanted to put him in his right place, you would hear, "Act crazy if you want to now, nigga. Ah'm 'gon show your ass who crazy!" Many a bad nigga stopped in his tracks with that daunting sign of hostility. Anyone could tell when a serious and final line had been drawn, separating a Black man known as a "bad, woofin' nigga" from a "nigga you don't play with," one who carried either a pistol, a switchblade knife, a straight razor, or all three. I often heard, in response to an incredulous or unbelievable statement or behavior, "Aw, come on, now, you're pulling my leg." Other times, unbelievable assertions, a shady statement, or disgraceful conduct would be responded to with the exclamation "Nigga, please!"

"Crazy niggas" were distinct from the two types of bad niggas. Crazy niggas are better described as being eccentric, odd, and strange but totally harmless. In fact, these characters were somewhat like safety valves in a pressure-packed situation. They were comical, entertaining, and playful—just a bit touched in the head, yes! But not testy or hot-tempered. We had our share of crazy niggas. However, these kinsmen were never put down. Their lifestyle—if they did not out-and-out bother anybody who cared not to associate with them—was theirs and the business of God. Despite being, sometimes, mind-numbingly irritating, they were treated like everybody else in the family, in the community. Some called our loving brother Irvin "one crazy nigga" in the manner that he was often compared to comedian Richard Pryor. "He's *our* crazy nigga," snapped one of my cousins, proudly and angrily, as she pointed her finger into the face of a man who had remarked, negatively, that Irvin was a crazy nigga. It was just as important how you say them—those two words—as it was if you said them and about whom you were referring, under what conditions, and in what context.

One particularly crazy nigga—a distant cousin of ours on Daddy's side—was always called Crazy John. John's signal zany behavior was to run around town "driving a car," which consisted of him holding the lid of a five-gallon lard can as though it was the steering wheel of a car. He mouthed the sounds of a throttling and gunning engine and a transmission changing gears as he sped along the narrow streets. He "scratched off" and "burned rubber," using his right hand and arm to act out changing gears and his left to signal lane changes and turns. He thrust his feet backward as he stood still, in neutral, and then he would blast off running and go around the neighborhood, through yards, up alleys, all at scorching speeds. In the summer, John was often shirtless, his big muscular chest flashing and dripping with sweat. Crazy John, dressed in tattered and torn jeans, a musty, filthy tee shirt, and often barefooted, always smelled "like a Bo mink" as Granny would say. To this day, I am still disappointed with myself for not asking Granny how to spell the name of this animal. Was it a *Bo* or a *Beaux* mink, and exactly why did she liken Crazy John's odor to a semiaquatic animal that favored a beaver?

Folks in the community would simply look at John and indulge him, shake their heads and smile, and give him food and a cool drink of water, and they would defend him from those bad niggas who dared to hassle John, who could barely speak. Whenever he pulled up onto our back porch, always around breakfast or supper time, Mom would say, "Leave John alone, he ain't bothering nobody." She would invite him in, make him wash up, give him a cool drink of water or lemonade in the Ball jar she kept just for him, feed him at the kitchen table, and send him on his way with a tender, maternal air. There were several "Johns" around town, including one known as Pee-Roy, the derivation of his nickname being obvious. He smelled more terrible than a Bo mink. Pee-Roy was viciously murdered by a widely known crazy nigga who, by legend, "come back from over there in World War II with a plate in his head." Such a rationale for eccentric, peculiar, and criminal behavior applied to several military veterans. As an innocent little kid, I would lie in bed and try to visualize who would put a plate in another person's head and how and why in the world they would do such a bizarre thing.

It is good that modern mental health practices did not find currency in the Black coal towns of Appalachia back then. If so, all our crazy niggas—like Crazy John—would have been defined as being severely neurotic and demented and probably would have been institutionalized; certainly they would have been ostracized—homeless, had there been such a category. We were taught to relate to them as being slightly out-of-the-ordinary souls, but, otherwise, they were quite normal and were treated with respect.

There were many, many men who went into the coal mines day after day, but on weekends, they were prone to fits of heavy drinking binges. But back then, end of the workweek blowouts did not put a fellow too far outside the boundaries of normalcy. There was quite a bit of pressure built up—and steam to be blown off—by the weekends.

Throughout the coal towns of central Appalachia in the 1920s, '30s, '40s, and '50s, Black adults who were otherwise upstanding citizens attended rent parties—where people were charged to come in—on Friday and Saturday nights. It was, for some, a time of high anxiety because weekends meant an uptick in activities that involved drinking alcohol and the associated trouble, when—as crooned by Chattanooga-bred

Empress of the Blues Bessie Smith—men would use "gunpowder to sweeten their tea." This line is from her 1930 hit song "Black Mountain Blues." On weekends in the coal towns, it was not uncommon to hear about whose razors and whose guns had sliced and punctured holes in whose flesh.

I know and have interviewed dozens of women like my mother who grew up in coal camps like Lynch and Benham in Kentucky; Norton, Big Stone Gap, and Stonega in Virginia; and Keystone and Gary in West Virginia—all girls-to-women who went to school as far as they could, married, and raised families from the 1920s through the 1950s. Many personally knew the life of Bessie Smith's many blues elegies. I never determined whether Smith's "Black Mountain" was in North Carolina, Nevada, or Maine, where at least four of the spaces in the United States are known by that name. But there is a town named Black Mountain that is located in Harlan County, Kentucky, near the Virginia border, fifteen miles east of the county seat, Harlan. I err on the side of believing that Bessie Smith's "Black Mountain Blues" was not just some imaginary, on-its-head place. She had to be referring to the Harlan County of folklore, of legend; she was describing the locale of well-known traditions, a place where there is substantial evidence that reveals that injustice was sometimes considered fairness and where faces were slit by straight razors. People, usually men, were shot in gambling rooms or another man's bedroom. Children were conceived in the county jail under the cover of unofficial conjugal visits. Booze—legal and banned—flowed like mighty streams. And love and sex were displayed in both orthodox and unusual ways and places, such as in the back seats of vehicles in well-known wide spaces along the highway leading up the mountain toward Virginia.

"Shame and Scandal in the Family," an enormously popular song with Trinidadian origins by 1950s-era calypso king

Harry Belafonte, had its version in central Appalachia coal camps. The song covers the experience of a certain boy who went to his father to identify the girl he wanted to marry; but his father informed him that the girl he had in mind was really his half-sister, the father's "love child" by another woman, not the boy's mother. When he told his mother of his dilemma—what his daddy had told him—she told him to go right ahead and marry the girl because her husband wasn't his daddy, but her husband didn't know.

Worldly music from Ma Rainey to Billie Holiday seeped from coal-camp house parties. Homes—the bootleggers' houses—where people crowded in for chatter and babble, to play card games and to buy and drink and get drunk off home brew or beer and store-bought liquor by the drink, were in every neighborhood in the colored sections.

Everybody—including the "law"—knew where these places were. The Whites had such gathering places, water-holes, too. I don't know where the White watering holes were because I had no doings in the White parts of town, and the only time I visited for any length of time in a White neighborhood was in the company of Dad when he had a handyman's job in some White people's home: carpentry, plumbing, wall-papering, or painting.

It does not sully the otherwise respectable reputations of my grandmother and my father, respectively, because they worked with a White man moonshiner, Mr. "Fats" Lawson, all during my early childhood years. Dad "ran," that is, transported, 'shine between its point of manufacture somewhere in a hollow near Jellico, Tennessee, and our home in Harlan County. He could have easily replaced Robert Mitchum in the 1958 benchmark film on distilling and distributing illicit liquor *Thunder Road*. My grandmother sold the moonshine that Dad transported to her house. I witnessed, firsthand, my neighbors as they lived out the lyrics of songstress Bessie Smith's "Black Mountain Blues."

I knew it verse by verse. The brutalizing labor of coal mining put strong young men on edge for brawls and speech and behavior that was, in turn, coarse, lewd, obscene, and otherwise acting a clown. Such manners were, however, the exception rather than the rule. Everybody recognized—and accepted—those Black men around town who could be seen slovenly drunk and outlandishly uncivil on weekends but who were reliable, hardworking, loving husbands and fathers the rest of the week. They often occupied the front pew seats in church on Sunday. Maybe a deacon or a trustee.

We saw adultery, gambling, people gossiping and bad-mouthing each other, folk who dabbled in illegal activities, rabble-rousing, and our fair share of trials, troubles, and tribulations. We heard vulgar language and waved in agreement with the sermonizing of a "jackleg preacher." We learned ourselves how to speak it and admired expert shit-talkers, and we knew something about lust and sexual desires, of the hankering and hanky-panky that caused husbands to cheat on their wives and vice versa. We learned to recognize those children inside the same family with different fathers. Some children suffered from abusive beatings, and occasionally, there were fist, knife, and razor-wielding fights, shootings, and a rare homicide. Colored people in coal camps in central Appalachia, after all, lived and died, much like everybody else in America.

"He's a girly boy!" is all Granny said when I asked about a burly, muscular, Sudanese-dark, and clean-shaven man with processed hair whom I saw about town. In the summer, he would often literally strut and swivel-hip about the neighborhoods, decked out flamboyantly in tight-fitting white shorts and a bright-colored shirt, which would be open down to his belly button, tied, like shoestrings, above his navel. He was always jovial, convivial, smiling, and swiveling with the most appealing, bright white smile; sometimes with lipstick and powder on his broad, handsome face; his eyelids shadowed; and smartly styled, processed hair. He and his friends were not avoided or rejected at all. They did not hide in some isolated spaces, and they attended high school and church as regularly as anybody else.

Despite the widespread use of homosexual slurs and the maltreatment of men and women elsewhere, the people who later came to be called gay and lesbian were received, generally, in a community-wide climate of social equality and impartiality. We all sat together at church and at school, and their "alternative lifestyles" were no big deal in the Black communities of our coal camps. Of course, there were the trash-talking, mean-spirited folks in the community who could be heard, occasionally, referring to some men and women using homophobic slurs. Ironically enough, it was those who badmouthed and disparaged those in what we now call the LGBTQ community who were disliked and cold-shouldered.

By the time I was old enough to discern the shades and tones and fine distinctions of such people matters, I had also learned that what went into you—your ears and consciousness, for example—wasn't as important as what you let come out of your mouth, in the form of bad-mouthing people or the way you treated your fellow human beings. The quote attributed to American historian James Truslow Adams was framed in black and white on the wall behind the desk of the librarian, Mrs. Gregory, in the Lynch Colored School: "There is so much good in the worst of us, and so much bad in the best of us, that it ill behooves any of us to find fault in the rest of us."

I have never asked a female friend with whom I grew up about when and from whom she received her instruction on the birds and the bees, but for boys along Looney Creek, sex was an open-book subject, especially at the Pool Room and in the locker room at school. Talking about sex was not taboo. The older guys talked openly about women with unusually strong sex drives, saying they had a "white liver." Logically, a "lily-livered" man was considered cowardly, timid, or unmanly.

I'd blush when the men in the Pool Room or some other gathering spot talked about a woman in town who lost two husbands by death because it was said that her inordinate passion had "killed 'em off." In politically correct retrospect, I must wonder how it affected us young boys to hear about men who were accused of being "whipped" by such women, which was just slightly worse than being called the woman's body part by which they had been whipped.

Sex—"it"—was not discussed as some fixation, even though this most human of issues was everywhere. It was the rhyme and reason that a lot of good things and bad things happened, as it did everywhere, as I came to find out later in life. Men fought, cut, stabbed, shot, and killed other men over it; and on rare occasions, a woman would slice the face and the jugular vein of her lover or husband with a razor or a knife, or shoot or take an icepick to him because he was chasing it or getting it from another woman, who might also be some other man's wife. I saw up and down the hollers as a young boy signs and signals and symptoms of Denise LaSalle's 1984 blues hit "Your Husband Is Cheating on Us."

I was flabbergasted when my dad answered two related questions I asked in the same breath when I was twelve: "Daddy, what is a cut buddy, and what do they mean at the Pool Room when they say of a man, 'He's helping the man out?' " *Cut buddy* referred to a man who was neither the formal nor recognized boyfriend of a woman but rather just someone with whom she had casual sexual relations with, and no special emotional attachments were involved; it was "just sex" and nothing more: "layin' in the cut." The Pool Room was the place where these stories were bandied about. "Who's yo' daddy?" was not a contrived question. And of course there was the rare, but most popular, ladies' man, a fellow who might have multiple women pregnant at the same time.

A *cut buddy* could also refer, in a more sinister way, to a man who "cut" into another man's space, in his bed, with his wife. Coarsely put, "He hit it in the cut!" Then there was the more benign type of cut buddy, the one who "helps the man out" who could not, for physical or other reasons, like advanced age, take care of his wife, especially if she was younger. In that way, "helping him out" came off like the moral duty of a Boy Scout if the helper did it with dignity and respect, avoiding, as far as humanly possible, public displays of the relationship. It ain't what you do, it's how you do it.

Well, on second thought, "it" was discussed, quite a lot, among the teenage boys, mostly in the Pool Room. A lot of the subtexts about the various and sundry—and sordid—ways and means by which people thought about, pursued, executed, and hid "it" from others I first learned while listening to those who were expert at playing the dozens—talking irreverently about another person's mother. The dozens, it turns out, played quite an important role to keep the lid on high-pressured questions and answers about everything from "Who's she giving it to?" to "Who's baby is it?" to a word I had from my father on it: "If you have to ask her for it, you probably won't like the answer she's going to give you, which by then you ought to already know." Simple enough.

Then there was the outrageously named spot where many colored boys in Lynch, if they chose, could go to learn about certain things that I am still trying to bring myself to tell my grown sons—let alone my grandsons—starting with the widely popular and commonly used name of the place. I still blush a bit when I hear or call the name of the often-congested get-together place for men, just four doors up from our house. I was never rebuked by my parents for my frequent stops and breaks taken at this place where the old men gathered. They didn't just laugh and talk about sex, but they also chattered about business, education, history, politics, religion, and sports, especially baseball and boxing.

In East Africa—from Kenya to Madagascar—one of the most distinct symbols of the physical setting, the environment, is the baobab tree, a hardy and seemingly indestructible breed. The baobab tree not only is known for providing excellent shade but also is central to the transfer of traditional legend and lore. In almost every village, the elders held meetings under the baobab tree with the belief that the spirit of the tree would guide them in decision-making.

On Second Street, four houses up the hill from ours, or roughly in the space in which six cars could park, was our neighborhood's most famous equivalent to the baobab tree, a seventy- to eighty-foot-high white oak tree. This quite common tree was the tallest, broadest, and most foliaged tree on the entire street. Between there and the Pool Room—six houses down the street the other way, at the bottom of the Second Street hill—one could hear all manner of conversations about the history of Black people in the town, all versions of the current rumors and gossip, and anything that pertained to the miners' situation, about the United Mine Workers of America. In Lynch, in virtually every section of town where the Black people lived, there were outside gathering spots where the old men congregated to play checkers or dominoes, better known as "bones." The regulars among the retired miners ended up at this hub of relationships in midmorning. Others dropped by some days, not on others, but anyone, any man that is, who wanted to simply pass the time, to shoot the shit, would stop by this big tree on Second Street. All my life, for the twenty years I lived uninterrupted on Second Street, I never saw a female under the tree, not even the lady of the house, Mr. Pollard's wife, Miss Idella. To this day, I never knew the real name of the noticeably quiet man who constantly had a bulging plug of Brown Mule tobacco in his left cheek, whom the kids called Mr. Polly. At the stroke of midnight on New Year's Day, like clockwork, every year, Mr. Polly would go into his backyard and blast off dozens of shots from what sounded like the biggest pistol in the world.

If you considered "shooting the shit" as a crude and artless activity, then you did not stop by this esteemed locale for uncommon, manly conversation. The name for this place used by all who knew it, and everybody knew it, derived from the fact that it was the preferred outdoor meeting place for mostly old, slow-walking, slow-talking, back-bent, former Black coal miners—retirees with blackened lungs who either continued to smoke Lucky Strike cigarettes, throw a plug of Red Man or Brown Mule chewing tobacco into their jaw, or put a pinch of Skoal snuff just inside the corner of their mouth, which would stick out like a grape-sized marble just left of the center of their mouths. These were evenhanded, good, timeworn Black men—country boys with prostate problems, which they described to each other with the straightforward expression, "Um havin' problems passing my water." They also small-talked, in code, about other incapacities related to sexual effectiveness, which they joked about freely, without embarrassment. Literally, the name of the meeting place translates into the unrefined name of the unresponsive male sexual organ.

Four two-by-eight-inch planks fashioned a table that jutted from the tree's trunk to form a card-like table, only much sturdier. A weather-beaten and broken-down, discolored La-Z-Boy lounge chair slumped to one side, and chairs were pulled from Polly's porch to accommodate those who didn't lean against the cars on the street, less than three feet away, or those who did not flop down on the four concrete stairs that led onto the sidewalk. The huge maple was on the left of the stairway. Others stationed themselves within earshot of the checkers or domino board in what was called "the Indian squat," where the man crouches and sits with his knees bent and his butt touching the back of his legs and the heels of his feet, also known as sitting on one's haunches, mixing it up, shooting the shit. "How yo' ham'mah hangin' dis mo'nin, Old Man?" was the standard greeting to any gentleman, a regular, who was ambling to his spot around the tree.

Two regulars under the tree were Mr. Robert Oliver, a steadfast deacon at Mount Sinai Baptist Church, and the ever-spitting, with a chaw of Red Man in his jaw, Mr. Monk Andrews, both of whom assisted Mr. Charles Green, our Boy Scout master. Lynch had the only all-Black official Boy Scouts of America troop in eastern Kentucky as part of the Boy Scouts of America Cumberland Council, and legend has it that the troop was organized beneath the shade of this tree. Dozens of Black boys, from middle school age through high school, spent a glorious, fun-filled week every summer at Camp Blanton—a Boy Scout camp built in 1934 under the auspices of the Civilian Conservation Corps (CCC) near Wallins Creek, Kentucky. I am sure none of us realized—as we hiked the densely shaded trails or sat around campfires roasting weenies and swam and canoed in the ever-cold waters of the lake—that we were in one of the most pristine forests in all of eastern Kentucky. I went to Camp Blanton in the keeping of my big brother Irvin for my first time in 1956, when I was ten. While Camp Blanton was less than an hour from

Jack Amos and Garmon Gregory play checkers while John Thomas (l) and Elbert Pollard wait their turn, beneath the famous tree.

Lynch, it seemed to be far, far away. Never less than three dozen boys would be ferried to Blanton Forest, packed like so many cords of firewood aboard a rickety old truck that had plywood siding and was owned by a very pleasant Black man, a coal miner who hailed from neighboring Lee County, Virginia, called Mr. Bonny Blue. Dad and several other men would follow the truck in cars to help the longtime scoutmaster Mr. Charles Green and his assistant Mr. Robert Oliver to get us settled into the rustic cabins and pitch our tents. I was involved in those annual camping trips through 1964, my senior year of high school, when the troop was disbanded. Baseball teams—from Little League to the semipro Lynch Grays—were, starting in 1934, organized, administered, and managed by men who met regularly around the tree.

The highly ritualized gathering usually began in midmorning after breakfast and went on until dusk from late spring to past Labor Day, every day except Sunday, for these senior citizens and their mentees, teenage Black boys. Some of the men played together for decades, even before they retired, when, presumably, their prostate glands and sexual virility worked perfectly, some since they "come up here outta Alabama."

I visit now in Houston with a Jamaican friend whose relatives are natives of Barbados and Jamaica, immigrant men who gather in their spot in Houston to play dominoes. Among these Bajan and Obeah men transplanted to the United States, I witness the same proceedings and rituals that took place beneath the seasonably verdant or amber waves of the tree back in Lynch, the same traditions and stuff bantered about and passed on. There is a coded language, a series of facial expressions and eye movements, indeed a subculture in this space.

The clearest present indication that the once-heralded, beehive-like coal mines in Lynch are idle, that the people—disproportionately the Blacks—are all but vanished, is the solitary feature of the space around the tree, which itself has been fading for the past twenty years, as though it misses its tenants. I watched the tree lose its hardiness over the years. The Pollard home has been vacant for more than a decade. The two houses next to ours, both duplexes between ours and the Pollards' homeplace, also reflect the decline of the space we called home. Although no one has lived in it for almost a decade, we maintain our homeplace neatly, but between it and the Pollards' house, the Amoses' old house is now vacant for almost twenty-five years. It is ragged and dilapidated while the adjoining side, where the band teacher of the Lynch Colored School Mr. Rawlins and his family lived, is in almost total decline, the roof with gaping holes. Farther on up our side of Second Street toward the tree sat a well-kept yellow and white double house that was once occupied by our third-grade teacher Mrs. Dallas and her husband Mr. Calvin and, attached to them, the house of a wonderful couple I only knew as Miss Monkey and Mr. Scrap Iron. It was flattened, demolished in 2018.

Ten years ago, I noticed that the tree itself was not as hardy and as fertile in the spring and summer as it was back in the day when it was a mirror image of those once ox-strong Black coal miners who ended their days in its dwindling shade. In a literal way, the tree, in the fashion of time-lapse photography, contracted, shriveled, and withered over the years, just like the men whose feet held down its roots and watered them with tobacco juice and liquid left over from the cups and cans and bottles of what they drank. The last regulars—Polly, Mr. Jack "Chewing Gum" Amos, Mr. John Thomas, and Mr. Garmon Gregory—are all long-since dead, literally. The tree fell, lifeless, sprawled across Second Street in the late winter of 2020. A few of us had vowed to hold a ceremony of reminiscence around the spot, our ground zero, when we gathered at home on Memorial Day 2020. Like everything else, such plans were scrapped "out of an abundance of caution" for COVID-19. Very few of us returned home for the annual Memorial Day get together. I am reminded often of one of Granny's witticisms: "If you want to hear God laugh, just make your own plans."

I asked Lynch native Walter Lee Peeples, who is still called "Buttermilk" by his homies, what he learned spending time as a teenager at this popular spot. Mr. Peeples referred to the location by its popular, insiders' designation, what virtually all the Black people called it:

> Damn near everything of what I learned about life, I learned it under the Dead Dick Tree. Big George Gnat Washington taught me how to move from one spot to another without

> moving your car so your old lady wouldn't know where you were at. He would get dropped off and walk to his spots. Seaboat and Mr. Jack could teach you how to squirrel hunt right there under the tree. John Thomas taught me how to fish—right under the tree. They were the kind of men who, when they were making a point about life and how to live, would tap you gently on the shoulder. Sam Cole, the local loan shark, would go back and forth home and bring back a different type of pistol each time. I have a license to carry a gun right now because I learned at the Dead Dick Tree: "Better the po'leece catch you wid dis gun den some crazy peckerwoods catch you without it!" But I don't have to worry if a policeman sees my weapon when I choose to carry it openly—Texas is Kentucky on steroids when it comes to crazy White boys!

Buttermilk, now in his mid-sixties, retired as a locomotive engineer after thirty-eight years with Union Pacific Railroad in Houston, Texas. Gordon Parks wrote *The Learning Tree*, which was adapted into a dramatic film in 1969, about the growing-up journey of a Black boy in Cherokee Flats, Kansas: stories of the boy's initiation into manhood, sex, love, death, justice, injustice, and, because he is Black, a fair measure of racial hatred. An assortment of that kind of learning took place under the Dead Dick Tree in Lynch, Kentucky. I learned a lot there, as did countless numbers of Black boys.

Appalachian coal towns had a goodly bit of dash and raciness, such as was the case in virtually all early twentieth-century frontier towns. After all, hundreds of young men—most footloose, if not fancy-free—were moving about the country in search of work. Defiled behavior, aggression, lawlessness, and everything that comes along and goes along with rootlessness were quite common early on when Blacks—and others—first arrived in the coal camps. The word *camp*, in and of itself, as in "Let's set up camp," denotes having little more than a roof over one's head or being in a space temporarily, maybe on an adventurous trip or passage. It took a generation, at least, for these coal camps to take on the qualities of settled, refined, and developed communities. Black people, new to the mountains, to Harlan County in 1900, having been torn from their roots and families in Alabama, were not much different from their counterparts who had been thrown together in the teeming urban areas of the North, like in New York City—Harlem. They were nothing more than industrial workers in a rural space. Nowhere to run to, nowhere to hide. All new stuff. The stuff of which the "Black Mountain Blues" is made. I learned to live and let live and not to bother myself, not too seriously, with the differences between people. I was raised to believe that "none is perfect but the Father."

I did not develop the habit—and nor do I practice it to this day—of the exercise of belittling, condemning, or judging people. The overwhelming majority of us in central Appalachian coal towns—as individuals and between our families—were much too codependent and mutually supportive. We displayed neighborliness, courtesy, humbleness, unpretentiousness, moral consciousness, and a deep appreciation for religious rituals and the sanctity of the earth itself; we were communal, and we possessed and practiced a keen and self-effacing sense of humor. These were our guiding values. Such is what Loyal Jones called Appalachian Values.

CHAPTER 10

In a Coal Mine, Everybody Is Black; Outside, Not So Much

MOST OF the White people in Appalachian coal camps have been notoriously pigeonholed in a negative manner. The degrading stereotypes that became the popular images of Southern mountain Whites—backward, barbaric, believers in "haints" and ghosts, irrational to the core—did not occupy Black people's thinking about their White neighbors. These unpleasant and offensive images of mountain Whites certainly did not govern the everyday relationships between Blacks and Whites.

When I moved to Lexington at the age of twenty in 1966, I began only then to hear regularly how middle-class Whites from outside the mountains thought of and treated "hillbillies." It was at the University of Kentucky, starting in 1966, where, for the first time, I was repeatedly bound to answer the question of my own origins, as it seemed that every conversation started with "Where you from?" My answer left a lot of jaws dropped.

It was there in Lexington that I first heard the phrase "I

didn't know there were any Black people in that neck of the woods." This proclamation came from students at UK who were from what we called "up North," as well as from Black and White students from other parts of Kentucky—those from central Kentucky and, of course, those from the state's only big city, Louisville. With a population of 328,000 currently, many, especially those from rural Appalachia, would consider Lexington to be a "big city" as well. I heard the encyclopedia of stereotyping about Appalachian mountain White people on the part of individuals who were not likely to have had any personal contact with the "hillbillies" they disparaged so easily, the folks I'd grown up amidst. I became acquainted with some of the more disparaging and abusive words and phrases and stereotypes used by non-mountain Whites when they referred to mountain Whites in my first few weeks in a dormitory named Haggin Hall, which was populated with three hundred or so White boys and three Blacks. Often I would walk away from these encounters, my head shaking, thinking, "Wow, if that's what these White boys think of the White people back home in eastern Kentucky, I wonder what they think of Black people from there?" I often avoided talking about where I was from and would sometimes say I was from New Jersey to avoid being seen through the Appalachian Mountains looking glass.

It didn't take me long, or much reading, to grasp the idea that if Africans had not been enslaved in America, these coal-field Whites, in the hearts and minds of these White folk from the lowlands, would have been America's "niggers." I was a "Black hillbilly" but not belittled and mocked like White mountaineers. To a person, it seemed remarkable enough that I made it to the state's flagship university from a subculture that they looked down upon. It hit me like a ton of bricks: the category "nigger," the Black "other," applied to White folks too. I did not feel any more special because they seemed to imply that there were some White people who were "no better" than me.

Jim Crow–like segregation, and the discriminatory laws that underpinned it, prevailed in the coalfields of central Appalachia up to the mid-1960s with no more, or less, effect than was the case throughout the American South. When I was in the ninth grade, in 1960, my father was ecstatic because a Black woman, Miriam Morris Fuller, became the first African American to be accepted for studies at Clinch Valley College in his home county in nearby Virginia. That same year, Blacks were admitted to the community college that opened in Cumberland, the one I attended from 1964 to 1966. I well remember in the same year when the city council of Cumberland, four miles from my home, chose to fill in the area's only public swimming pool with concrete rather than to allow Blacks to swim in it. Whites in Lynch could swim at the Lynch Country Club. When us Blacks were not swimming in Looney Creek, we went, never more than once a month all summer, to the "colored only" swimming pool in Harlan, thirty-five miles away. Harlan County Blacks, led by Rev. John Hannah, founded a chapter of the NAACP in 1965 and mirrored locally, in a comparatively muted way, the protests that were on the national news. When Black citizens tried to enter the "Whites only" public pool in Harlan in the mid-1960s, they were turned away, the pool filled with rocks and paved over.

But certain special conditions prevailed in some of the company towns, which may explain why Blacks were eager to take work in the region and why they were considered valuable assets by the companies that employed them. In the highly capitalized coal towns in eastern Kentucky—like Lynch, Benham, Jenkins, and Wheelwright—Black miners were paid the same as Whites; they lived in the same standard, company-owned houses; and their schools and health care and burial grounds were on par, for the most part, with the Whites'.

Of its town that opened for business a couple years before neighboring Lynch, Wisconsin Steel—through its subsidiary, International Harvester—announced in its 1915 corporate brochure of Benham: "The town was built as a circle, around which were situated the mine offices, company store, hospital, theater, clubhouse, school, church, and bandstand. These facilities provided the high-quality schoolteachers, clergy, medical staff, consumer products, entertainment, and recreation. Families worked, played, worshipped, and went to school together. Quiet rows of neatly painted houses and manicured lawns obscured pay differences."

However, the Black and White families in Benham did not play, worship, or go to school together. The houses occupied by Blacks, in the physical spaces reserved for them, such as Smoky Row and Machine Shop Hollow behind the coke ovens—where my mother was born—were significantly and conspicuously inferior to the houses in which most of the Whites lived.

Segregation in coal towns, therefore, was a relative issue. Discrimination based on skin color in a locale where everybody depended on the benevolence of the company was, largely, a moot point. Most of the White people lived under the same relative transience and temporariness of their work as did the Black people. The all-powerful company treated the Blacks and the Whites pretty much the same. If a White man missed a shift at the mines, the company-sponsored law enforcement official visited the house to find out why. The same company doctor verified claims of illness and disability among all miners. And it didn't matter if his name was John Vicini, who had arrived in 1920 via Ellis Island from Italy, or Johnny Jones, who came to Lynch in that same year having been born and raised in Ensley, Alabama, which is in the city limits of Birmingham, then a company town virtually owned by US Steel. Regular absenteeism would mean that the miner—Black or White—was out of work. Period. Exclamation point! No appeal.

In the 1920s and 1930s, all miners in some coal towns in the region were paid in company-issued money called scrip, a forerunner of today's government-issued food stamps. Imprinted with the logo of specific companies, scrip was worthless except in the stores owned by the issuing company. Different coal towns were connected to one another—distinguished only by what company owned the land—and their mine and security and business units cooperated to the extent that they had you coming and going! Whites, no less than the Blacks, owed their souls to the company store!

For the most part, except at meetings of the United Mine Workers of America, there were no integrated practices or customs or rituals—outside the mines—that brought Blacks into any regular contact with White people. Black and White miners worked alongside each other, but the bathhouses were partitioned off, Blacks on one side and Whites on the other. We lived in our part of the coal towns, and the Whites lived in theirs.

Except for the White insurance man and the occasional company maintenance workers who came to "fix something" in the company-owned house, we had virtually no contact with White people. Whites sat downstairs in the company-owned theater houses. Blacks and Whites passed each other—with civil courtesy—moving to and from in the common spaces of the towns, such as the company-owned store and post office and filling station and the neighborhood convenience stores, which were also owned by the company. There were mom-and-pop stores in some of the houses, where one could purchase candy, homemade baked goods, and soda, which was also known, unless it was a Coca-Cola, as "pop."

Harassment and beatings and crude racial incidents and the ultimate dread of Southern Blacks, lynching, were not as much a part of the culture in Appalachian coal towns as was the case in the Black Belt South, specifically in Alabama and Mississippi.

That noted, 3,500 White people showed up to witness the hanging of Floyd Frazier, Black, on May 19, 1910, in Whitesburg, in neighboring Letcher County, Kentucky. Mable G. Condon, in her book *The History of Harlan County*, reported the 1896 hanging of Buford Overton, a Black man who was accused of killing an old White couple who peddled wares through the mountains somewhere around Martins Fork Lake. Though unsubstantiated, Condon also mentioned a triple hanging of Black men in Harlan County "in the late 1880s."

Rarely, if ever, did the grapevine in Harlan County report White-on-Black violence that came to wide attention. The "redneck" or "cracker who went for bad" knew that any given Black mountain man, like the ones who hung around the Dead Dick Tree, was likely not a garden-variety docile Negro, not the kind to frivolously bother, goad, or pester, not without a good fight; or worse, the White man might just have randomly encountered a "crazy nigger" and would have experienced a brutal retaliation by a knifing or a shooting. Handguns were concealed everywhere, especially in the pockets of many otherwise friendly and congenial Black men walking with a stick cane to his garden—armed to the teeth with a snub-nosed .38 Smith & Wesson or a Colt .45. "Every shut eye ain't asleep!"

Racial violence, based on the sometimes-commonplace variety practice of a White man's privilege or a group of White men actually picking on a randomly selected Black man—the kind of racist aggression born of the perpetrator's so-called inherent bitterness towards Blacks—was minimized by the absolute control of the company, which framed the understanding of community solidarity. That is, there was no place for the Whites who were so inclined to play out their racist inclinations. In such a densely populated space, burning crosses were hard to conceal. Also, the population of Lynch represented a racial and ethnic diversity that contrasted widely from the population profiles of most of the coal towns in the same general area of eastern Kentucky. For example, Blacks were notably absent in parts of Harlan County, such as in the towns of Bledsoe, Hulen, and Wallins Creek and in nearby Leslie County, in coal-town settlements like Hyden. Lily, a town near Corbin and London in Laurel County, is still 99 percent White. Black people stayed away from "lily-white Lily," as we called it.

Black men—and those coming of age—knew the "sundown towns," and they also knew how to code-switch in order to avoid, or to redirect the direction of, "nigger moments" in a nanosecond when survival required it. In our day, White people's spaces—and Black people's spaces—were clearly marked off. It was less perilous for a "strange" White person to enter a Black space than vice versa. The dangers faced by a Black person, especially a Black male—a teenager or a grown Black man—crossing over into a White space were tangible.

While visiting Pine Mountain Settlement School in the fall of 2019—more than six decades past my teen years when I was instructed to avoid such places—I experienced a shortness of breath and hasty heartbeats whenever a car behind me seemed to be following me too closely. The settlement school, though breathtakingly beautiful, is in Bledsoe, in Harlan

County, Kentucky, along Pine Mountain, where the last public hanging of a Black man took place in 1929. Black people deliberately avoided that side of Pine Mountain, where Hyden and Leatherwood, Kentucky, are located. "Don't be caught dead around those peckerwoods over there near Leatherwood," Dad would tell us somberly.

Walking into public spaces in the Hydens and Leatherwoods and Corbins of central Appalachia was met with that unmistakable "What are you doing in here?" look: "What right do you have to be here, nigger?" It is an unmistakably condescending, sneering look. I still watch for it, subconsciously, now seven decades removed from Corbin-like places, which I have found to exist almost everywhere I have visited in the United States. I deliberately take my teenage grandsons to the mall to practice how they should react to being racially profiled and what to do when they encounter acute disrespect based solely on being Black. I could teach a college-level course titled "Nigger Moments 101."

When I was ten, in 1956, on a fishing trip that I remember like it was ten minutes ago, my father grabbed my hand when we entered a dilapidated gas station in Corbin, Kentucky, along Highway 25W. "That scene looks just like that gas station we went into in Corbin when I was a little boy," I reminded him when I took him to see the movie *Deliverance* in 1972, when I was twenty-six; he was then fifty-five. We didn't look at each other.

A half dozen grisly looking White men, unshaven and grimy, were jam-packed around a potbellied stove on squat stools and cane-bottomed rocking and straight-backed chairs in the dimly lit store, their creepy gathering place. When we walked in, time seemed to freeze; even the clock that wasn't on the wall stopped. It was like they were in a boardroom on this cool spring morning, characters there in what the welcoming sign noted was "The Home of Colonel Sanders' Famous Kentucky Fried Chicken." We—the colored people—had always heard that the "secret recipe" had been concocted by one of Sanders's cooks, a Black man named Russell McKee.

On the wall behind the cash register was a sign that read, "Nigger, if you can read this sign, run! If you can't read, nigger, run anyway!"

Dad looked directly at the glowering and meant-to-intimidate faces of a half dozen or so White men, all in one sweep. To this assemblage of the very embodiment of hillbillies and crackers—one country bumpkin, two clodhoppers, a single hayseed, two hicks, and a very old yokel—he said, softly but confidently, "How you men doing this morning? Good day for a Harlan County coal miner to take his boy fishing, ain't it?" We walked out uninjured, safe and sound. I later learned that such signs were literally everywhere between Corbin and Birmingham. "They probably can't read that damned sign." That's all Dad ever said about it.

By the tender age of ten, I had been taught Corbin's infamous reputation, of its place among the hot spots in the so-called American Red Summer of 1919, when terrorist attacks by White supremacists on Black communities were like sporting events. In Corbin that year, virtually all the African Americans of the town, about two hundred men, women, and children, were rounded up and herded onto overcrowded railcars and sent south to Knoxville, Tennessee.

According to longtime Black Corbin resident John Turner, who is no relation to us, "They swore at us and said, 'By God we are going to run all niggers out of this town tonight.' "

Several of the single Black men who were run out of Corbin ended up in Harlan County but an hour away, where they found refuge—and new lives. Mr. Diamond, also known as

"Candy Man," took his Alabama-born cousin into his home in 1919, two weeks after the purge. The Diamond home was on the Kentucky-Virginia line, northeast of the city of Harlan in the coal camp known as Black Mountain.

As Audre Lorde put it in her 1982 lecture "Learning from the 60s," "I learned that if I didn't define myself for myself, I would be crunched into other people's fantasies for me and eaten alive."

The story of my Appalachian mountain people is no blackface version of G. C. "Red" Jones's classic *Growing Up Hard in Harlan County*, although like Mr. Jones, we know a bit about adversity, mettle, perseverance, and overcoming the odds. Unlike the histories of many White mining town families with Appalachian roots, ours are not really *that* deep, not when compared to the large numbers of Scots-Irish and German settlers who began to flood into what is now considered southern Appalachia, reaching southwestern Virginia, western North Carolina, and upper East Tennessee a century before the Civil War, the time during which Black people in the United States, for the most part, were enslaved.

We have no records that go back to the seventeenth century in central Appalachia; the furthest way back I have searched finds our maternal great-grandmother born in Lee County, southwest Virginia, in 1833. Nobody Black I know throughout the landscapes that my network covers in central Appalachia left an oral or a written account of how they were enticed by a smooth-talking coal-company agent into selling the rights to the ground beneath their family's feet for a few dollars, a small number of pigs, a mule, or a rifle or shotgun: "Did you know that if we'd a' not been hoodwinked out of our land by them coal-company shysters in 1902, we'd a' had billions of dollars in coal royalties by now, our family set forever?"

I never heard or read that line applied to any Black

Appalachians, although it is part of the historical narrative of many Whites, a tale told from Jellico Mountain, on the Kentucky and Tennessee border, to Kayford Mountain, located near Cabin Creek, West Virginia. "Broad form deed" was not a phrase spoken beneath the Dead Dick Tree.

A family that emigrated into eastern Kentucky from Syria—the Dawahares—were prominent merchants in nearby Cumberland, the non-company-owned town of the Tri-Cities that anchored the commercial zone closest to Lynch and Benham. Srur Dawahare was born near Damascus in 1880, roughly a decade before Blacks were arriving to the rapidly developing coalfields of central Appalachia. Following his Ellis Island entry, Srur became a peddler and traveling merchant, eventually opening his first store in 1917 in the town of Neon, near Whitesburg in Letcher County, Kentucky. By the time—a century later—that the big box stores and Amazon swamped such mom-and-pop enterprises, the Dawahares owned more than thirty department stores in eastern Kentucky, southwest Virginia, and southern West Virginia. Until the 1970s, Dawahare's was one of the leading retail clothing businesses in all of Kentucky, including in Lexington, almost two hundred miles distance from the coalfields.

The presence of Eastern European immigrants in the coalfields, particularly in Lynch, is legendary, almost mythological. They were Czech, Polish, Yugoslavian, Croatian, and Hungarian. People with Eastern European surnames, like Hoska, Popovich, and Stankovich, were plentiful. There were the Italians with names such as Bianchi, Palko, Stagnolia, and Vicini. In the census of 1940, thirty-eight nationalities were counted in Lynch.

But generally, the Black people looked at these White ethnics just as they did the other (native) White people, those with Irish surnames, such as Caudill, Flannery, Smith, Johnson, and Williams. To Blacks, ethnic European Whites were indistinguishable, maybe except for their thick accents, from any other White people, even though they did not all look alike or—among the first wave—speak the same language. I did not know them as such while growing up, but our grandmother knew many dark-skinned people who were neither Black nor White. She called her Melungeon friends—the Mullinses and the Mises—"gypsies," and they told her they came into the area from eastern Tennessee. In the mid-1940s, the wide assortment of the nearly 12,000 residents in Lynch included around 4,100 African Americans.

There was an undeniable—even if a peculiar—kind of social cohesion and community spirit between Blacks and Whites. Without a doubt, it was the commonness of the drudgery, the risks, the low pay, and certainly the ill-health effects of being a coal miner that bonded us and them with the sense that, despite being Black or White, native or immigrant, in coal country our destinies were what Dr. Martin Luther King Jr. described as "inextricably intertwined."

That is not the same as saying that there is any evidence that most mountain Whites would agree with Dr. King or act in terms of a shared consciousness of social and economic class unity with Black people. Race capped class in the coal camps, even as there was unanimity among the United Mine Workers of America across racial lines. "We're all the same color underground" is still an often-repeated saying among coal miners. But most coal towns, unlike Lynch, were not pro-union districts—not even close-by Benham, which Lynch people always described as being "just across the ditch."

A photo of John L. Lewis, national president of the UMWA for four decades starting in 1920, hung on our living room wall when I was a boy. I also saw the same UMWA-issued photo in the homes of many of our neighbors and next to the

Farmer's Almanac calendar in the barbershop. Dad and his fellow miners were zealous trade unionists, card-carrying members of the UMWA. The photo of John L. Lewis displayed in our home above Mama's piano in our living room came before the one of Dr. Martin Luther King Jr., naturally, in chronological order. John L. Lewis's headshot photo—showing his round of puffy white hair parted down the middle and his eye-catching, caterpillar-like eyebrows—was sometimes positioned, in many Black homes, next to Jesus. Photos of two White men, eight by ten. "I know John L. Lewis is a White man," Dad once wisecracked, "but I also know Jesus don't look like that, not where the Bible says he's from."

After the March on Washington in 1963, Dad framed similar-sized photos of Dr. Martin Luther King Jr. and President John F. Kennedy—taken from *Jet* magazine—to join John L. Lewis. This holy threesome graced the wall in Dad's man cave, his DIY basement dugout where he kept his fishing and hunting gear and his tools. Times had moved on.

The local Black undertakers, Mitchell's Funeral Home in Cumberland and Simmons's in Harlan, buried the Black people, almost exclusively, up until roughly the same time the Black schools were terminated. Linked to the Black funeral home businesses in eastern Kentucky was the Lincoln Life Insurance Company, based in Louisville. Twice a month, a very pleasant and most professional man named Mr. Owsley came to town to collect the five dollar a month premium on the insurance policy our parents had through Lincoln Life. The all too familiar profile of President Abraham Lincoln was on the cover of the thin gray cardboard sleeve in which Mama kept the policy payment record, in a shoebox with other such "important stuff," under the cabinet next to the flour tin.

Seasonally, a Black-owned barbecue stand sprouts up in

the Harlan Walmart parking lot. If a Black-owned brick-and-mortar structure existed in my youth besides the undertakers or the small shopkeepers in or around the perimeter of the central business district anywhere in eastern Kentucky, I would like to have my memory jogged of it.

Our neighbor and Mama's best friend, Mrs. Eula Mae Moss Hammonds, a Black woman, stands out for being the head of nursing at the Appalachian Regional Hospital in Harlan from the late fifties through her retirement in the late seventies. Now, that was something to go in the section of *Ebony* magazine titled "Speaking of People." While her singular achievement did not make *Ebony*, she was profiled generously in the *Tri-City News* section called "Colored News," the weekly feature written by Mrs. Mattye Knight, the English literature teacher and all-around sage at the Lynch Colored School. Mrs. Dorothy Morrow of Lynch was also a Tuskegee Institute–trained registered nurse who worked in the Notre Dame Hospital of Lynch. To the delight of all who knew just how special it was, the late Ricky Pack, Lynch-born and raised, Black, spent the early part of his medical career—in the 1980s—serving in Harlan County.

There was no shared sense among Blacks to hold animosity against White people. And those Whites who harbored hatred and hostility toward Blacks—the KKK types—must have been way back in the woods someplace. There were no active White racist agitator groups in the towns, but Black people seemed to know from prior experiences how quickly the tide could turn. What effects racial distinctions, bigotry, exclusion, and the attitude and propaganda of White supremacy had in the coal town of my youth were at best benign and at worst undetectable. These beliefs and thoughts and creeds were like the big rattlesnakes that lived deep in the mountains that surrounded us: we knew we weren't likely to see them come out in the open, but we kept a wary eye out for them, even the little ones, just in case.

The place of race in life was taught to us informally, off the record, so to speak. But in our tightly intertwined communities, we never thought a bit about being inferior—or superior—in relation to White people. Whatever benefit White mountain people had that was directly tied to their being White was not all that apparent. Ultimately, it could have been asked: "If a White man thought himself superior, why would he be doing the same 'nigger' work and living under the same conditions—in a coal town—with Black people!?" We were all locked between these high mountain walls in a narrowly hemmed-in area, far from the weighty and consequential racial troubles of the world, which included the mainstream current trends and leadership of the civil rights movement. The bombing that occurred on September 15, 1963, at the Sixteenth Street Baptist Church that murdered four little Black girls in Birmingham, Alabama, was not discussed at our church the following Sunday. I was eighteen, and had it been discussed, I was quite old enough and politically conscious enough to remember it. Of course, we talked about it at home and at the Pool Room, but the catastrophic event was not discussed at school, not at the White school, where Black students had been for just a month. The otherwise earth-shattering news of the Birmingham church bombing of 1963 did not smash the business-as-usual quietude in and around Black Mountain.

Concerns about race and the civil rights movement in the 1950s and 1960s did not get through to Black mountain people, certainly not in the way trade unionism—the Coal Wars—consumed them in the 1930s in Harlan County. The brotherhood of trade unionism did not cross racial lines, not when it came to purely racial matters and social justice. Whites and Blacks working together to earn a living was one thing, but working together toward racial equality in general was quite another. When it came to the infringements on Blacks' human rights, the protest song "Which Side Are You On?" by Florence Reece was not heard. The Highlander Center, a training resource for labor and civil rights activists from across the United States from the 1930s to the 1960s, might well have been ten thousand—not just one hundred—miles from Harlan County, Kentucky. When Dr. Martin Luther King Jr. and other civil rights leaders left the Highlander Center in the mid-1950s and 1960s, they went south, into Alabama, Mississippi, Georgia, and the Carolinas—the virtual Sahara Deserts of America's sweltering heat of racial injustice. Strategically, it was not beneficial to the movement for them to go northward through the Cumberland Gap into the coal towns of central Appalachia. The mountains were high, and the country's political and economic domains were far away. Sequestered as we were, it was like the civil rights movement never even happened, not in the coal camps of eastern Kentucky. On the other hand, in the urbanized areas of West Virginia—as in Charleston and Huntington, where there were critical masses of Blacks—the tactics of the civil rights movement were demonstrated.

The civil rights movement, while in full bloom in the state of Alabama from where most Blacks in the interior of central Appalachia migrated in the early years of the twentieth century, was neither developing nor active in the coal camps. Yet, a Black person did not have to live in a metropolis like Birmingham, for example, to figure that out. They knew through word of mouth and contact with relatives back home in Alabama, but they were limited in the ways that they could react to their hardships based on racism in the mountains. After all, they lived in company-owned towns, and the preachers there could not lead them, not openly anyway, to defy Caesar.

They rendered unto Caesar what was Caesar's: things were governed by Caesar's business. The coal company, in our case, US Steel, was Caesar.

The news of the murder of Emmett Till in 1955 flashed through the community like wildfire. The cover story of *Jet* magazine's coverage of the funeral that September fanned the flames. But on the other hand, for reasons I cannot dislodge from my head, there was no doomsday discourse around The Tree about it. Nor about the Supreme Court decision in the *Brown v. Board of Education* case a year earlier. Was it that the Black people in the coal camps at the time were not sophisticated enough to understand and to resist the implications of the *Brown* decision, say, for example, on the future of—the control of—Black students' education and, specifically, what was surely to happen to Black students without a critical mass of Black teachers? I doubt that. I think, rather, that they, the older ones especially, had enough experience and were canny and astute enough with the ways of White folk to keep what opinions they were considering to themselves. They had no history of picking public policy fights in the coal camps. It was then, and it is now, about options, or the lack of them, that were available to Black people in the coal camps and elsewhere. In the coal camps, there were few, if any, options. It was what it was before it became what it is today, and not much has changed politically.

The local papers—the *Harlan Daily Enterprise* and the *Knoxville News-Sentinel*, the two most widely circulated newspapers in Harlan County—covered the murder of Emmett Till, the most heinous act of White supremacist terrorism to enter my consciousness at the time, in a rather casual, humdrum, and unemotional way. No blaring headlines. No breaking news or interruption of classwork with an announcement from the principal blared through the school's loudspeaker. Were it not for *Jet* and *Ebony* magazines, which came by mail to a few homes, like ours, or Black newspapers such as the *Louisville Defender*, the *Chicago Defender*, and the *Pittsburgh Courier*—which hung on slotted three-foot sticks with handles in our school library—Black people, in general, were kept in the dark about the civil rights movement. The mountain was high, the emperors lived far away, and only a few Black families had televisions.

On nights when the weather conditions were perfect, rhythm and blues and rock and roll music floated over the mountains and into radios from the fifty-thousand-watt AM station WLAC originating in Nashville, Tennessee. Including a raucous, Tarzan-like howl to start the show—most likely the brainchild of some bright White promoter to draw us Southern colored folks in—WLAC featured three White DJs: Bill "Hoss" Allen, Gene Nobles, and John Richbourg. WLAC's White DJs gave Black listeners throughout the South the option to buy all manner of personal-care products, like "Royal Crown hair dressing, Baby," or to receive by mail "a dozen live baby chickens, just in time for Easter." When I was ten, in 1956, a generation of Whites were being introduced to Black music through the televised medium of Dick Clark's *American Bandstand*.

Depression, despair, and suicidal thoughts came through the desolate and melancholy voice of Ruth Brown, Mama's favorite R and B artist, whose music she played often on our Victrola. I still own the original 78 rpm of classics like Ruth Brown's "Trouble in Mind." But as soon as I would wonder what captivated Mama about such a gloomy song as "Trouble in Mind," Mama would turn and play Ruth Brown singing "Fine Brown Frame," then smooch up to Dad and coo. "Punkin, you're crazy as hell," he would say grinning, pushing her away as the five of us laughed. We did not have a television, but our mama could play a piano just like Eubie Blake or Fats Waller, and we learned to sing along to all the popular music that Mama kept up with by reading *Jet* and *Ebony* magazines. Thank God for Mr. John Johnson, the founder of those culture-carrying platforms for colored people.

Our relatives in New Jersey would mail us 78 and 45 rpm records like "Sixty Minute Man" by Billy Ward and the Dominoes. Even the old guys around the tree grinned at those lyrics. In jest, a few of us young teens would serenade a beautiful girl across the street from our house named Claudine Mae Hall: we did the hit by Lloyd Price titled "Lawdy Miss Clawdy." We did a jig as Mama banged out Big Mama Thornton's "Hound Dog" on her piano long before we ever heard of Elvis Presley. Dad considered the Midnighters' "Work with Me Annie" as lewd and lascivious, but he liked "Ain't That a Shame" and "Blueberry Hill" by Fats Domino. Sam Cooke's 1964 hit "A Change Is Gonna Come" was clairvoyant, far-sighted. "A Change Is Gonna Come" was not only a beautiful ballad, but it was also politically important to us, as 1963 was the year they integrated the schools in Lynch. Change *sho' nuff* did come, and the changes totally transformed the lives of Blacks in central Appalachian coal towns, and change has remained the only constant since, as it always has. Not insignificantly, President Barack Obama used Cooke's immediately recognizable vocals on "A Change Is Gonna Come" as the theme of his presidential campaign in 2008.

Even though Nashville, where WLAC's signal originated, was close to the epicenter of the civil rights movement, it carried more loudly, reliably, and consistently the voices and messages of blues legends like B. B. King than it did the voices and messages delivered by the likes of Dr. Martin Luther King Jr., let alone that of the self-proclaimed and highly venerated

Black nationalist freedom fighter Malcolm X. The Black Muslims, as they were called, did not grace the airwaves of mainstream media.

Like our Black counterparts throughout the coalfields of central Appalachia, our local radio station broadcasting from nearby Cumberland, WCPM, offered up a listening menu that was primarily country and western, twangy Grand Ole Opry standard bearers like Roy Acuff, Hank Williams, the Carter Family, Johnny Cash, Merle Haggard, Dolly Parton, Loretta Lynn, Buck Owens, and Willie Nelson. WCPM operated a weekday morning show called *The Trading Post* and a Black religious program, replete with a sermon and local-based a cappella quartets singing gospels, sprinkled with announcements specifically targeted to Black people, which ran as we prepared for Sunday school and church service. That format was the extent of local Black media. There were no Black voices on local radio Monday through Saturday.

I was in the tenth grade in 1962 when we got indoor plumbing. A television arrived the next year, just in time for the March on Washington. The outside world was precisely that—outside the mountains. Appalachian Black coal miners were trying to make a living for their big families, and one of the most important objectives was to raise their kids the right way and see to it that they got the best education possible. After two generations in the coal camps of eastern Kentucky—by 1950—it was a foregone conclusion that most of those born in these hills, including in Lynch, "the Cadillac of coal towns," and certainly the next generation of children, would make their living outside the mountains. I do not remember ever hearing a father tell a son that he wanted him to grow up to be a coal miner, just like himself. Instead, it was, "You gotta do better than me!"

For the period between the time Blacks arrived and settled

in these coal towns and up through the 1950s, most of them developed a positive feeling about themselves and toward their neighbors. Coal towns were highly regulated environments, the forerunners to today's planned, gated communities—or campuses, as they are now called—like the Googleplex facility in Mountain View, California, where my nephew Justin Turner, with an undergraduate degree from Stanford and an MBA from Columbia, lives and works—for Facebook.

The company officials were patrons, in the sense of how fiefdoms were run in the Middle Ages, and they were not too unlike benevolent slave masters. It was, simply, the way the system worked. Those who went along with the system found employment—that is, if the system (the mines) provided work.

For most of the twentieth century, the mountains of eastern Kentucky—because of the absolute control of coal companies—sheltered Black people from the racist acts that were regularly practiced in the Southern Black Belt. On the other hand, the highly regulated coal-mining spaces repressed whatever urges Black people might have had to participate in civil rights demonstrations. It was a rather perverted version of the old question, "If a tree falls in the woods and there is nobody there to hear it, does it make a sound?"

Underneath the mountain of historical records about the pervasive poverty in the coal towns in central Appalachia lie the answers to two important questions: How does one explain the level of optimism, resiliency, and intergenerational upward mobility among working-class Blacks (the migrants) from these places? Why do we hear so little about Black Appalachians exhibiting the desperation and depression that marks the current regional opioid addiction among many Whites?

The drive to succeed on the part of many working-class Blacks with roots in central Appalachian coal towns is in stark contrast to reports about many poor Whites from the mountains, like the ones J. D. Vance sketched in the 2016 *New York Times* best-seller *Hillbilly Elegy*. Even poor Whites are granted at least a minimum status of privilege that is associated with simply being a White person in the United States. Black people with a deep history of responding to race-based prejudice, discrimination, and caste-like economic structures came to know—and passed on to their descendants—that they had better never take anything for granted. Nothing!

CHAPTER 11

School Integration Was Worse than a Kick in the Head by an Alabama Mule

SCHOOL—specifically the Lynch Colored Public School—was, without the shadow of a doubt, the brightest feature of life for Blacks growing up in Lynch, Kentucky, during the middle of the twentieth century. I also have no doubt that this sentiment applied to all Blacks who attended the segregated schools throughout the central Appalachian coalfields.

In practically every colored section of every coal town—and in urbanized non-coal-producing regions like Bristol, Kingsport, and Johnson City, Tennessee—there were colored schools that were, for the most part, first class—that is, as far as what was meant by the contradictory and incongruous proclamation "separate but equal."

Schools established for Blacks in southern West Virginia—such as in McDowell County locales like Bluefield, Keystone, Welch, Gary, and Beckley—were some of the best Black schools in the nation. So weighty and consequential was the presence of Blacks in West Virginia that Bluefield State College and West Virginia State College were established with

Author's granddaughters Africa and Amani Turner at Lynch Colored Public School in decline, 2019. William H. Turner Collection.

the express purpose of educating Blacks in the southern part of the Mountain State. Keystone, West Virginia, and Lynch, Kentucky, rivaled New York City and Chicago as “melting pots” in the early twentieth century. Bluefield State, in West Virginia, is listed as a historically Black college, but, consistent with the out-migration of Blacks from the coalfields over the past half century, 90 percent of the students, faculty, and administration at Bluefield State are White. Correspondingly, at the once all-Black West Virginia State University near Huntington, Whites far outnumber Black students, 80 percent to 20 percent. Kentucky State University, also an HBCU, is not far behind in those demographics.

Early on, young Black children were educated in Black churches in the coal camps, but in the late 1920s, structures were erected specifically as colored training schools on the Booker T. Washington model. Large, quality structures, always relative to the buildings constructed for Whites, containing grades from primary to senior high and with excellent teaching faculties—with names like Douglas, Dunbar, Langston, Lincoln, Rosenwald, and Washington—could be found up to the early 1960s in Benham, Lynch, Harlan, Hazard, Jenkins, and Wheelwright in eastern Kentucky. In southwest Virginia, Blacks for a fifty-mile radius around Appalachia—including Big Stone Gap, Coeburn, Dante, Pennington Gap, Saint Paul, and Stonega—converged at Bland High in Big Stone Gap for high school.

In virtually all of the so-called segregated colored schools like the one I attended, the study of Mr. Booker T. Washington and Dr. Carter G. Woodson—both raised in West Virginia—was unavoidable. Their lives blossomed during this golden era of Blacks in Appalachia when King Coal reigned as the dominant economic activity.

Mr. Washington was born into slavery (1856) twenty-five

miles from Roanoke, Virginia, and his autobiography, *Up from Slavery*, was published in 1909 at the pinnacle of the first major migration of Blacks out of the Black Belt South, which included the relocation of critical masses of them into the central Appalachian coalfields. Washington, until his death in 1915, operated out of Alabama from the Tuskegee Institute, a teachers' college that became the model for Blacks' education. He was supported enthusiastically by Northern White industrialists, politicians, and philanthropists like Julius Rosenwald and John David Rockefeller. His pledge that Blacks would accommodate themselves to work, live, and develop separately from Whites—and not demand the right to vote—made him the most powerful African American opinion leader, even in death, until the modern civil rights era beginning in the 1950s.

Carter G. Woodson, born in 1875 between Charlottesville and Richmond, Virginia, but raised in Huntington, West Virginia, thought that recalling prominent individuals and milestone happenings in the history of people of African descent was especially important. He spent his life—after graduating in 1903 from Berea College in Kentucky and earning a doctorate in history in 1912 from Harvard—promoting his writing (*The Miseducation of the American Negro* and the *Journal of Negro History*) and organizing agencies such as the Association for the Study of Negro Life and History all to codify and celebrate what has come to be known as Black History Month (February), which is recognized annually in the United States and Canada and has more recently has been observed unofficially in Ireland, the Netherlands, and Great Britain.

Booker T. Washington is solely responsible for the teaching philosophy and styles that characterized these colored schools. For most of the twentieth century, Kentucky State College—along with Bluefield and West Virginia State, as well as Knoxville College in Tennessee—supplied most of the teachers to schools for Blacks in the central Appalachian coalfields. There were other historically Black colleges in central Appalachia, such as Storer College in Harpers Ferry, West Virginia, and Morristown College in East Tennessee.

At the February 13, 1947, Parent Teacher Association (PTA) meeting at the Lynch Colored School, all parents present were given a list of *What the Teachers Expect of the Parents*, signed by "Teachers of Lynch Colored School":

1. To send to the teachers a clean, healthy, properly fed and properly clothed child with necessary tools with which to do the work.
2. To check graded papers and report cards regularly for progress, absences, and conduct and investigate any serious drop in grades.
3. To provide a quiet place in the home for study and require the child to study before the following school day.
4. To frequently appear unannounced in the classroom and observe the child's work.
5. To cooperate fully in matters of discipline and regular and prompt attendance at school.
6. To discuss problems concerning the child with the teacher and not with the child.
7. To see that the child gets the proper hours of sleep and comes to school with the proper frame of mind.
8. To bring criticisms to the teacher and the school instead of discussing and making criticisms in front of the child.
9. To attend the PTA.
10. To cooperate with or support all school activities.

11. To encourage the child to obey the teachers and respect both the teacher and his fellow students.
12. To commend the good deeds of their children as well as criticize the evil ones.
13. To think seriously of permitting children to attend unchaperoned house parties.
14. To insist upon good conduct when going and coming from school.
15. To train the child not to make hasty criticisms of other students.
16. To cooperate with the teachers in developing good habits, such as broad mindedness, honesty, dependability, and self-reliance and consciousness.

Mr. Booker T. Washington's practices and ideas for the way the colored schools were run flowed from his headquarters at the Tuskegee Institute in Alabama. In what became known as his "Atlanta Compromise" speech, delivered in 1895, he urged Blacks and Whites in the South to realize that their mutual interests were best served, and that interracial harmony would be maximized, so long as social segregation allowed for Blacks to acquire education and economic security.

There was a strong emphasis in our school on practical subjects and discipline, although ironically, shop class was not taught at the Lynch Colored School. Home economics was taught to the girls. Some were taught Latin and the classics. Schooling was the central thread in the quilt that covered the lives of Blacks in coal-company towns. The school building was the biggest structure to which Blacks laid claim as exclusively "theirs," even though all buildings—right down to the outhouses—were owned by the company. The colored school in Lynch and the one in the city of Harlan—home of

Lynch Colored Public School, c. 1950. Southeast Community College Appalachian Collection, Cumberland, KY.

the Rosenwald Red Devils—were the largest school buildings for Blacks in the entire region. Where the Harlan Rosenwald School stood majestically is indicated now by a relatively unremarkable and hardly noticeable three-by-four-foot tombstone-looking marker beside the highway that obliterated what once represented the heart of the Black community in Harlan. The Harlan Renaissance is not remembered in the form of public shrines.

The cluster of Black homes in the city of Harlan—mainly shotgun houses and businesses and the Harlan Colored Swimming Pool—was in what was known as the Georgetown section. The entire district, a ghetto to some, was demolished in 1974 when the course of the Cumberland River was changed for the purpose of what authorities called "flood abatement."

"Yeah, right!" many Blacks thought, knowing how urban renewal also applied to rural areas. Where Blacks had lived for nearly a century was pressed flat. I always wondered where all those displaced people went, not to mention how they were not party to the decision to displace them. The city of Harlan later built a then state-of-the-art athletic complex on the site. The recreational area still exists, having been improved several times since it was erected in what was otherwise designated as a floodplain. "Didn't It Rain?" a gospel song popularized by both Sister Rosetta Tharpe and Mahalia Jackson, took a caustic and mocking twist in the Black community of Harlan. In the month of January 2020, the area, despite the flood-abatement plan, was inundated, the flooding so extreme that school buses were underwater.

It was not uncommon to find teachers in the colored schools with degrees from the outstanding private Black colleges such as Fisk in Nashville; Wilberforce in southern Ohio; Hampton in Virginia, where Booker T. Washington studied; and, of course, Tuskegee, the university Washington founded that was well known to the Blacks in mining towns with roots in "Sweet Home Alabama." Significant numbers of the teachers held master's degrees, which they earned in summers at such prestigious colleges as Columbia University in New York City. They gloated—and let their students know frequently—that they were well educated and that they were, in fact, much better educated than the teachers at the White school. Nobody, at least in the Black community, ever questioned the veracity of this boastfully proud claim.

Any pattern of absence or irregular attendance from school might as well have been the father's nonappearance at work. "Problem children" in colored schools were the same thing as "problem parents," and fathers and mothers were straightforwardly summoned before the company superintendent to "explain" and change their children's abnormal behavior, such as truancy and uncleanliness. Immoral or decadent behavior and consistently poor performance in school reflected on the whole family. The teachers—mostly Black women whose husbands were miners—toiled watchfully with the families over schoolchildren to avoid the consequences of delinquent behavior on the part of children.

Home visits by the teachers occurred almost naturally because—by company design or pure coincidence—a Black teacher lived on every street in the Black neighborhoods in Lynch. One of the unintended good consequences of racial segregation was that Black students virtually couldn't get away from their teachers. Early on, in the 1920s through the 1940s, single female teachers boarded in the homes of married couples, such as our granny Ran.

Inside half a mile of our house, for example, I delivered the morning newspaper—the *Knoxville News Journal*—from the time I was twelve years old until I was twenty to the home of our high school principal as well as to my first-, fourth-, fifth-, and tenth-grade teachers. One of them, Mrs. Mary Davis, a very stern teacher, was mockingly called "Blackjack" because of her very dark complexion. She taught fifth grade for forty-two years and would often find sanctuary in our home or our granny's home whenever her oft-drunk, hot-tempered "bad nigga" husband, a fellow everybody detested and called "Florida Kid," would attack her. Nobody was afraid of him but her, and her neighbors would step in whenever he went into one of his frequent wine- or whiskey-induced outbursts.

Because Lynch and Benham were more highly capitalized and subsidized—by US Steel and International Harvester respectively—than all the other company towns in Harlan County combined, the schools and teachers were, as the choice of words went, "the best money could buy."

Much more so than preachers, the teachers—most of whom served for a lifetime—exerted great and lasting influence over the entire Black community. Several of my teachers taught all my brothers and sisters—the case for most families. My mother's first-grade teacher, Mrs. Henrietta Sweatt, was the same first teacher encountered by every Black student who passed through the Lynch Colored School from 1930 to 1970. Mrs. Sweatt and most of her colleagues stewed in, and skillfully applied, the Latin phrase *in loco parentis*, a reference to a person who takes on the same functions and responsibilities of a parent. Her word was law. I saw Mrs. Sweatt reprimand—rather, make that haul over the coals—and then paddle a disobedient first-grader in front of his mother and grandmother, both of whom stood aside and smiled approvingly. It was the boy's first day of school.

Mrs. Sweatt and other elementary teachers set the standards, which were organized around three basic values: (1) practicing good manners, (2) displaying common sense, and (3) being a disciplined person. Of these three, it was discipline—ritualized and repetitive drills in reading, writing, and arithmetic—that lay at the heart of their mode of instruction. Teachers had free rein to use a black strap—a two-foot-long, half-inch-thick strip of rubber cut from a mining conveyor belt—to enforce their rules, which were often set in real time.

Our parents trusted our teachers unquestionably and unconditionally. An inferior or mediocre student was expected to behave well, despite his or her lack of academic sharpness. That is, you might not have any book sense, but if you learn to simply act like you have some common sense, you will still be able to get some kind of job. The teachers were concerned and dedicated, and they looked for and found the switch that turned every student on. They pushed us awfully hard and constantly talked aloud about potential. And when a student was punished—especially if a whacking at school was deserved, and it always was—the parents were told afterward, and a second "whoopin" at home was almost certain to follow. A critical mass of those in my grandparents' generation—those who came to Lynch from the cotton patches, the sharecroppers—had little formal schooling. They were, on the other hand, fully aware of the importance of their children and grandchildren taking advantage of the opportunities for learning that they did not have.

Mrs. Sweatt was quoted in a 1987 piece titled "Black Home in Appalachia" in the Louisville *Courier-Journal* as having said, "Sometimes I spanked them and sometimes I told their parents, and they came and spanked them too. That is how we got it done. Black kids were pushed harder than the white ones. I believe the black teachers were more conscientious than the white teachers were, more concerned and dedicated. Some folks made history out of that little crowd that I taught. We had to assimilate good manners and common sense."

Character, in fact, could compensate for most scholastic or other shortcomings or handicaps that were academic, mental, or emotional. In another way, having some common sense was a natural by-product of having good manners. After all, not everybody was bright or brilliant in schoolwork, but any nincompoop—any "village idiot"—could be taught to exercise good judgment and everyday awareness so that they could, at least minimally, take care of themselves, get a job, have a high probability of finding someone to marry, raise sensible children, and live a productive life. Later, this approach became known as "tough love." In the case of children with academic disabilities, the remediation came to be known later as "special education." The education dispensed at the Lynch Colored School and its counterparts that dotted the coal camps was special, period.

I was in college in the mid-1960s when I heard for the first time the phrase "special education classes." "Slow learners" and the "educationally disabled" were not operative terms in the way the teachers then taught students who had academic, behavioral, health-related, physical, or other "special" educational needs. "Deaf and dumb" and "retarded," however crude and politically incorrect those terms were, were in retrospect the most-used expressions to identify students with learning disabilities and to include some who clearly had mental and emotional frailties. Children with Down syndrome did not attend our school. Some kids who could not hear or were hard of hearing went away, to Danville, to the Kentucky School for the Deaf, which, even in the days prior to the *Brown* decision, was open to all hearing-impaired students in Kentucky, irrespective of race. I do not recall any students who used wheelchairs in my school days.

There were no resources, no specific provisions or services or alternative instructional classes, for educationally disadvantaged children. It was as if everybody just knew, and the teachers certainly knew what to do with those students whose limited use of language was evidence enough of their limited thinking, reading, writing, or mathematical skills. There definitely was no educational tracking system that dispersed the school population to courses according to the students' scores on an intelligence test that supposedly determined if he or she was above average, normal, or below average. No students were assigned to classes with other students whose overall academic profile was the same as their own; that is, there were no such things as gifted and advanced classes. The brightest student in the class might be sitting next to the student who was educationally disadvantaged or, in the lingua franca, "as dumb as the day is long," as Mrs. Sweatt often said, aloud, of students who tested her patience.

On the wall of the library in the Lynch Colored School was Douglas Malloch's famous inspirational poem "Be the Best of Whatever You Are."

> If you can't be a pine on the top of the hill,
> Be a scrub in the valley—but be
> The best little scrub by the side of the rill;
> Be a bush if you can't be a tree.
>
> If you can't be a bush be a bit of the grass,
> And some highway some happier make;
> If you can't be a muskie then just be a bass—
> But the liveliest bass in the lake!
>
> We can't all be captains, we've got to be crew,
> There's something for all of us here,
> There's big work to do, and there's lesser to do,
> And the task you must do is the near.
>
> If you can't be a highway then just be a trail,
> If you can't be the sun be a star;
> It isn't by size that you win or you fail—
> Be the best of whatever you are!

I often heard, "So-and-so ain't gonna never 'mount to shit, because she ain't got no damn common sense, even if she *is* smart!" Worse yet was to have it said that you were nothing more than "an educated fool," which was shorthand for a person with innate ability who did not use any common sense, also known as native, or mother, wit. In school, the first order of business was order. There was a clear chain of command. Everything fit into a tangible pattern, triggered by bells that rang with the same regularity as the coal train whistles that blew routinely, calling our daddies to work. Seats in classrooms were always arranged, and there was an almost seasonal-like sequence to things: the whole system of learning was very ritualized and results-oriented.

Always sparklingly clean and with its dark mahogany floors shiny with oil, our school featured a pictorial tour of Black people's history in America on the walls of the main corridor. From the first grade on, every school day, at every class break, we passed by more than two dozen elegantly framed portraits done up in the style of American Realism. These glass-encased portraits, uniformly three feet wide by three feet long, were framed in shiny oak, and they lined each side of the first- and second-floor corridors at the Lynch Colored Public School.

In the style of Harlem Renaissance photographer James Van Der Zee, the photographs, each with a summary biography of the subjects, included West Virginia coal miner and Berea College graduate, the father of Black history, Dr. Carter G. Woodson; Dr. Mary McCloud Bethune, educator and civil rights activist who founded Bethune-Cookman College in Daytona Beach, Florida, and who was cofounder of the United Negro College Fund; Dr. W. E. B. Du Bois, Fisk graduate who was the first African American to earn a doctorate at Harvard and who was a founding member of the National Association for the Advancement of Colored People (NAACP); Dr. George Washington Carver, agricultural scientist at the Tuskegee Institute in Alabama, inventor, and the most famous Black scientist in the world, known as the "Peanut Man"; and Marian Anderson, singer of classical music and spirituals who sang outside before an audience of seventy-five thousand at the Lincoln Memorial in Washington because Constitution Hall, which was owned by the Daughters of the American Revolution, refused to host her, owing to the color of her skin.

There was the angelic countenance of Madam C. J. Walker, who focused her entrepreneurial skills on hair-care products for Black women, becoming, by the time of her death in 1919, the wealthiest self-made woman in America; Ida B. Wells, the devoted antilynching proponent and feminist who was one of the cofounders of the NAACP; the first African American to play in Major League Baseball, signing with the Brooklyn Dodgers in 1947, Jackie Roosevelt Robinson; Marcus Mosiah Garvey, among the Harlem Renaissance period of Blacks who advocated for separatism from the Whites and the formation of self-governing Black communities—his ideas came to be known as Garveyism; Ralph Johnson Bunche, who was involved in the formation of the United Nations and was the first Black to receive the Nobel Peace Prize in 1950 for his efforts in the establishment of the modern state of Israel; Harriet Tubman, who was born into slavery in 1822 but escaped and made some thirteen undertakings to rescue dozens of enslaved people through a network of antislavery activists and safe houses known as the Underground Railroad; and Paul Laurence Dunbar, who was born to parents who were enslaved in Kentucky and who became one of the most famous playwrights and poets of the late nineteenth and early twentieth centuries. The pictures also included Sojourner Truth, abolitionist and women's rights activist who was born Isabella (Belle) Baumfree but who renamed herself in 1843 and, at the 1851 Women's Rights Convention held in Akron, Ohio, presented what is recognized as one of the most well-known abolitionist and women's rights speeches in American history titled "Ain't I a Woman?" Mrs. Mattye Knight regularly assigned that speech during her almost four-decade-long tenure as a teacher at the Lynch Colored School. During the Civil War, Truth recruited Blacks for the Union side. After the

Mattye Guy Knight, longtime literature teacher at Lynch Colored Public School. William H. Turner Collection.

war, she also tried unsuccessfully to secure land grants from the federal government for former slaves summarized as the promise of forty acres and a mule.

There was, of course, the photo of African Americans' most dominant leader between 1890 and 1915: Booker Taliaferro Washington. Booker T., as he was called reverentially, advised the president of the United States as well as the heads of corporations, such as US Steel's Andrew Carnegie and Sears and Roebuck's Julius Rosenwald.

The unstated but well-understood reason for these Black luminaries being in front of us each day was to convey that we too could be a credit to our race, and to the human race. The teachers, their specialties aside, planted and drilled in us the academic and principled seeds that they knew we were going to need later, as Mrs. Knight would say, "when life jumps out at you!" If you did not study Marian Anderson while you were in high school, you would not appreciate how to handle rejection. We were made to read about George Washington Carver because, besides being an accomplished scientist, he overcame polio and other adversities; his life was an object lesson in resilience and character. They threw the Booker T. and Rosenwald story at us to demonstrate the value of compromise and cooperation to achieve goals. So ingrained were the stories of these Black people of distinction and achievement that I assumed that everybody in the world knew who these people were and what they did. The appreciation of Black history was not just a February affair, as it is in the school life of Black children today. Black History Month occurred every day in our school.

I still cringe every time I think about the decision to remove these portraits from the walls when the school was repurposed as a middle school in 1964, when the two schools in Lynch were "integrated." I distinctly remember seeing portraits of White men on the walls of the school into which we were supposedly assimilated. I have no memory of who these men were, but I do remember that there were no Black faces to be seen among the grand portraits on the walls of the integrated Lynch school system.

Our principal, Mr. John V. Coleman—and before him, Mr. Benjamin Shobe—studied at Kentucky State College for Negroes. His roommate, Henry V. Cheaney, who was awarded a doctorate in history from the University of Chicago, made the rounds to every Black mountain school in the 1950s and 1960s to lecture, often speaking at the commencement exercises at Benham, Lynch, Harlan, Jenkins, Middlesboro, and Hazard—all in the same season.

The Harlan and Middlesboro Rosenwald schools came into being under the sponsorship of the Rosenwald Fund, which was set up by Booker T. Washington's patron, philanthropist Julius Rosenwald (1862–1932), part owner of Sears, Roebuck and Company. Mr. Rosenwald donated millions in matching funds to support the education of African American children throughout the rural South. In Harlan, Kentucky, in 1918, the Black people of the community undertook the responsibility to raise five hundred dollars for the construction of a building, and with the contribution of four hundred dollars from the Rosenwald Fund, a new two-room school building opened in 1920. The last students and teachers left four decades later, absorbed into the Harlan Independent School System.

At the high school level, the teaching corps, all exceptionally well-prepared disciplinarians, offered a rich curriculum. Classical literature, music, art, foreign languages (French, German, and Spanish), science, math, history, and biology were standard curricula. The typical Eurocentric set of social science and humanities courses of study (Burns, Browning, Keats, Shakespeare, and e. e. cummings) was complemented by an Afrocentric one. For example, it was required of us to read and analyze the poetry of Paul Laurence Dunbar and James Weldon Johnson alongside that of the top names of the Harlem Renaissance Black poets, playwrights, essayists, and novelists such as Dorothy West, Langston Hughes, Countee Cullen, and Richard Wright. I heard about Zora Neale Hurston at the Lynch Colored School when I was in the eleventh grade, in 1963, when Mrs. Knight also had us reading James Baldwin's *Another Country.*

Ebony and *Jet* magazines were displayed as prominently in our school's library as *Look*, the *Saturday Evening Post*, *Reader's Digest*, and *Life*. Norman Rockwell's America did not overshadow what we saw—in our colored schools—in the works of Black artists such as Henry Ossawa Tanner and Aaron Douglas, whose paintings hung as prints prominently in most of the schools that coal-camp Blacks attended.

Monthly, the schools held student talent showcase productions that were nothing short of public exhibitions in excellence. We performed all manner of plays and recitations, called "operettas"; many of them were Eurocentric in content and style, but most were taken from works by writers like Paul Laurence Dunbar and Lorraine Hansberry. Most parents, especially the mothers, devotedly assisted in these productions; the men helped to build sets, and our mothers made special costumes for the productions. Attendance at these theatrical and dramatic shows was substantial, seemingly mandatory for adults, the parents, and grandparents; families were deliberately seated together. We sang, soliloquized orations and readings, and performed various histrionic presentations with a level of seriousness that surpassed the intensity of competition in athletic events between the colored schools.

A company town's reputation and honor were heavily hinged on successful sports programs, both in the high schools and, in some cases, with the company-sponsored baseball and basketball teams, the latter of which were listed as semiprofessional. It was rumored, and not uncommon in the 1930s and 1940s, for young single miners—otherwise grown men—to play as high school students on Friday nights in basketball and football games. Some were recruited by the coal companies—scouted, so to speak—because of their ability to play baseball. Like today's corporate tycoons, the winning ways of a coal camp's teams were just behind coal tonnage produced in terms of a town's bragging rights.

Little annoys or nags me more than the widely held stereotype that Appalachian people are a bunch of ignoramuses. In my home, I was taught to be troubled by the assumption that Black people, as a rule, neither could nor wanted to—even when given the opportunity—amount to much. Many of us worked harder just to contradict that stereotype. To be called "a credit to your race" was a high honor.

The landmark decision of the US Supreme Court in *Brown v. Board of Education* (1954) was based on the noblest intention, to put schoolchildren, no matter their race, in the same facilities for learning. The elimination of "separate but equal" facilities was one matter, but there is no doubt, in retrospect, that the educational outcomes of Blacks diminished measurably and noticeably after the *Brown* decision was put into operation. Integration became the handmaid of disintegration and evisceration.

Our school was separate, built just for us by the US Steel Company, as evidenced by the name of the school, which is still etched on the facade for all to see: Lynch Colored Public School. The two-story red-brick building was in no way equal to the building the company erected for the White students. Their school was constructed using native limestone and granite and was located in the solidly White part of town, on Main Street, on what was called "the upper end of town." The (White) Lynch Graded and High School had no color-coded adjective carved into the facade of their main buildings. The colored and the White schools were separate physically—and culturally—from each other. They were not equal in terms of the cost and outlay for construction and upkeep, not in the least. Even so, us Black people cherished our schools. Our schools were the vital spark plugs of our communities, places where yearn-to-learn fires were ignited and fanned, and then they lit up the futures of Black families that were just one generation removed from sharecropping in central Alabama.

Schooling took on a sacred-like importance to most people in the coalfields, especially Blacks. People knew, as plain as the nose on your face, as the expression went, that mining jobs had dried up in just one generation after the influx of Blacks to the coalfields—between World War I and World War II. By the onset of the Great Depression, Julius Rosenwald had overseen the opening of almost five thousand schools for Blacks in his name. Just as Lynch was opening as a coal town (1917), schools separated by races sprang up in all the coal-producing counties. And those with a critical mass of Blacks remained open, as "colored schools," until the mid-1960s. Lynch had the highest number of students of all colored schools in the region.

How well I remember the competitiveness and jealousies between the Lynch Colored School and her counterparts in Benham, Middlesboro (Lincoln), Pineville (Roland Hayes), and Harlan (Rosenwald) or London High, Dunham in Jenkins, Liberty High in Hazard, Perry Cline in Pikeville, and Somerset High. There were roughly only six dozen teachers in these schools, all college graduates, primarily from Kentucky State College for Negroes.

Schools just for Blacks could be found within a seventy-five-mile radius from Lynch into southwest Virginia and eastern Tennessee—the Tri-Cities of Bristol, Kingsport, and Johnson City—and all had virtually the same mission: to educate Blacks separately from Whites. These Black schools from the Tri-City area were athletic rivals. Each year, Lynch would play against Gary Negro High School in Gary, West Virginia, which was also bankrolled by US Steel.

There was considerable loss when these schools were desegregated. I do not use the word "integration" because the schools were not "combined" in the authentic sense of a mutual, shared, collective, well-thought-out convention for bringing together otherwise unrelated and contrasting people and their institutions. Far from it. The White authorities simply implemented it the way they saw fit, exercising *their* interests and priorities, especially in terms of hiring decisions. Such is the meaning when it is noted that the United States did not really abolish slavery, but simply repurposed it.

The Black schools, unfailingly, got educational materials, like books, after they were discarded by the White schools, at which time the White students got new provisions and materials. I recall telling Paul Turner, a White boy I came to know after being at the White school for a few weeks, that I felt like I knew him already because his name had shown up several times over the years in the books I would get at our school, recycled from their school. Paul laughed, but it was not funny to me, not in the least.

The principals of the colored schools in all the coal camps of eastern Kentucky were the most powerful Black people, an equivalent for Blacks to the mayor in every town. Few Black men wore a white shirt and tie every time you saw them, but the Black principals did. It was as though the Black principal was required, by custom, to be aloof, aristocratic, ever the model of decorum, refined and reserved, a credit to his race. Even when in his yard on a Saturday morning cutting his grass, our principal, Mr. Coleman, called "Fess" informally, would be dressed just so, always embodying dignity, self-respect, and authority.

In an *Atlanta Journal* article published in 1992 under the headline "Memorial Day Reunion Draws Kentuckians Back to Their Roots," Kenneth Mapps—who was then fifty-six but who died in 2019 at the age of eighty-three after spending forty years as a driver and later as a manager with Greyhound Lines based in Atlanta following a six-year stint in the army—said of his coach and later his principal at Lynch Colored Public School Mr. Coleman: "Fess taught me to do it good and do it hard and this has helped me throughout. Of course, you want to be a man, like your coach and your father."

Mr. Coleman did it good, and he did it hard. After all, he was constantly under surveillance, so to speak, by the superintendent of the Lynch Independent School District. At least two or three times a year, in the manner of a fire drill, the superintendent, Mr. Sam Potter—a White man, of course—would show up at our school.

In what felt like a military-style inspection, he would walk around with Mr. Coleman and give the building—and us—the once-over, reminiscent of the way Mrs. Ruffner, the lady for whom Booker T. Washington worked as a teen, would do. She would run her white-gloved hand over places Booker T. had been instructed to dust. A day or so prior to the White superintendent's visit to our school, the word got around, mockingly, that tomorrow would be "white glove day." Mr. Charles "Chief" Cross, the longtime school janitor to whom I served as an assistant for six years, like many older Blacks, referred to the White men in charge of things with the scornful slang name "Mr. Charlie"; his female equivalent was "Miss Ann." Down deeper, Mr. Charlie was called "a cracker" by the older Blacks, a reference, a racial epithet, for White slave drivers, the one who cracked the whip. The scenario during Mr. Potter's visit was an exercise in "putting on Mr. Charlie."

We'd go to school a bit more shined up than the day before, and the building was burnished and buffed, the banisters wiped down, the windows cleaned, the rows of chairs in the classrooms in perfectly straight positions, the glass in the trophy cases shined. When the superintendent of the Lynch Independent School District came to our school, everything was made spick-and-span.

I still see the twinkle, an almost half-wink, in Mr. Coleman's eye when he knew Mr. Potter had arrived. Chief, the janitor, broom in hand, had been on the lookout out in the front of the school, giving a signal to Fess who was in the window of his second-floor office, just beneath the "Colored School" concrete badge. When Mr. Potter left, there was a collective sigh, for once again, we had successfully put on the bossy, the dominating, and the high-and-mighty Mr. Charlie, the White man! No doubt the scenario was repeated in colored schools all around, since the politics of segregated education was the same throughout central Appalachia. It was like playing out Baldwin's book *Blues for Mister Charlie*, which was loosely based on the murder of Emmett Till.

Skinning and grinning, behaving in an insincerely cheerful and subservient way, even going so far as faked flattery, has long been a mode of survival for Black people in America. Going well, going hard. Without question, the principal spoke for and visibly represented and embodied the best in the Black community to the White power brokers—the company bosses and the school board and the big-store agents.

The most disgraceful drunkards, the so-called tough guys, and even the "bad niggas" showed respect to the principal of the school. Everybody wanted the best for their kids, so the logic went. How else could a Black man get to be the principal of the school unless he were the best, which sometimes required the art of faked sincerity? Indeed, the principals of the Black schools were in a class all unto themselves. When they were de-professionalized—demoted and literally run out of town in the name of integration—a collective gulp, a feeling of collective disbelief, roiled across the Black community.

If Mr. Coleman could be dismissed so summarily, what does that signal to the rest of us?

Without fail, if asked to recall their experiences at any of the Black schools in the coal camps, former students in my generation gush enthusiastically with wistfulness and child-like reminiscence. If indeed the principals of the Black schools in the area were the tip of the spear in terms of community influence, the school itself was the bull's eye in the Black community.

For all of us, the school was a centering point, a safe place, a place where no matter what was going on at home, we knew that the school was the leveling ground, like a canopy or a dome under which one could mellow out, a cooling-out space. At "the White school," which was how the older members of the community called the integrated school for decades after the closing of the Black schools, Black students were placed, almost automatically, in lower tracks, their aspirations and expectations lowered by the White teachers. Frieda Dianna Hopkins Outlaw, one of my high school classmates—our mothers had gone to the Lynch Colored School together—tells of how the chemistry teacher said to her when we went there from the Lynch Colored School in 1963, "You don't need to take this class," implying that it was beyond her ability level or the level of expectations he had already set for Black students. She took the class anyway, excelled at it, and went on to Berea College and majored in nursing. Today, at seventy-four, after a distinguished career in health care, Frieda, with an earned doctorate in educational psychology from Catholic University, is a top consultant to the American Nursing Association.

When the center of the community—the school—was closed, many of the Black students lost their way. There were fewer or no Black role models; the living magnets who drew them into their sacred orbit each and every day, and who drew every good and noble thing out of them, were gone just like that! The place to which they looked forward to going was replaced by an unfamiliar environment and by White teachers and staff who—at least in that first year—seemed to "try" being courteous. I was there in the first so-called integrated class, and I saw it and felt it with my own eyes and spirit. Most of the White teachers seemed stiff and pretentious and uncomfortable with us. And naturally so, for this was a path not taken before. Some were outright brusque and gruff and mean-spirited and dispiriting. Unlike the highly visible and full-of-zip students that their older siblings were at the colored school less than a decade earlier, most Black students at the integrated school, except the exceptional athletes, became invisible. The rate of Black students who went to college dropped off precipitously. At the White school, the portraits on the wall might as well have been Martians in the eyes of the Black students. More than sixty years later, I cringe whenever I think about what happened to the portraits that decked the halls of the Lynch Colored School. They—the decision-makers involved with detailing the process of integrating the Black into the White school—trashed them. On my personal account, I do not know what I was thinking to allow that to happen. After all, I was at home when the drama and details unfolded, and I was still there for a full two years after 1964. The process by which the Lynch Colored School was closed, and the outcome that followed, was an out-and-out tumultuous and devastating social whirlwind.

That the teachers at the Lynch Colored School were caring and loving, almost naturally, can never be contradicted. Most of them came to teach in Lynch in the 1930s, some when the school opened in 1926, and they not only knew their students personally but also taught many of their students' parents, at least the mothers. After integration, Black students no longer saw all their teachers as they walked down the streets in the neighborhoods in which they lived or in other places where Blacks congregated. White teachers, after all, did not go to the Black churches and did not belong to the organizations that fastened the Black community to itself.

The Lynch Colored Public School band was disbanded, literally, and in the so-called integrated setting, fewer and fewer Black students took up clarinets, drums, flutes, French horns, oboes, trumpets, trombones, and tubas. There were no more Black teens piecing together their musical skills to make up a rock and roll and a rhythm and blues ensemble. Bands like the Jive-A-Dears of the Lynch Colored School, which was organized and managed by the music teacher and marching band director Mr. Howard Rawlings from 1955 to 1964, disappeared. Such talented ensembles evaporated and have not existed among Black youth since. There were a number of music groups that played at sock hops in the colored school gyms and in the juke joints and music halls that then dotted hillside Black communities, like Shorty's Joy in Norton, Virginia, or the Veteran's Club in Cumberland, or The Hall in the Georgetown section of Harlan.

The rate of Black students who went to college after graduating from the mountain-area high schools fell precipitously after integration. And even as Black athletes proliferated like so much kudzu—dominating the football and basketball teams—even a smaller proportion of the star Black athletes went on to college as compared to the athletes who graduated from Black high schools two and three generations before the mid-1960s. This fact remains, even though the number of Blacks in the traditional college-age cohort (eighteen to twenty-four)—as a percentage of the total population—fell by a factor of 70 percent between 1960 and 2010. The title of an old and transcendent hymn "Will the Circle Be Unbroken?" applies. The circle, the network that consisted of Black teachers seeing to it that their students went to Knoxville College or to Kentucky State College, was broken.

The faculty and administrative ranks in schools, from kindergarten through twelfth grade, became almost totally White throughout eastern Kentucky—indeed, throughout central Appalachia—once integration "matured" so to speak. The prediction and cautionary expression the janitor of the colored school Mr. Cross had made in the summer of 1963, about how integration would "set colored folk back farther than a kick in the ass by an Alabama mule," took on real-life consequences. By 1966, while I was in my second year at the local community college, the analogy my father had made long ago that featured a frog being boiled alive struck my awareness again. We had, like the frog, been placed in room-temperature water, and now it was boiling, if but slowly. For all practical purposes, the students at the colored schools—the frogs—were cooked to death, some never realizing exactly when we lost consciousness. I also could not forget Granny's warnings as to what happens when Black people "lose their stuff."

The school was the thread that held the Black community together; in fact, it held entire families together. At one time, in 1952, I was in the first grade, my sister Evelyn was in the second grade, our brother Irvin was in the fourth grade, our sister Marie was in the fifth grade, and our oldest sister Peggy was in the seventh grade. The five of us walked to school each day, together, through our grandparents' yard. Our mother had been taught in the first grade by the same lady, Mrs. Sweatt, who also taught each of us in first grade. The Lynch Colored School served the same purpose for many big Black families—and the not-so-big Black families as well.

When the schools integrated, the Lynch Colored School was repurposed as the Lynch Middle School. Older siblings left for the Lynch High School, parting ways from their young siblings and going to the all-White part of town. The Black community began to crack with these new tracks.

Only God knows what happened to the untold number of trophies—cups, medals, medallions, plaques, plates, and shields—that once filled the five six-foot-tall, multishelved, glass-enclosed, oak-framed cabinets that lined the main and second-floor hallways of the Lynch Colored School. Other records of the students' academic and athletic achievements were kept in Principal Coleman's office and in the library. They too were gone, blown away, as it were, with the wind of absorbing the Black students into the White school! I hope it is not true, but I was told by a reliable source that a garbage truck was loaded up with "all the stuff they didn't want to keep." If that is true, it is an outstanding example of "the stuff" Granny said Black people lost, or threw away, or what White authorities considered to be worthless "Black stuff" and therefore could be justifiably and excusably disposed of.

By contrast, there is a very distinctive space in Lynch that is specifically dedicated to preserving the history of the school that absorbed the Lynch Colored School. Situated in the iconic Lynch Depot building—in the nexus of the tourist attraction known as Portal 31 on Main Street—the Bulldog Room is home to hundreds of pictures, jerseys, and trophies that the brochures say "paint a picture of a culture that was, and in many ways still is, deeply-rooted in Appalachian pride." Framed photographs lining the walls in the Lynch Depot include Black faces of athletes, but there is absolutely nothing among the exhibits that indicates the existence of the Lynch Colored School.

In *Acting White: The Ironic Legacy of Desegregation*, author Stuart Buck narrates stories of the reactions of Blacks throughout the South in a chapter titled "The Closing of Black Schools." He recalls:

> In Tuscumbia, Alabama, the former principal of the black high school said that when the buildings were torn down, "I saw a lot of people standing on the street crying. And it was like somebody had died." . . . A former teacher said, "It just kills me dead. . . . We used to raise money to keep that school up for years, selling ice cream and hot dogs [to build the black school]." When the school was closed, black students lost their school colors, their symbols, and their mascot.

When Rougemont, a Rosenwald School in Durham County, North Carolina, closed, Buck notes:

> One of the teachers recalled that she "cried for almost a week. It was just like you were losing a friend." A community resident said: "It hurt the community; everybody. We had one of the best schools in [the city]. We had good teachers. Why did they want to change it?" Another resident noted: "Many students from the area stopped education after integration came. There wasn't a strong push. Things seemed to have broken down."

In countless interviews over a four-decade span with graduates of the colored schools within an eighty-mile radius of Harlan County, words and expressions such as "flabbergasted," "disgusted," and "heart ripped out" and a variety of feelings such as animosity, anguish, despondency, and rage peppered the responses to the question, "How did you feel about the closing of the colored school?"

Psychologically, the most overriding factor that made the so-called integration of the schools such a bitter and hard pill to swallow, at least for Black people, was the extent to which segregation had the effect of compelling them to be self-reliant, self-sufficient, self-respecting, and self-contained. Up to that point, Black people did not have to concern themselves with what White people thought about them, about their intelligence or their potential. Not really, not directly. "I ain't stud'n 'bout what no cracker thinks about or says about me, 'long as they don't fuck with me." Integration changed that viewpoint. The water was on the stove, room temperature.

Within five years, the lion's share of the Black teachers, most in the prime of their careers, were gone from the Lynch school system. Our coaches—with winning records in the segregated days—were demoted to junior high jobs, made assistants to the White coaches or eliminated entirely, which was most often the case. The Black teachers in the county who were close to retirement and did not wish to move to Lexington, Louisville, or Indianapolis stayed in place. To say that "things haven't been the same since" is shorthand for Janitor Cross's prediction about the adverse effects of integration on Black people: This same endpoint befell all the colored schools in the coal camps of central Appalachia. One takeaway: change is not always progress. Blacks traded the relative degrees of independence and self-determination that they possessed inside the framework of racial segregation—especially where the schooling of their children was concerned—for what the racial integration of the schools promised, and now we have neither.

CHAPTER 12

The Principal of the White School Became a Lifelong Friend

IN EARLY August 2018, exactly fifty-five years after the absorption of the Lynch Colored School into the Lynch High School, which is still called "the White school" by the handful of Blacks around the area who are over seventy years of age, I received a phone call from Mrs. Faye Isaacs, the wife of Mr. Lonnie Jackson Isaacs, better known as "Jack," who in 1963 became the first principal of the merged schools in Lynch.

"Bill," she whispered retiringly, "Jack is extremely ill, and we are bringing him home for hospice care." After she shared that it probably wouldn't be long, we talked a bit about how close Mr. Isaacs and I became in the half century that had passed since the two schools were combined in 1963. I reminded her about my last lengthy conversation with the man who always insisted I call him "Jack," which I could not and would not do. In November of 2017, he ranted during a phone conversation we had about President Donald Trump, whom he described as "contemptible, disrespectful, deceitful, misogynistic, narcissistic, and racist!"

"The other day, among the last things he said before he could no longer speak, he reminded me that he wanted you to say some words at his funeral services," Mrs. Isaacs said. Over the years—especially between 2002 and the last conversation we had—whenever Mr. Isaacs and I talked, I made an entry about the exchange in my diary. I brushed off the thought of speaking at his funeral the day he said to me—while he and Mrs. Isaacs were guests at our Lexington home for dinner—that he wanted me to have a speaking role at his final rites. At the time, 2005, I was vice president for diversity at the University of Kentucky. Thirteen years had passed. We talked many times by phone and in face-to-face visits over those years.

At Crestwood Christian Church on Bellefonte Drive on August 31, the place and date of Mr. Isaacs's memorial service, I was, again, like the proverbial fly in the buttermilk, or standing out like a hair in a biscuit. Those are expressions my granny Ran used to describe when a Black person was the lone Black person in a space full of White people. I had grown used to this feeling since going to college, from the time when we left the Lynch Colored School.

Mr. Isaacs, born in 1934 in Lynch, graduated from the Lynch High School and later returned to teach history. He became principal in August 1963, when he was twenty-seven and I was seventeen. We were in that first so-called integrated class. Mr. Isaacs was a very reflective, deep-thinking person, and his slight stutter made him seem even more deliberate in expressing his thoughts and ever so meticulous in choosing his words.

My grandparents—who lived on First Street and from whose front porch the red bricks of the two-storied Lynch Colored Public School looked like a wall—knew Mr. Isaacs's

Mr. Lonnie "Jack" Isaacs, first principal of combined Lynch Colored Public and Lynch High Schools, 1963. Southeast Community College Appalachian Collection, Cumberland, KY.

parents who lived on Main Street, less than half the length of a football field away up from the Lynch Colored Public School. He held a newspaper route during high school, which helped him get to know just about everybody—"everybody

White, that is," he said. "I guess that came in handy, I think. It facilitated my acceptance as principal of the school, for what that was worth." Mr. Isaacs and I had that paper in common: my older brother and I—and our three younger brothers—all delivered the *Knoxville Journal*, though we did it to colored homes only. The paper routes were as separate as the housing.

Our grandfathers worked in the same coal mine. He lived the typical life of an intelligent—even if slightly eccentric—White boy in Lynch, graduating with honors and obtaining a BA from Cumberland College, a fundamentalist Baptist-affiliated institution in Williamsburg, near Corbin. He took his master's from Eastern Kentucky State University and completed all but the dissertation for the EDS at the prestigious Peabody College of Education at Vanderbilt University in Nashville.

While I was attending Southeast Community College five miles from my home, then a branch of the University of Kentucky, Mr. Isaacs and I talked occasionally. I did not, as a matter of choice, attend sports events at my alma mater, so I had no physical context in which to socialize with him. One of our shared memories was how it was very tense the first few weeks of school in August 1963, not least because the opening coincided with the March on Washington, which we did not talk about. We laughed about how I was summarily dismissed, without him knowing about it, during the first week for an "unspeakable remark" I made to two White girls. I was having a gulp from a water fountain between the change of classes when I overheard one say to the other, "Do you think we should drink behind him?"

"I don't give a fat rat's ass if you die of thirst," I remember saying, walking away, wiping my mouth, not even looking back at them. It was a combination of my resident "crazy nigga" and the "Punkin moments" that also lived in the subliminal sector of my mind.

I was told to "go home" by someone in Mr. Isaacs's office who claimed to have overheard the remark, which I did, not even stopping in the principal's office. But not fifteen minutes after I had taken the half-hour walk home, Mr. Isaacs was knocking on our door, explaining the "misunderstanding" to my mother, who, not to his knowledge, gave me the impression that she was proud of me for taking a stand. Mr. Isaacs rode me back to school, talking to me in such a sensitive way as to give me the unforgettable feeling that he liked me and that he cared very much for me, for all his students, Black and White. Not to worry, he said to me, adding, "This will pass, William." In passing, without going into any detail, he told me about one of his own experiences in high school, how a certain teacher told his girlfriend that she was wasting her time with him because he would likely amount to nothing. "I am now her boss!" he told me. I felt better right away. I felt good about him from that moment on.

The next week, I was elected secretary of the senior class of 1964. Small consolation: I had been the vice president of my junior class back at our old school; now my plans for being president of my senior class were dashed. The senior class president at our old school was called, lightheartedly of course, the Student HNIC—the Head Nigga in Charge! My younger brothers—Tony, Karl, and Jeffery—made up for it. Each of them turned out to be an officer, president, or vice president in their junior and senior classes at the integrated school—Lynch East Main, as it was officially known.

I glossed over those backstories before getting into the thick of my remembrances of Mr. Isaacs at his memorial service. I tried consciously to keep my eyes mainly on his children and grandchildren, and I relayed to them, with raw emotions, sniffling and shedding tears liberally, what Mr. Isaacs called "the almost heartless and insensitive way" the mixture of the two schools unfolded in Lynch. I had a sense of how he felt about the whole thing as he had told me of his refusal to join the Lynch Country Club—an invitation that came only after he became principal. "I told them I could not and would join their club out of respect for my father because he would have never been asked to join," he said. "They only asked me because I was the White principal, now an elite!"

I remembered to them how Mr. Isaacs gave me details of the school board meetings—the official and off-the-record ones—that he attended as the detailing of decisions unfolded: everything from who would be the principal to which biology teacher would stay and which would go. "Except for Mr. Coleman, who himself was not invited to every meeting the school board held leading up to the announcement, there were no other Black people in the room," he told me. In 1963, Lynch was still a company town—US Steel's town. US Steel's White managers were the core members of the school board; they made the decisions. There were no Black people on the school board. There was no input from most of the townspeople on what would be done in the name of integration, who would do it, or why and how it was to be executed—not to mention seeing around the corners, those unintended consequences of their otherwise rational decisions. I simply heard, like most Black people, that something was going down, and we would have to abide by it. Characteristic company-town politics.

Mr. Isaacs told me countless times over the years some of the essential things he was required to say and not to say—and do—by the superintendent, the mouthpiece of the company officials, presumably from the Pittsburgh headquarters of US Steel through the Gary, West Virginia, district office down to the general superintendent of the Lynch works. Absolutely, the company undertook combining the two schools in 1963 with the same centralized, top-down social engineering principles and practices that they used when they conceived of and then built the town less than a half century earlier. What the company did was always shrouded in secrecy, and as things were hidden or masked, the people's reactions were concealed in an environment of repressed curiosity. You did not question the company. If anything, you questioned yourself for thinking about questioning the company.

Were you crazy, Mr. Isaacs?

The people were reliably silent, consistently. It did not matter what people—Black people at least—thought about civic and community-wide affairs; they avoided talking aloud about it. Either they were not invited, or they chose to sidestep public meetings, and they certainly didn't engage in any activities like protesting. There was nothing they could do, and there was nowhere they could go: no one and nowhere to turn to, nowhere to hide. Black Mountain was an exceedingly high wall, all around.

I told the mourners about Mr. Isaacs's musings on how the merger of the two schools required many sacrifices, material and nonmaterial, and that the major losses fell on the Lynch Colored School. This so-called integration was a one-way change. The Pirates were wiped out by the Bulldogs. That is not possible in the natural world.

"That doesn't require much of you," said the pig to the chicken who had recommended they have bacon and eggs for breakfast. "For me, it's a piece of my hide," sighed the pig. I compared the Black administrators, the teachers, the coaches, and even our school's janitor, Mr. Cross, to the pig; they lost their hides. We lost our place. We lost the backbone and lifeblood of our community. Suddenly, it seemed like Granny and Mr. Isaacs were talking through me.

Mary Lynn Williams and Frieda Diana Hopkins—whose grades qualified them at the Lynch Colored School for recognition as valedictorian and salutatorian—"weren't even considered when that conversation came up in a meeting early on in the school year," Mr. Isaacs told me, adding a note about his "sunken-stomach" feeling as he looked at the high school teachers in the room, particularly Mrs. Mattye Guy Knight, who had by then taught English literature at the Lynch Colored School for three decades. Those of us who were considered excellent students at the Lynch Colored School—the Beta Club members, for example—were not grandfathered into the same groups at the so-called integrated school. He knew Mrs. Knight had taught us something from the major themes in Shakespeare to the Victorian era, but more importantly, he mentioned being a bit intimidated by her over-the-rim-of-her-dark-glasses glare—surely a glower or scowl to him, as he was less than half her age. Mrs. Knight was known to rattle off from the deep body of African American literature she taught us, from spiritual slave elegies and chants to Booker T. Washington, W. E. B. Du Bois, and Gwendolyn Brooks. And to think the grades we brought from the colored school did not count! Upper-level students, White and Black, lost a lot in that initial year; for one thing, Mrs. Knight, at first, was reduced to teaching ninth graders only. Not just Mrs. Knight but virtually all the highly dedicated Black teachers from our high school had the air taken from beneath their wings in the new setting. It just was not the same anymore. I remember stepping foot only once in the library at the school into which we were supposedly integrated. I noticed that there were no Black newspapers. Ironically, when we went there in late summer 1963, the month of the March on Washington when Dr. King told the world about his "dream" for America, I read, at Mrs.

Knight's recommendation, a 1958 book titled *Things Fall Apart* by Chinua Achebe. How taunting was that?

At the so-called integrated Lynch High School, Blacks were more tolerated than genuinely incorporated. The Black boys with high-demand athletic skills were taken care of, as it were, but the average Black Joe or Jessie Mae—let alone the below-average ones—were, as Mrs. Sweatt used to say, "like a lost ball in the high weeds of Georgia." That was another way of her telling a Black student what he or she could expect if they put forth low effort and had second-rate skills in a racist world. The curtain came down on such straight talk. But I was able to remind a lot of people of those shades of gray on that hot August afternoon.

Mr. Isaacs's most challenging personal issue was his full knowledge of how the school board favored him over Mr. Coleman to be the principal of the combined schools. "It was a farce," he told me in 1967 as we sat in the Toddle House restaurant near the University of Kentucky campus in Lexington, where I had arrived a year after he had left Lynch. He served as principal in Lynch—or as he professed, using a curse word for the first time in my presence, "suffered through the bullshit"—for less than two years. That is a typical Isaacs turn of irony; fact is he also was "actively recruited" by the Lexington-Fayette School System, having been publicly recognized by the Lynch Independent School System for his "exceptional contributions to the integration of the schools," as documented on his obituary.

US Steel and the Lynch Independent School Board—which were essentially the same governing bodies—gave Mr. Isaacs an outstanding achievement award for "leadership in integrating schools in Harlan County." I told him how they should have played Ray Charles's 1961 hit song "Hit the Road Jack" at the awards ceremony.

In 1966, he left Lynch with what he called "a lot of pull but much more push." He had been heavily recruited—as much for his brilliance as for the success he achieved in Lynch—to an administrative position in Lexington at one of Kentucky's most prominent high schools, named for the nineteenth-century statesman Henry Clay.

Ironically, Mr. Isaacs was recruited to Fayette County because of the award he won for leadership in the integration at Lynch. He was recruited to become the principal at Henry Clay, but as he explained, "In a strange twist of fate related to the politics of the consolidation of the county and city governments, I was blocked, and I had to assume the role as associate principal at Henry Clay."

When I reminded him that Henry Clay enslaved more than six dozen Black people on his rural Lexington estate named Ashland, and that Clay played a prominent role in strengthening the Fugitive Slave Act, Mr. Isaacs burst out laughing, exclaiming, "You had to have learned that at the Lynch Colored School." Without a doubt, of course I had!

We never witnessed cross burnings in Lynch; that's not to say that cross burnings did not or could not happen—somewhere out of sight, quite nearby possibly. Neither did I ever see or hear of White men in blackface at the all-White Lynch Country Club, where the Lynch High School usually held its proms. But I would not be surprised if I came to learn that such scenes occurred there. White men in bib overalls didn't sit whittling with their Barlow pocketknives in front of the big store in Lynch, staring or sneering at Black people the way the ones who came down from the hollers did in front of the Harlan County courthouse on Saturdays in the 1950s. Was it that Lynch White folks were more polished and genteel? Or were their relations to their Black neighbors, like everything else, framed by the boundaries set by the company? Harlan was not a company town, and to Black people, most of the outlying areas beyond the Harlan city limits were known as "sundown towns." And the sun went down real early in many places behind the high mountains.

Looking directly in the eyes of one of his grandsons, I quoted Mr. Isaacs: "You can't imagine how I felt when it fell on my shoulders to tell you kids that there would neither be a senior prom nor a senior class trip." The entire situation was so "Lynch-like," by which I mean the cancelation of the prom and senior trip was like the stiff politeness that characterized civic dialogue in general. There was no public clamor, no protests or demonstrations. The disgusting feelings I have for the faceless White custodians of those racist traditions that denied us an important rite of passage—a senior prom and trip—lingers after all these years. At the Lynch Colored School, the senior prom was a community extravaganza, an out-and-out spectacle like the Oscar awards pageant in Hollywood. These almost sacred ceremonies were thankfully revived the year after we graduated.

The taboo of interracial dating, or even the prospect of it, lay at the belowground level of why we did not have a prom or senior trip. The Whites' abhorrence of "race mixing" was at the bottom of whatever justifications they made for denying the class of 1964 a prom and a senior trip.

Beneath the surface level of civility, which was company-driven and enforced, the company officials—the boss class, the Silk Stocking Row residents—maintained a climate of strict racial separation. The nine-hole Lynch Country Club, carved from the forest at the eastern edge of town, was the best example. Except for the Black people who cooked or kept the grounds there, Black people never went near the place. "Most of them ain't, at heart, no different than them Mississippi segregationists," my father often said around the supper table. "We wouldn't even be in these out-of-the-way hollers if the US Steel had been able to find enough local Whites to work the mines."

In the short space of one year—between 1966, when I left home for good and went to Lexington to attend the main campus of the University of Kentucky, and 1967, when I met with Mr. Isaacs at the Toddle House—I became heavily involved in civil rights, anti–Vietnam War, and women's rights activities, both on campus and in the city. I also left Lexington on many weekends to participate in organized protests led by the Southern Christian Leadership Conference throughout the Deep South. Mr. Isaacs seemed, then consciously, to want to mentor and advise me; it was as though he was intent—through me—to compensate for some of the "bullshit" with which he had "gone along with to get along with" back in Lynch.

By phone and on visits when he would drive to the edge of campus and pick me up, he gave me advice, and we talked about my involvement in the founding of the UK Black Student Union. He showed great concern for my safety when I led pickets outside UK basketball games in protest of the all-White Kentucky Wildcats in 1967 and 1968. He'd say, "You know what you're doing is equivalent to denying the existence of God or burning the American flag, don't you?" Then, in the same breath he would declare, "I am proud of you, William, for standing up for what is right." I reminded him how my grandmother used to say, over and over, when it was a teachable moment, "Ain't nothing in the middle of the road but white lines and dead possums!" He promptly recollected that his grandmother had taught him the same thing. We would laugh together, aloud.

He promised to come for me, so that Mama and Daddy wouldn't worry, if I got put in jail for these protests and demonstrations, which I led continuously from the time I went to UK in 1966 through my graduation in 1968. That year, the National Conference of Christians and Jews recognized Mr. Isaacs for his "audacious leadership which enabled the integration of the schools of Lexington, specifically Henry Clay High School," also noted in his obituary.

Mr. Isaacs was present at UK on the night of April 7, 1968, when I stood in for Muhammad Ali, who had canceled his long-planned and widely publicized speaking engagement in order to go to Atlanta following the assassination of Dr. Martin Luther King Jr. on April 4. Muhammad Ali, a Louisville native whom I had met a couple times the year before when he visited Kentucky State College in nearby Frankfort, was a hero of mine—he and Malcolm X. The year before in April 1967, Ali, a Muslim, cited religious reasons for refusing to be inducted into the US Army, declaring, "I ain't got no quarrel with them Vietcong." He was immediately stripped of his heavyweight title. Almost to the day a year earlier, April 4, 1967, Dr. King gave a speech at the Riverside Church in New York City titled "Beyond Vietnam." He linked the civil rights movement with the antiwar movement and came out against the war. I was in complete accord because the UK Black Student Union, of which I was president, was supported by the anti-Vietnam groups, such as Students for a Democratic Society (SDS), and vice versa. It all made a lot of good sense to me; either that or I was just too naive to know how "dangerous" my thinking and alliances were at the time. Anyway, there I was, just two years removed from Harlan County, at twenty-one, speaking on the topic "I Am Willing to Die," substituting for Muhammad Ali on the occasion of the death of Dr. Martin Luther King Jr.

Mr. Isaacs met me outside and drove me back to my dormitory after I gave my speech, for which I got a standing ovation from more than ten thousand people packed into Memorial Coliseum, Kentucky's basketball arena, which was dubbed "the house that Rupp built." How ironic, since it was my first time inside this sanctuary-like building, which I had only been close to earlier when we picketed the home basketball games, protesting coach Adolph Rupp's decision not to recruit Black basketball players. Mr. Isaacs gave me twenty-five dollars, knowing that I was leaving for Atlanta the next day, bringing the total of all the money I had in the world up to thirty dollars. Along with my closest allies in the UK Black Student Union—Theodore "Fuzzy" Berry and Jim Embry—I was invited by the Student Nonviolent Coordinating Committee (SNCC) to be a marshal in Dr. King's funeral procession. In that hallowed role, I literally looked in the south end of the north-bound mules that pulled the wagon holding the remains of Dr. King. What an honor!

In that same memorable spring of 1968, Mr. Isaacs wrote a letter of recommendation and made a call on my behalf to Mr. Galen Martin, a Berea College graduate and one of Kentucky's most prominent civil rights advocates. Mr. Martin was the executive director of the state-run Kentucky Commission on Human Rights (KCHR), and the call was for a job, which to Mr. Isaacs, seemed only natural for me. I became a field representative with the agency and got in the thick of things—as an advisor—when my father and several other Black miners in Lynch filed a class action suit against US Steel for employment discrimination. The last straw for Dad came when a White boy in Mr. Isaacs's generation, whom Dad described as not having "enough sense to pour piss out of a boot," became his supervisor in the mine. The proceedings of the class action lawsuit, handled efficiently by the KCHR, resulted in a "finding for cause," and Dad and his compatriots became, in 1971, the first Blacks promoted to supervisory positions at the US Steel Lynch works. Mr. Martin and I became lifelong friends from the brief time I worked for the commission: he spoke at the graduation ceremony when I was interim president at Kentucky State University, and I had the honor of being asked by the family to say a few words at his funeral in 2006.

Here are a few lines from Mr. Isaacs's obituary as it was printed:

> Lonnie Jack Isaacs graduated from Lynch High School where he later returned to teach History and become a Principal in 1963. In 1966 he came to Fayette County Public Schools to Henry Clay High School and after 39 years as an educator retired in 1995 from the Fayette County Public School System as one of their most dedicated administrators. He constantly sought to make a difference and had a passion for helping his students. He was a firm believer in the inherent worth of each child and especially proud of his work integrating schools in Harlan County for which he was recognized with an outstanding achievement award.

Lonnie Jack Isaacs left our hometown under pressure because he wanted to—but couldn't—"do right by all the students, Black and White." He was plainly far ahead of the times in Lynch compared to the company officials, the school board, and most of his fellow White citizens in town. But in Lexington, he came out as a liberal and was able to bring many Black students like me under the canopy of his influence and guidance.

One of Mr. Isaacs's Henry Clay students, Anthany Beatty, was the only other Black person present at his funeral on that hot day in Lexington's Crestwood Christian Church, more than a half century after Mr. Isaacs and I had met at Lynch High School.

In 2001, at the age of fifty, Anthany became the first African American chief of police in Lexington. A Lexington native, Beatty had been with the department for twenty-seven years, having joined the force in 1973. He earned his master's degree in public administration from Kentucky State University and his bachelor's degree in police administration from Eastern Kentucky University. In 2007, Beatty retired from the Lexington police department and became assistant vice president for public safety at the University of Kentucky.

"Mr. Isaacs never told me that he did the same for you as he did me," Chief Beatty said to me as we embraced and cried together after the service. "Mr. Isaacs was the father I never had growing up in the projects." Like Anthany, and while we both dislike the description, we achieved lots of "firsts" from the time we first met Mr. Isaacs until the last time that we saw him.

For me, my friend and mentor Lonnie Jack Isaacs—Mr. Isaacs—was much more than the first liberal White person I met. He also had a lasting impression on me, and I tried over the years to model his way to students whom I taught. I took time to get to know them personally and went out of my way to support them, to give them confidence. Indeed, as the saying goes that is attributed to Henry Adams, who was descended from two US presidents, "A teacher affects eternity; he can never tell where his influence stops."

I had two great high school principals: Mr. Coleman and Mr. Isaacs.

CHAPTER 13

Not Bad for Some Colored Kids from Harlan County, Kentucky

E PLURIBUS UNUM: one out of many. The motto of the United States of America.

Benham, Kentucky, native Bernard Bickerstaff: *e pluribus unum*.

Bernard Bickerstaff, seventy-seven at the time of this writing, has basked in the sunlight of a nearly half-century career as a National Basketball Association (NBA) head coach and front-office executive. Indisputably, Bernard holds the highest national status of anyone Black—that I know of—from the eastern Kentucky coalfields.

In 2020, Bickerstaff was a senior advisor for the Cleveland Cavaliers; his son John Blair was the head coach. As head coach of the Charlotte Hornets, Bernie worked for owner Michael Jordan; in Los Angeles, he coached Kobe Bryant, and he won a championship as part of the front office in Cleveland when NBA superstar LeBron James played for the Cavaliers. To borrow a phrase from the dialect of the old timers like his grandfather, an Alabama-born coal miner in Benham, who came to the area out of Alabama in 1919, "That boy done been in tall cotton a long, long time!"

Bernie climbed the ranks to the summit of his profession—the head coach of four NBA teams and general manager and president of two organizations—in part because he had been a self-assured, high-stepping drum major and maturing basketball star at the Benham Colored School, graduating in 1960. He is best remembered in Kentucky for scoring forty-nine points one Friday night against one of the state's powerhouse teams, Taylor County Industrial High School for Negroes, in Campbellsville, Kentucky, whose star player, Clem Haskins, went on to a hall-of-fame NBA career. Bernie's team played their home games in the all-White Benham High School gym because the colored school he attended had no gymnasium. Other than that, the chief differences between the Benham Colored School and the Lynch Colored School was the half mile that separated them and the fact that the Lynch Colored School had a gym.

The similarities between the two schools are striking in terms of the geographical backgrounds and the academic preparation and relatively long tenure of the faculties at both schools. For that matter, the same can be said of all the colored schools in eastern Kentucky from the 1920s up through the desegregation of the dual school systems in the mid-1960s. Mr. Matthews, the principal of the Benham Colored School, was no different in style, temperament, image, and the respect he commanded in the Benham community than was the case of Principal Coleman in Lynch. Same for Bernie's most inspiring teacher Mrs. Constance Ellison, counterpart to Mrs. Mattye G. Knight of Lynch. Besides his grandparents who raised him, Bernie said of those who influenced him, his role models, mentors, and guides: "I am who I am because of the influence of those in that community."

Speaking at his induction in 2018 into the Kentucky Sports Hall of Fame, he acknowledged his upbringing. "I want to share it with the people of southeastern Kentucky and Benham," Bernie said. "Because without them, it just wouldn't have happened." As if that were not enough to underscore the indelible imprint of the environment that nurtured him, he added, "There is no doubt about it: that was the most influential time of my life. When you talk about the nurturing and the genuineness and the discipline and the navigation through the racial barriers that were very prevalent at that time. Just the consistency of the people."

The City of Benham renamed US Highway 160 after Bernie in 1991, thirty-one years after he left for college. The half-mile stretch of US 160 that was renamed Bernard Bickerstaff Boulevard runs through the only Black neighborhood in Benham, right past the space where the house he grew up in used to sit before it was demolished after standing vacant for more than two decades, like more than half of the houses along what some locals call "BBB." International Harvester shut down its Benham coal-mining works in 1971, less than a decade after Bernie left home.

Starting from childhood, through high school and college, and over a period of four decades of professional work and community service, I have maintained contact with many people whose backgrounds are like Bernard Bickerstaff's. To profile and mention how Bernard Bickerstaff overcame the odds runs the risk of making the mistake that comes with recognizing just one person, or just a handful of people, when the room is full of people about whom the point applies.

Therefore, Bernard Bickerstaff, *e pluribus unum*, is just *one* out of many, to transpose the Latin. He is a powerful example of how many of us—a disproportionate number of us—relying primarily on a bit of common sense and a measure of discipline, navigated unchartered waters and still arrived at destinations that are considered extraordinary and unexpected based on our origins. Fact is, over the last half century—which is the time frame during which coal-mining jobs in central Appalachia began to decline precipitously—a surprisingly and disproportionately high number of high-achieving individuals have emerged from the African American neighborhoods of Harlan County and the contiguous coal-producing counties of eastern Kentucky, southwest Virginia, and southern West Virginia. In scores of interviews, Black natives say directly, or they imply, that in one way or another their success goes back to the principles and practices of the Booker T. Washington–inspired philosophy that was drilled into them in their colored schools: self-respect, self-help, racial solidarity, and persistence in the pursuit of goals. They learned to focus on goals that would elevate themselves, and they possessed a strong work ethic; they helped others, especially family. For them, happiness was not to be measured solely in terms of material prosperity, although that was primary; more importantly, success in life was achieved by strong family ties, responsibility in community affairs, and a passionate spiritual and religious grounding.

There are many high-achieving Appalachian African Americans—literally hundreds now between the ages of fifty and eighty—who comprise the second and third generations (the children and grandchildren) of those Blacks who came to the coal camps within a seventy-five-mile radius of Harlan County between 1890 and 1930. I have identified and interviewed many of them. Like Bernie, these Blacks with central Appalachian coal camp roots became successful because they, like he, showed adaptability, creativity, courage, faith, hope, integrity, perseverance, and strength of character. Many of our families had the same economic roots in central

Appalachian coal camps as those of families like the ones J. D. Vance depicted in *Hillbilly Elegy*. Many of us experienced the same level of upward mobility as he did, but I never heard anyone in my network gloat about overcoming a bad Black mountain culture. Just the opposite: they were pushed by the belief that greatness comes from adversity.

I know how most of them grew up because I grew up the same way. Their narratives go back through the beginning of the twentieth century, when Jim Crow segregation was highly formalized. They became physicians despite studying in make-do chemistry labs in colored schools, where the labs consisted of a half-dozen beakers and a match. They rolled their eyes from the "colored section" in the balcony at twenty-five-cent Saturday matinees played at the company-owned movie theaters while Johnny Weissmuller—starring as Tarzan—subdued lions and crocodiles and African people who looked just like them.

The older ones—like Bickerstaff—used colorized restrooms, and some of them waited for their mothers and grandmothers to come home to fix their supper after she left the home of the White family who paid her six dollars a week to cook and clean. We all knew exactly which filling stations along US 25—in Corbin, Kentucky, for example—had "No coloreds allowed" squibbed in barely legible English on their entry doors. Most of them. My mother, born in Harlan County in 1924, was fairly tentative when she used a public restroom for the first time at a service area on the Pennsylvania Turnpike as we were motoring to New Jersey in 1960.

"Turn your head this way, boys," Dad would say to me and my brother when Mom or one of our sisters had to relieve themselves as we drove on a Sunday after church to our grandmother's in Virginia, or to the colored swimming pool, thirty-five miles away, in Harlan. They would squat on their heels, dresses pulled up or pants pulled down, between the open car doors on the side of the road, winter, spring, summer, or fall. On one such occasion, as we were returning to Lynch from our grandmother's in Virginia—at the top of Black Mountain near the entrance to the mine where Dad worked—he pulled over after nature's call to our oldest sister Peggy. As she climbed back into Dad's 1957 Ford Country Squire station wagon, our brother Irvin, the recognized "family clown," asked of her, hilariously, "How do y'all do that without pissing on your feet?" I understood better, "when I got older," as I was often told I would, what sociologist Antonin Obrdlik meant when he said, "Gallows humor is an index of strength or morale on the part of oppressed peoples."

I have recalled in these pages much more than personal responsibility tropes or what could be interpreted as conservative talking points about Appalachian Black people overcoming racism and poverty. Far from my intention. The very existence of Black people is one of the main features of central Appalachia that commentators are always "getting wrong," to use the words in the title of Elizabeth Catte's dazzling book *What You Are Getting Wrong about Appalachia*.

Nowhere here have I written of any of those "stubbornly ingrained cultural" elements—as Erin Keane puts it in *Salon*—that countless writers, like J. D. Vance in his *New York Times* best-selling book, have attributed to the White people of Appalachia: "poor and under-educated, even lawless and violent. And what's more, largely content to stay that way."

The exceptional individuals I profile did not overcome any innate cultural deficits. Nor did they "just decide one day that they didn't want to act like poor people anymore," as Vance implied that he did on his own journey. Most of the people I lived among never acted as if they were poor, whatever than means and looks like. Lacking resources and surviving and thriving in the face of racism is not a performance.

In the summer of 2016, when Vance's book hit the *New York Times* Best Sellers list, I started from my newly adopted home in Houston with a stop in the elegant home of Dr. Frieda Outlaw, my high school classmate, who now lives in suburban Nashville. The chief administrator of a state health agency, Frieda took her BA from Berea College, her master's in psychology from Boston College, and a doctorate in psychology from Catholic University. Frieda and I were born two weeks apart in the hospital of Notre Dame in Lynch, Kentucky, in the summer of 1946. During our visit, we phoned and chatted with her sister Rita, also a Berea grad who later earned a master's degree in mathematics from Michigan. Rita recently retired after a long, distinguished career with IBM. I told Rita—who almost won the big prize on *Jeopardy!* a few years back—how all the home folks in Harlan County were still amazed with her Harvard-grad daughter Skylar, who made a perfect score on the SAT and who now works for the National Security Agency. During that same conversation, I told them how Frieda's friend and fellow Berea grad Jim Branscome had brought *Hillbilly Elegy* to my attention. "Don't you get tired of reading that crap about mountain people?" Frieda asked, deadpan. Not a question.

During my visit, Frieda's husband, Lucius Turner Outlaw Jr.—who holds an undergraduate degree, Phi Beta Kappa, from Fisk University and a doctorate in philosophy from Boston College and who is a tenured full professor of philosophy and African American studies at Vanderbilt University—took me for a spin in a Diamond DA40 aircraft outfitted with Garmin G1000 avionics. Lou hails from Starkville in Oktibbeha County, Mississippi, which is an Appalachian Regional Commission–designated Appalachian county. Not the same as an Appalachian coal camp, but, hey, we went up, up, and away from slavery to the freedom that is symbolized by flying one's own private aircraft.

I next arrived in the Washington, DC, region to visit with other childhood neighbors, starting with the Freeman brothers—James Jr., "Junebug" (deceased as of August 2019), and my classmate Willie, better known back home as "Tank"—both army veterans and retired DC policemen. We talked again of how their father was one of those who left Lynch in the middle of the night to avoid the bill collectors from the company store. After being laid off at the US Steel–owned mine in Lynch in 1958, their father—whom we all called Mr. Jerry, although his name was James—migrated to New York City. We laughed about the government-issued bologna and cheese they survived on at that time and how later, when they left the military service, they purchased a home in Washington for their parents and younger siblings.

In nearby Maryland, I visited with Betty Freeman-Reed, eighty-four as of this writing, who is the sister of the Freeman brothers. Betty is a retired coordinator of high school counselors for the school system in Aurora, Colorado. After graduating from the Lynch Colored School, Betty moved on to receive a degree in education from Tennessee State University. After forty-seven years in Denver, Betty moved in 2017 into a premier planned community—National Harbor, near Oxon Hill, Maryland, and right next to a casino—to be near her brothers and her own grown daughters. The extended family is committed to "take care of Mama in her golden years."

Delecia Eller, Betty's oldest, is completing a doctorate this year, while the youngest daughter, LaDoncia, is an administrator for a federal cybersecurity agency. Betty emphatically expressed her views about the next generation in a 2016 interview with me: "I expect the same high achievement from my six grandchildren." Betty's fellow 1958 Tennessee State graduate was yet another Lynch Colored School alumnus named Willis "Bunny" Thomas, now deceased. Bunny was an all-American basketball player at TSU and on the starting team for more than a decade with the Harlem Globetrotters, then led by Meadowlark Lemon.

How well I remember—I was fourteen at the time when dozens of us Black kids gathered at the bottom of the street from my home, in front of the Pool Room and juke joint—when Bunny came home in a brand-spanking-new white 1960 hard drop-top convertible Ford Thunderbird, decked out with full-range, three-inch, whitewall tires. He was *somebody*, the personification of the Black role models covered every week and month in *Jet* and *Ebony* magazines. We were, to be sure, isolated in Harlan County in 1960 from the rest of the world, but we had home folks who came back regularly whose lives of accomplishment let us young ones know that we too could be somebody. Fact is that every one of the eleven Thomas children—their dad an Alabama-born-and-raised Methodist preacher and US Steel–employed coal miner—graduated from college.

Another person from the generations of Mr. Vance's grandparents, General Pearson (his given first name), left Lynch Colored School in 1950 to study and graduate from the Howard University School of Medicine in the nation's capital. A few years ago, I interviewed General Pearson's Lynch-born-and-bred sister Christine Pearson-McCord, who spent thirty years as a principal of two high schools in Nashville, Tennessee.

I arrived back in Texas where my childhood friend Rev. Dr. Franklin Callaway, seventy-two, from Benham, and a neighbor of Bernie Bickerstaff, ferried me from the airport to his enormous home in the Woodlands, a tony, upscale section of the most diverse city in the United States. Dr. Callaway, called "Frankie," is the senior pastor of Yehoshua Missionary Baptist Church in Spring, Texas, a Houston suburb. A Vietnam-era US Air Force veteran, Franklin is a 1965 graduate of Cumberland High School in Cumberland, Kentucky, and he earned a bachelor of arts degree in Christianity and speech from Houston Baptist University in Houston, Texas, a master of divinity degree in urban evangelism from Southwestern Baptist Theological Seminary in Fort Worth, Texas, and a doctor of ministry degree in church leadership from Southern Baptist Seminary in Louisville, Kentucky. He has also studied business administration at Kentucky State University in Frankfort, Kentucky, and sociology and religion at Texas Christian University in Fort Worth, Texas.

We connected in a three-way call with his brother-in-law Kevin, a vice president at Verizon in Atlanta, and his brother Tony, owner of an in-home health-care business in Raleigh, North Carolina. We talked about Tony's daughter, Trish, who graduated from Harvard Medical School a few years back. Trish would visit with me and my family while she was an undergraduate at Wake Forest University studying for a chemistry degree. In the summer between her junior and senior years, she left her Volkswagen Bug in our driveway. Tony's wife and Trish's mother, Patricia, wrote her doctoral dissertation in education for the University of Kentucky, which was based on attitudinal and cultural values that influenced Benham Blacks. In her dissertation titled "Don't You Fall Now: Resilient and Academically Successful African Americans' Literacy and Family Involvement Practices," Dr. Callaway summed up the upward mobility journeys of four Black Benham-raised siblings in the Frison family, who lived across the street from the fifteen Callaway siblings.

Erskine, the oldest son, graduated in 1956 from East

Benham High School, which was originally named Benham Colored School. Kentucky State was his next stop, where he majored in mathematics, and then he taught math in Danville, Kentucky, in its colored school, Bates High. He left teaching in the mid-1960s after the superintendent of Boyle County schools, a White male, notified him that he would not be assigned to teach in the integrated high school because the board thought it would be inappropriate for a young Black man to teach White high school girls. Erskine moved to Cincinnati and launched a career as an industrial engineer for Admiral Electronics, from which he retired after thirty years.

Eddie, the next Frison son, followed big brother Erskine's footsteps from the same school, East Benham, to Kentucky State University, then transferred to Tuskegee Institute, and ultimately walked proudly away from the University of Dayton with a degree in electrical engineering with a stint in the air force in between. He retired from General Motors as a senior electrical engineer but is still talked about in Benham for returning home for three weeks one summer and volunteering his time and money to wire his home church, Rising Star Baptist. The same church house hosted African Methodist Episcopal Zion (AMEZ) parishioners on alternate Sundays, and the two congregations worshipped together on months with a fifth Sunday. In an interview, he reminded me, "Sister Punkin, your mother, played piano for both flocks for more than four decades."

Dorothy, ten years younger than her brother Erskine, was the first of the Frison children not to study at East Benham High School and the first in the family to complete all of her preprofessional studies in Harlan County. "Dot" graduated from Cumberland High in 1966 and achieved her lifelong dream of becoming a registered nurse by combining studies at Southeast Community College and the Harlan Appalachian

Regional Hospital. Following in her brothers' footsteps, she migrated to and settled in southern Ohio, near Dayton.

The Frison family has a Berea College graduate in David Earl, also known as the look-alike of his namesake, his father, whose first name was King and whose middle name was David. The family patriarch, Mr. Frison, whom everyone called "Buster," was the chairman of the deacon board of Rising Star Baptist Church. He and his wife were regulars in our home, as Miss Vivian and our mom were what were called "ace boon coons"—best buddies. To some, David Earl was known as "Devil Earl," because he, in the manner of his idol, rock and roll legend Little Richard, walked his personal journey unfazed by those who might have looked askance at him—an eccentric nonconformist—because he sometimes chose to wear a red sleeveless dress and five-inch, high-heeled pumps. David Earl studied chemistry but died early, before he reached thirty-five, while working for DuBois Chemicals in Houston.

"Baby Sister," as Audrey was called, grasped the family's get-an-education baton and took it to Cumberland High School, Eastern Kentucky State University, and past a master's level degree in hospital administration at Xavier University in Cincinnati.

The Frisons' adopted baby brother, Paul Gaffney, a basketball star at Cumberland High School in Harlan County, studied at Tennessee Wesleyan University on a basketball scholarship, where he was the captain of the team in his junior and senior years. Paul went on to be the lead player and voice—his generation's Meadowlark Lemon—for fifteen years with the Harlem Globetrotters. I noted in an article written in 1990 how unique it was for Harlan County to count three of its native sons on the roster of the world-famous Globetrotters: player Willis "Bunny" Thomas; Bernie Bickerstaff, who served as coach and front-office consultant; and Paul, who has been inducted into the Tennessee Wesleyan University's hall of fame and the Naismith Memorial Basketball Hall of Fame with the Harlem Globetrotters.

In our conversations about "whatever happened to so-and-so from Benham," we brought up the name Jeffrey McDonald, also Frank Callaway's boyhood neighbor. Jeff, who lives in St. Louis, holds an undergraduate degree from Kentucky State and an MBA from Boston University. He retired two years ago after a successful thirty-eight-year career as director of worldwide financial operations for DuPont Chemical Company, also working stints for Monsanto and Ralston Purina. Jeff's younger sister Bettye McDonald Powell is vice mayor of Trotwood, Ohio, which is but a stone's throw from J. D. Vance's home ground of Middletown. These two McDonalds were inspired by their aunt Frieda McDonald. A Kentucky State graduate, Ms. McDonald taught at East Benham for twenty-five years and took a master's degree in education from Union College in Barbourville, Kentucky, two hours away, where she studied on weekends. The strong-willed and high-energy octogenarian relocated after her retirement long ago to the family homeplace in Tuskegee, Alabama. Home again!

After our exchange with Kevin and Tony, Frankie and I then teleconferenced with my younger brothers—Tony, Karl, and Jeff—who live in Cincinnati, New Orleans, and Indianapolis, respectively. Tony, whose birth name is Mark Anthony, and who has owned his CPA firm for almost four decades, graduated from Western Kentucky after spending his freshman year at Notre Dame. Karl is married to Cecily, a Vassar grad and Vanderbilt University–trained pediatrician. Their sons Lawliss and Justin were raised in New Orleans and earned their bachelor's and master's degrees at Morehouse College and Kentucky and at Stanford and Columbia respectively. Justin, mentioned earlier, is an executive at Facebook and lives in Los Angeles, California. Lawliss works for the Office of Economic Development for the City of New Orleans.

Karl holds a bachelor's degree in philosophy from Fisk University and a master's in diplomacy and international economics from the University of Kentucky. Before going into business and co-owning a thriving seafood import/export company, A La Carte Seafood, with his Chinese American business partner, Karl was vice president for development at Xavier University of Louisiana and the first African American executive director of the Louisiana Seafood Promotion and Marketing Board.

We all joked about how our youngest brother, Jeff, sixty at the time of this writing, has sold each of us a Mercedes-Benz over the years, "exporting" them to our various homes from Indianapolis where, for the past three decades, he has been among the top salespersons in the Chicago-area market. He has sold a Mercedes to his Lynch High School classmates Kenny Austin, an anesthesiologist and pain-management specialist in Fort Wayne, Indiana; Ricky Pack, MD, deceased, another of Jeff's classmates who practiced medicine in Louisville; and Dwayne Baskin, a University of Kentucky grad and senior executive with Southwire, one of the world's leading producers of wiring, cabling, tools, and assembled electrical components. Dwayne is chairman of the Eastern Kentucky Social Club in "Naptown," or Indianapolis, the "Crossroads of America"—a destination for a critical mass of African American miner and migrant families.

During these calls, Paul Gaffney's name came back up. Paul, who now lives in Chattanooga, reminded us of Larry Kirksey, from Harlan, who had just retired as lead receivers' coach with the Houston Texans. Over three decades in the

National Football League, Larry coached, among other premier players, the San Francisco 49ers Hall of Fame wide receiver Jerry Rice. We chatted as though we had been together the week before, although most of us had not seen each other in several years. When we got Larry on the line, he reminded us that his son, David, was lead scout for the Tampa Bay Buccaneers; like Bernie and John Blair Bickerstaff, Larry and David were a father-and-son team at the top of the mountain in professional sports.

Willis G. Meeks, eighty-six, now retired in Rancho Cucamonga, California, volunteered his service into the air force two days after graduating from Rosenwald High in Harlan in 1956. We call Willis a "real rocket scientist" for his air force career (1956–1964) as a missile guidance systems specialist, followed by a twenty-year career with the Jet Propulsion Laboratory, serving as network controller for NASA's Deep Space Network.

I started this section noting that while NBA coach and front-office executive Bernard Bickerstaff of Benham in Harlan County undoubtedly has the highest national profile of a Black person I know from any central Appalachian coal camp, he is, at the end of the day, *e pluribus unum*—one out of many, or better yet, just one of many.

The record of flourishing and successful Black people from coal camps in central Appalachia brims from all parts of the region. What these people did with their lives—what might be called the path of their pilgrimage—after leaving behind their coal-town shanties in neighborhoods called "Black Bottom" or "Sanctified Hill," after leaving behind their colored schools and their African Methodist Episcopal Zion, Baptist, and Pentecostal sanctuaries, speaks volumes not only about their families, teachers, and faith leaders. Their accomplishments also call attention to their own agency, their individual steadfastness, and their dogged determination to make it despite the odds.

I thought I had seen and read every negative stereotype drawn from the century-long use of the label *hillbilly* until I read J. D. Vance's 2016 book, *Hillbilly Elegy*. At the end of reading and analyzing it, I concluded that he took a roundabout route to say, "This should not happen to White people in America."

If history offers any lessons, it is that there are extreme, isolated, and individualized examples of values and behavior and outcomes within any marginalized group. This is not to say that Mr. Vance's hillbillies are phantoms, but they are not representative of all poor Whites. Similarly, if he had referenced the lives of even one single poor Black family in his narrative, their woes or triumphs should not be taken to represent the entirety of Black Appalachian migrants. The fact that he did not mention the experience of Blacks in Middletown—those who migrated from the same region as his family—shows that he sees racial discrimination as both understandable and something even to be expected. But when the same financial inequality and attendant insecurity applies to Whites, even those making the wrong choices, the narrative becomes incomprehensible and is looked at as an unendurable, existential threat of the first order.

Most Black people I know from central Appalachian coal towns, such as the ones I talked to during my travels in 2016, are not trying actively to run away from their culture, and their families are not in crisis. I would be the first to acknowledge that there are also some pure lunatics and some outrageous, crazy, foolish, and harebrained Black people—just like in Mr. Vance's family—who migrated from eastern Kentucky's coalfields. Like Mr. Vance, I too know—in my own extended family and among families in my network—individuals and families who may be worthy of derision and pity, people who cannot be helped because they refuse to help themselves to America's opportunities. But I also recognize the impact on them of systemic, racist, capitalist oppression and the impact of economic transformations over the past half century.

Historically, a far higher percentage of African Americans than Whites have been and remain working class. In Appalachian settings like the ones from which my family and Mr. Vance's grandparents migrated, African American coal miners were at the very bottom of the working hierarchy: they were the last hired, the least likely to be promoted, those largely excluded from unions, and the first displaced by the mechanization of the mines.

In the 1950s, African Americans shouldered the worst of the advent of the laborsaving mechanization of the coal mines, and they went off to Ohio, to places such as Cincinnati, Cleveland, Columbus, Dayton, and Middletown, or to Chicago, Milwaukee, Louisville, Lexington, Flint, Pontiac, Detroit, and beyond, where many have stayed. In Michigan and Ohio, Black migrants from Appalachia once again faced racism and were confined to the positions that proved to be most susceptible to mechanization. When cities like Detroit began to show signs of desertion as imported cars invaded the United States and the auto plants moved to the Pacific Rim and Mexico, Blacks were yet again the first to suffer.

Most Blacks who left coal camps after they lost their jobs and migrated to areas similar to where Mr. Vance's grandparents did kept their hopes alive and pursued the American Dream. Karida Brown's book *Gone Home: Race and Roots through Appalachia*, for instance, shows that Black working-class people from the eastern Kentucky coalfields were able to adapt to negative shocks and keep going; they code-switched with the rhythms of a long history of hard times, discrimination, challenges, and sacrifices.

In reviewing an essay I wrote in 2018 titled "Black Hillbillies Have No Time for Elegies," Professor Ron Eller commented on its main point: racism and structured, institutionalized inequality and disparities are the reasons why some working-class Blacks exhibit higher levels of optimism about the future than poor Whites, why the Blacks are less likely to exhibit desperation, depression, and commit suicide, a fact recognized long before Mr. Vance set to paper the crisis of Appalachian Whites.

In an email to me, Eller reflected:

> I have long wondered why some poor whites fail to have higher expectations for themselves and their children and become fatalistic about their condition while some blacks with a deep history of persecution and the absence of privilege can be driven to succeed? Is it in fact a product of racism itself that white privilege appears to grant some status to poor whites, and when they fail to succeed (because of class and the capitalist system) they accept their condition and develop a failed identity (blame themselves) while finding others to blame for keeping them down? Thus, does systemic racism also prevent poor whites from recognizing their own political and economic injustices? And for mainstream whites, the failure of poor whites from Appalachia to succeed must be a product of their own individual decisions and culture (thus their hillbilly culture in Vance's terms) since, as whites, they ought to be able to achieve the American Dream but choose otherwise. The "racialization" of Appalachia as white

> (our contemporary ancestors) not only sustains a larger apartheid system in America but sustains an unequal form of capitalism within the society as well.

My generation of Black coal-camp natives never had an expectation to inherit anything, but we were inculcated by our elders with high expectations, hopes, and big dreams, which were passed down. They passed their values—"I can get ahead"—on to the next generation, and I have done the same to my own adult children, born outside Appalachia and who are now in their thirties and forties, Mr. Vance's age.

Mr. Vance ignored African American working-class people, and by excluding them, he missed a critical point of reference because their experiences could have given his family a warning as to what was coming and how to survive it. As Dr. Martin Luther King Jr. famously said, as though he too had been raised in Harlan County, "I've been to the mountaintop. . . . And I've looked over. . . . I may not get there with you, but I want you to know tonight that we, as a people, will get to the Promised Land."

Hillbillies like the ones Mr. Vance remembers—and eulogizes—can and will reach the Promised Land. That is, only if hillbillies, and those who seek to understand us, do not take too seriously these craftily though deceitfully written premature autopsies of Appalachian people, like the one written by Mr. J. D. Vance.

CHAPTER 14

King Coal Leaves the Throne

WHEN MY grandmother born in 1895 was coming of age in Georgia, cotton was plunging from its throne as king of the Southern economy. She, like millions of other Black migrants, left the Black Belt for central Appalachia, where coal mining was the dominant economic activity.

In April of 2015, the US Energy Information Administration (EIA) provided statistics and analyses showing that coal had lost its spot as the nation's top electricity source for the first time on record. Nonpolluting energy solutions like solar and wind—and not-as-clean solutions, like natural gas—had shoved coal from its century-long seat dominating the nation's energy sector. Electricity generation and fossil fuels are contradictory terms in today's world while the phrase "post-coal economy" has become an almost pedestrian slogan, the mantra throughout central Appalachia. In the same year as the EIA report on the death of coal, Google announced the opening of its newest data center, a plant powered 100 percent by renewable energy at the site of a soon-to-be-retired Tennessee Valley Authority (TVA) coal plant in Alabama.

Not insignificantly, the Alabama-based Google data center is in an Appalachian Regional Commission–designated county—Jackson—where Scottsville is the county seat. The county was named for Andrew Jackson (1767–1845), who was known as "Old Hickory," a general in the United States Army and, afterward, president of the United States of America. Jackson took a hard stance against Native Americans, forcing them to choose between assimilation or relocation with the Indian Removal Act, which authorized Jackson to remove Native Americans in the Appalachian sector of East Tennessee and North Carolina to federal territory west of the Mississippi River so that White settlers could occupy the ancestral lands of the Cherokee Indians, for example. The Trail of Tears made certain the deaths of vast numbers of Native people as they were marched off to Oklahoma to reservations that exist to this day.

By the time I was in high school, in the mid-1960s, machines were swiftly pushing the workers, especially Blacks, out of the mines. From the start, the large coal companies—the highly capitalized and the vertically integrated corporations like US Steel—engaged in research and development to save on labor costs: that is, to increase production, and thus profits, with the smallest possible number of human laborers. Mining machines that would operate continuously, 24/7, were just around the corner. Not insignificantly, these were called *continuous* miners. And just like that, machines continued to mine coal while masses of people stopped being coal miners.

Families were leaving the area by the hundreds, and the mines—as a place to make a living—were far from the minds of most young Black people in the coal towns. Granddaddy and Daddy had worked in the mines. Clearly, most of us born after World War II—like me—would not. I did not. My father did not want me to. It was very straightforward! Neither is it coincidental that none of my three sisters married a coal miner. They left the region, never to return to live, just after high school, between 1958 and 1963. Our oldest sister, Peggy, who lived and worked for three decades in the Richmond, Virginia, public schools, insisted that her ashes be interred at the foot of our parents' graves, a request to which we adoringly consented in 2006.

Black people have all but disappeared from the landscape of coal-town Appalachia. The push factors—good wages and the new way of life that brought Blacks and European immigrants to the coalfields—have been bushwhacked by market factors in a globalized economy that has virtually put Appalachian coal and its laborers down on their knees. Ironically, while coal production is at all-time record highs, miners—especially Black ones—have become an endangered species. Machines do the work in the mines that our grandfather did for almost a century. Also, using coal as the main source for producing electrical energy—for dams operated by Duke Power or the Tennessee Valley Authority—runs against a new worldview that opposes burning fossil fuels because it pollutes the environment so awfully, specifically increasing the greenhouse effect that is the bottom line of global warming.

Additionally, coal mined in the western United States has a much lower nitrogen oxide emission content compared to coal from central Appalachia. And coal from the state of Wyoming is cheaper than that to be found in Wyoming County in southern West Virginia.

In Lynch, for example, the decline and downturn took a major nosedive as far back as 1984, when US Steel sold its operations there to Arch Minerals of St. Louis. Sixteen years later, in 1998, Arch shut down its *entire* operation in Lynch. Neighboring Benham, which International Harvester of Wisconsin owned, has not had an operating coal mine since I was in my mid-twenties, in 1971. By 1970, the production of coal had been totally transformed from an industry that required strong backs to one run largely by machinery. "The Demise of the Black Miner" is the final chapter in Ronald Lewis's book *Black Coal Miners in America.* As Lewis wrote, "Between 1950 and 1970, the white work force fell from 483,818 to 128,375 men, a decline of 73.5%. The effect on blacks was even more devastating as their total in the coal-mining work force plunged from 30,042 to 3,676, a reduction of 88% in twenty years."

Last hired. First fired.

About 45 percent of the Black adults in six eastern Kentucky coal counties were unemployed in 2015; in addition, 26 percent were not in the labor force, not looking for work. In the coal towns of eastern Kentucky, southwest Virginia, and southern West Virginia, the unemployment rate of Blacks in 2015 was nearly eight times the national average. Blacks' per capita income in 2015 was only 65 percent of the per capita income of Whites in the region. Fully half of the Blacks in Bell, Floyd, Harlan, Knox, Letcher, and Perry Counties in eastern Kentucky lived below the poverty level in 2020. Writing in the *Journal of Southern Churchmen* nearly fifty years ago, James Branscome, a Berea College graduate wrote:

> One group of Appalachians who are consistently overlooked and underserved by the institutions of the region is the blacks. While the percentage of blacks in the region is low, about eight percent, they make up the entire population of many isolated small hollows and ghost coal towns abandoned by the corporations and welfare and poverty agencies. Because the backbreaking jobs that brought black imports into the region are gone and because of the discrimination and competition with mostly poor white people for jobs and welfare funds, their existence is a poor one indeed. As yet, no agency or journalist has

> documented the presence and needs of these people, let alone described the culture of a minority group in the midst of another cultural minority.

Two decades ago, Ron Eller, then the director of the Appalachian Center at the University of Kentucky, wrote, "It's a common theme running from Kentucky through Virginia and the West Virginia coalfields. The populations that still live in the coalfields continue to struggle with both a lack of physical infrastructure—especially water and sewer—and they also lack job training opportunities and quality educational facilities and resources."

Once the coal is gone or companies find more economical ways to extract it—using as few workers as possible—they leave, leaving behind nothing but dependency. Many people in the towns are now left entirely dependent on social security, welfare, retirement income, or some other form of transfer payments. Or worse, they live—and die—off the newest underground economy, the sale and distribution of opioids and other illicit drugs.

In cooperation with the Kentucky Department of Travel Development and the Department of Tourism, Benham and Lynch have turned to tourism in seeking a new economic base. A twenty-year-old plan unfolded in 1994 when the Kentucky Coal Mining Museum opened in Benham in a building that housed the old International Harvester company store. A quarter century ago, Benham's (White) school was converted into a unique lodging property called the Schoolhouse Inn. Nearby, the restored Benham Theatre rounds out the coal miners' museum.

The economic forces that pulled Blacks into the coalfields of Appalachia have now been replaced by market factors that have pushed them out. For example, between 1955 and

1975, West Virginia lost nearly 65 percent of its Black population. For the last half century, major downsizing has marked the coal-mining industry. Almost naturally, the jobs held by Blacks were in the most labor-intensive categories of mining, and, with the coming of the mechanization of coal mining, Blacks felt the brunt of job displacements.

An example is the coal operation in Lynch, described when I was born as "the jewel of all coal towns," with the largest power plant and coal tipple the world has ever known. At its peak, around 1935, about 11,400 people lived in Lynch, nearly a third of them Black and the rest divided between local Whites and ethnic immigrants. Today, there are fewer than 500 people in the town, about 260 of them Black. In late 2019, Lynch was number three on a YouTube-produced list of the "Top Towns Destroyed by the Loss of a Single Company."

Today, since no economic activity has replaced coal as king, the Black families are equally divided between those living off social security and other mining-related pensions, such as black lung benefits, and those in the grinding clutches of poverty who live on the economic margins on welfare programs such as social security and Supplemental Security Income (SSI) payments that replaced paychecks that came from jobs as coal miners, which averaged $58,000 per year in Lynch three decades ago. In an area known for its endemic White poverty, blackness makes one poorer still.

Quality of life measures and the population dynamics of Blacks in Harlan County are representative of the situation of Blacks in just about any of the former central Appalachian coal towns. All things considered, their churches, even though the membership rolls are very, very low, are the sole entities representing Black life in the sense of bricks and mortar. But if all the Blacks who attend the two dozen or so mainly Baptist churches in Harlan County were to combine into a single congregation, which is not likely to happen, that "mega-church" would not number three hundred members.

Weddings—the formation of families—and children born by married women are rarities today among Blacks in the coal camps of central Appalachia. This fact of human geography in coal towns can be explained, in part, because the number of Black men is much lower in the population than that of Black women. One of the last weddings in Lynch took place a decade ago between our now seventy-seven-year-old sister Ree and her recently deceased husband, Benham native Billy Kirk, who was seventy when they married at Mount Sinai Baptist Church. It was a big deal. The marriage of these late baby boomers also mirrored the aging of the population of Black people in Lynch, which was, a half century ago, one of central Appalachia's most vibrant coal towns.

When work disappears, when the company leaves the town as US Steel and Arch Minerals did in Lynch, it affects *everything*, and their leaving puts all matters, material and nonmaterial, into a funk. Time was when Lynch looked like a model, gated, intentionally built, thriving, and tranquil town. Now some of the streets in town—most of the remaining streets in the once all-Black neighborhoods—look like areas in a war zone. Many ramshackle and decaying, windowless houses with roofs collapsed dot the landscape. Where hundreds of houses used to be present has been reclaimed by nearly mature trees and haphazard overgrowth—unnamed plant life, milkweeds, and cattails. The "World's Largest Coal Tipple" is in shambles. There is no Pool Room, no common space or place where Black people go after school or work. The Tree disintegrated slowly and stood as a hazard until it was blown down in a recent winter storm. No more self-help organizations, nor even formal burial coordinators. The once plentiful and highly visible Black civic clubs and associations and community-spirited organizations no longer exist in Black coal towns. No longer are Boy or Girl Scout troops organized in the handful of Black churches that are left. In Lynch, a Christian organization, Meridzo Ministries, founded twenty years ago by a White married couple that returned home, controls the narrative and the actions that are meant to build hope among the people and guide the post-coal transition. Christian missionaries, combatting long-term poverty and its effects, have, for all practical intents and purposes, replaced the company.

There is no coal-mining work anymore hardly anywhere in the Appalachian coalfields. Of course, there are no more Black schools. There are no places, not even in each other's houses, where Black people go on Friday or Saturday nights. Fridays and Saturdays are no different than Wednesdays and Mondays. Black teens don't cruise around looking for a house in which to meet friends, eat hot home-cooked fried whiting fish sandwiches covered with copious shakes of Texas Pete hot sauce, tap their feet and clap their hands, and maybe, just maybe, witness the scene of a boy and girl clasping each other's hands and dancing and lusting after each other—anticipating maybe, as they used to say they did, a "smooch" in the backseat of a 1960 Pontiac Bonneville.

Now the out-of-control cover of kudzu conceals the glut of long-uninhabited homesites—in the Black and White neighborhoods—as well as those revered memory spots like the now abandoned Rising Star Baptist Church in Benham, where our mother played piano for nearly forty years from her teen years until she died in 2001. The vegetation has choked out the trees and is so thick that it covers entire houses in Benham. The ivy, with those purple berries that we knew not to eat, is everywhere. Walking no more than twenty-five yards from the back door of our homeplace in the fall of 2019, I wished aloud that there had been as much staghorn sumac in our backyard when I was kid as now. It competes with bramble bushes, or blackberry vines, which are as common now as small, grassy lawns used to be. A carpet of trash covers the footprint of every long-abandoned homesite.

Many Blacks who used to return home regularly on Memorial Day, also known as Decoration Day, say they can hardly bear to return anymore because the physical space is so faded, the old homesites of many in lethal decay or torn down, or because there are no places close by to stay and eat, so few amenities. The running joke is that one is more likely to see and encounter black bears in Harlan County than Black people.

What mining crews still exist consist mainly of a labor force of a few White men driving big trucks to haul coal extracted by explosives and loaded from a massive scoop called a dragline. Fewer people than ever before are going to the face of the coal seam in drift mines, into those now seldom-seen hillside tunnels in a mantrip. Instead, the mineral is mainly extracted now through a controversial process called mountaintop removal mining, also known as surface mining. The land, the mountain, or what the coal companies call overburden, is blasted away and pushed into the valleys to get to the coal seams. Once relatively pristine creeks full of hornyhead chubs now run over discarded tires, often pooling with slimy blue and green and orange-colored film in built-up ponds where we used to swim.

No miners are seen piling into—or out of—a car or pickup truck, like daily clockwork, clutching an aluminum lunch pail, either going to or coming home from the mine. No women hanging clothes on the rope strung between poles fifty feet apart in backyards, a sight that used to trigger one boy to quip to another, "I saw your mama's big draws on the line." Gone is the convenience store and deli section of the Pool Room where shimmering pink pigs' feet floated in an oversized glass jug, where the glass containers nearby were crammed with pickled boiled eggs, either pink or purple, floating in vinegar or brine. No place to buy a Coke to fill with Planters peanuts and sip while watching couples slow drag—or to find your own girl to slow drag with. No more jokes about the last time a guy from Harlan that everybody called "Snake" asked the cousin of his targeted date from Lynch if he had "a raincoat" that he could borrow.

Those souls who remain—those who left their Black mountain homes between 1960 and 1990 and came back home to live there later, those who came back home in the nineties after their blue-collar jobs in Detroit were eliminated by automation or globalization, and those who never left—have become accustomed to "doing nothing." And in any case, they have become conditioned to the causes and consequences of living in a state of routine nothingness. Such is what results when the company leaves the company town. There are virtually no Black teachers in the schools in today's central Appalachian coal towns. We—my generation, the ones who lived in company-owned coal towns during the golden era—were beneficiaries of what I am calling the Harlan Renaissance.

The Harlem Renaissance, centered in New York City between World War I and 1940, drew attention to the achievements of African American creative artists and writers and to the vitality of political and cultural movements experienced by millions of working-class Southern Blacks. By comparison, the almost century-long Harlan Renaissance represented an extraordinary period of enhanced lifestyles, self-esteem, and upward mobility for two generations of Blacks, complete with evidence of the intelligence, strength, perseverance, and resilience of those who migrated to central Appalachian coal towns. The dramatic shift in the population structure nowadays is best illustrated by looking at the small numbers of Black people in the working-age group (eighteen to sixty-five) as compared to that of the much larger percentage of Blacks over sixty-five in the coal towns today.

When I talk to young Black people in the mountains today, conversations about the future are laden with expressions of skepticism and pessimism. No more "No matter what, I'm going to make it!" but more often, I hear voices screened through a rather passive refrain: "It is what it is—ain't nothing to do!"

Blacks helped to convert isolated woodlands into thriving communities where the work they did transformed the United States from an industrial and mechanical power to a post-industrial superpower. Now, with the transformation of the national economy that no longer depends on coal as a source of energy, Blacks in the once-bustling coal towns of Kentucky, Virginia, and West Virginia have transformed into an economically depressed class, a powerless and abandoned and fast-disappearing people. The story of Blacks in coal towns is an important chapter in the industrialization of Appalachia. Their present situation and projected future mirrors—if not predicts—what happens anywhere when blue-collar, working-class jobs disappear, when the company abandons the company town.

Even while regional development organizations, like the partners in the Just Transformation Fund (JTF) and the Mountain Association for Community Economic Development (MACED), attempt to raise hope and an expectancy of a new beginning in the post-coal economy, few Blacks can be seen in the meetings that these groups hold for public comment. Black faces are not seen in the offices of these organizations in Berea, Hazard, or Pikeville. One could literally count on one hand the number of Black faces at the 2019 meeting of the highly visible regional organization Save Our Appalachian Region (SOAR), where, according to its website, "more than 1,300 people attended" the summit and "over 90 businesses and organizations were represented."

I know many leaders of these organizations throughout the central Appalachian region who are well-meaning and who express sensitivity to the needs of, and the commonality between, White and Black people, but it appears that they do not go far out of their way to involve Blacks as equal partners in the transition from the coal-based economy. Either that, or the lack of Blacks' involvement can be explained by the possibility that Black people simply do not care to be involved, for whatever reasons, including lack of trust or their memory of what happened when the White power structure merged the schools.

The relatives of those who have moved away—now for two generations—help their relatives and friends back home in ways that were not available before. Young Blacks in the coal towns today are not as isolated as their forebears were, and they can learn from our experiences. The technology that is available—once they learn to use it—gives them opportunities for leadership in the future of their communities. Their history and cultural heritage provide beacon lights to enrich their sense of what is possible. But Blacks in today's central Appalachian coal towns also need to be more actively involved in the broader community if they are to benefit from their rich history. Their outlooks cannot be dominated by what used to be. But the Blacks, and other lifelong residents of the area—having always been accustomed to and comforted by working for a benevolent and patronizing company—will have to overcome their long-ingrained mental dependency and learn to manage, rely on, and fend for themselves.

The Center for Research and the Eradication of Educational

Disparities (CREED)—a project at Kentucky State University directed by Middlesboro native Dr. Roger Cleveland—reaches out to expose Black youth in Kentucky Appalachian counties to futuristic thinking and educational opportunities.

Today's Black mountain youth are in a uniquely different position than their ancestors. Despite the digital divide between central Appalachia and the rest of the nation, unlike their great-grandparents, one of the tools they have—the internet—puts them in a better position to anticipate and see the future in real time. They are in a place to proactively prepare for future events and trends. The mountains are not so high; the valleys are not so isolated. The stories of many in my generation should empower and inspire them.

For young Blacks in the mountains today, the future is not as uncertain as it was for their great-grandparents, grandparents, and parents. They should—even if they don't—know more of what can be known. They have shoulders to stand on from which they can see a much wider range of possibilities and opportunities. Through the efforts of the deeply rooted media group Appalshop, located in Whitesburg, Kentucky, and their partners in regional advocacy and organizing at the Highlander Center in New Market, Tennessee, a purposive effort has been underway for over a decade that is focused on bringing an end to the Black—and White—brain drain in central Appalachia. In conjunction with the High Rocks Educational Corporation in Hillsboro, West Virginia, and from out of a meeting of the Appalachian Studies Association in 2008, Stay Together Appalachian Youth (STAY) emerged. Out of concern that the membership of STAY was distinctly homogeneous—White—a conversation about the necessity for diversity and inclusion emerged. With "systems of racism and economic injustice" in banner headings on a shared website, the Black group looks for "connections to guide our celebration of blackness and our strategy for change." While "creating a dignified and autonomous space for Black youth," the network seeks to answer the question: "What does it mean to live here, be young, and be Black?" They seek to:

1. define Black Appalachian joy and identity for ourselves
2. begin a restorative process for Black leadership in regional youth networks such as Stay Together Appalachian Youth (STAY)

   and
3. celebrate the many shades and melodies of our existence

Just as there is nothing new under the sun, this Black Appalachian Young and Rising group is not the first organization aimed at drawing attention to and combatting Black invisibility in the mountains of central Appalachia. In 1969, partly in reaction to the failure of the Appalachian Regional Commission to recognize and respond to the plight of Black Appalachians, the Black Appalachian Commission (BAC) was formed by Carl Johnson of Asheville, North Carolina, and Jack Guillibeaux of Montgomery, Alabama. Edward J. Cabbell detailed the history, evolution, and dissolution of the BAC in a 1980 piece in *Appalachian Journal.* The same commentary, titled "Black Invisibility and Racism in Appalachia: An Informal Survey," was the lead essay in our 1985 coauthored book, *Blacks in Appalachia.*

The Black Appalachian Young and Rising assembly can look to another precedent in the work of the Black Mountain Improvement Association (BMIA), which was formed at Berea College in 1989 and operated through 1995. The W. K. Kellogg Foundation supported the BMIA to focus improvement work in central Appalachian African American communities. It organized the communities to tutor middle and high school students, to work on health issues and education, and to provide technical assistance to community leaders—capacity building. An additional component was the Black Mountain Youth Leadership Program, a summer program at Berea College for African American youth.

Black coal-camp youth must envision how mountain history and the dynamic unfolding of their lives fit into and influence their standing in the globalized economy. They must understand how the way of life and the work available to their ancestors has been permanently transformed, and they must also be assisted in figuring out how to apply the values and practices that drove their ancestors toward a better life. One thing is for sure: Blacks in Appalachian coal towns have an extraordinarily rich future. They need only apply the lessons of their past to a new Appalachia—an Appalachia after coal.

CHAPTER 15

The Graying of the Eastern Kentucky Social Club

IN 2004, scholars and community activists Thomas E. Wagner and Phillip J. Obermiller of the University of Cincinnati documented the stories of hundreds of Blacks who left the eastern Kentucky coalfields in their book *African American Miners and Migrants: The Eastern Kentucky Social Club.*

In spite of how I have inclined—sentimentally and nostalgically—toward making the case for exceptionalism in the examples of my in-group and how many of them triumphed over seemingly overwhelming obstacles, I agree with Wagner and Obermiller when they point to the millions of African Americans who migrated from the Black Belt South after World War I who did exactly the same thing: they too made it past some form of the crushing effects of racism.

Like other Black Appalachian migrants—especially southern West Virginians—Blacks from eastern Kentucky formed organizations at the endpoints of their exodus during the Great Migration from Appalachia between 1945 and 1980. This group migrated to such cities as Cincinnati, Dayton,

Detroit, Cleveland, Columbus, Chicago, Indianapolis, Knoxville, Los Angeles, Louisville, New Haven, New York City, and Milwaukee.

The Eastern Kentucky Social Club (EKSC) was formed in 1969 in Cleveland, Ohio. It shares much with "homecoming" get-togethers, thousands of affinity groups that can be found across the United States, no matter the racial or ethnic makeup—a shared heritage and consciousness of kind. The gatherings are a combination of a class reunion, a family gathering, and an old-fashioned church revival all in one.

Two decades after the EKSC came into being, a similar group, composed of Whites with roots in another eastern Kentucky coal town—Wheelwright—organized in Lexington, Kentucky, to commemorate their mutual past in their temporary community at what was to be an annual celebration. In her 2011 book, Lisa Perry chronicled the memories and folklore of Wheelwright in *Reimagining Camelot*, a metaphor based on King Arthur's palace and court, a setting of sublime contentment. In no small way, in their heydays—their respective golden ages—coal towns like Lynch and Benham and Wheelwright in Kentucky, Stonega and Norton in southwest Virginia, and Keystone in southern West Virginia were all Camelots. Perry examined the demise of the reunions of the White out-migrants of Wheelwright, a lesson for the Eastern Kentucky Social Club. According to the promotion of Perry's book, Wheelwright, founded as a coal camp, was, like Lynch, intentionally brought into being "to serve the needs of the mining industry and intended to last only as long as the coal." Chicago-based Inland Steel Company purchased the town in 1930 from Elk Horn Coal Company and began a period of community development that ushered in an era that some today refer to as Camelot, a golden age when all one could want existed within the confines of a two-mile-long hollow in eastern Kentucky. By 1965, just like many such central Appalachian coal towns, Wheelwright shrunk when the population dropped by nearly 50 percent as people left with the latest coal bust.

My father used to talk a lot about what happens to people when they become too psychologically comfortable, adapted, and habituated to working for, renting from, and depending on the benevolence of a company from generation to generation. "Don't you boys even think about working for this coal company," he said. "Hell, coal don't grow on trees year after year like apples!" He was also very uneasy with the authoritarian oversight and patronage of the company, even if the company made it seem like they really cared that Lynch was a model town and such an incredible place to live.

In Wheelwright and other look-alike coal towns, the once-attractive hamlets became sullied and rundown when the companies left their company towns. Perry chronicles how those who lived in Wheelwright during its golden age came together to organize a reunion: over five hundred people gathered in Lexington, Kentucky, to commemorate their past tranquil and untroubled days. It was the way the people kept the memory of Wheelwright alive.

Black people with roots in Lynch kept coming back to Lynch on Memorial Day weekend; that is, up until a decade or so ago. These homecomings confirmed the importance of their simple values. Accountants, business owners, educators, health-care professionals, physicians, lawyers, military retirees, and ministers returned every year with pride, many having planned their annual vacations from Los Angeles, New York City, Chicago, and Houston around this special time "back home." The whiff of barbecue cooking met the morning's fog ceiling in this narrow strip of bottomland below Black Mountain. Over a seventy-two-hour period, a close-knit community was much more than a cliché as the migrant merrymakers reveled in stories repeated—deliberately in front of their children and grandchildren—that gave emphasis to their reverence for the place and the school and churches and community organizations that sustained them until they realized success in the places to which they migrated. Here, at home on a short trip, they were, again, in the land where their mothers and fathers lived and died.

The reunions of the Eastern Kentucky Social Club are not much different than what is unique in large family gatherings typical of Blacks in the southern sections of the United States; they're only magnified in numbers. The annual gatherings are a festive time that people can spend with their own kind: familiar friends, former neighbors, and relatives. That they all descended from, or are married into, families of Black coal miners is the element that makes the difference. It is neither a self-help nor a benevolent organization, and certainly, the EKSC is not a political entity like the National Association for the Advancement of Colored People (NAACP).

Generally, attendees at the Eastern Kentucky Social Club reunions, now active for more than a half century, are those with a lived experience in the coal camps back in Lynch, Benham, and Cumberland. It is not an all-encompassing eastern Kentucky club per se. In general, one will not find a critical number of attendees at these reunions from Hazard, Wheelwright, Pineville, Pikeville, Middlesboro, Harlan, Evarts, or London—all places located in eastern Kentucky that had a critical mass of Black citizens during the halcyon and prime days of the Harlan Renaissance.

Nor has the leadership of the various chapters (there is no central governing body) stressed organizational discipline and management practices based in modern technology—that is, the internet or social media. Correspondence announcing the reunions is still sent out by the US Postal Service and word of mouth. Officers of chapters have said to me that they respect the fear many of the older members have of putting their personal and financial information online, even though that would make announcements, registration procedures, and other record keeping so much more efficient. There are no newsletters or blogs to which one can subscribe on the internet, but there is an Eastern Kentucky Social Club page on Facebook. There are no marketing practices designed to grow the organization or to reach out to the descendants of the first migrants—the grandchildren and great-grandchildren of those who entered the coalfields of central Appalachia between 1900 and 1945.

The annual gathering of the Eastern Kentucky Social Club is framed, albeit rather loosely, around nostalgia, reminiscence, melancholy, commemoration, and celebration. Some version of the following statement can be heard time and time again at the gatherings: "We're all like family, our neighbors back in coal camps; if not by blood, we are bound by our common experiences, happy times and hard times." Old stories are retold, and photographs are pulled out among small, intergenerational sets of essentially the same individuals and families who have been present since the founding of the club. Lots of selfies are taken.

One glaring sight at the reunions of the EKSC, at least over the past twenty-five years, is the noticeable absence of young people, individuals in the generation of my children ranging from thirty-five to fifty who are offspring of the second generation beyond my grandparents, people not born in the mountains of eastern Kentucky.

The mission, goals, values, and modes of operation of the club have not been spelled out and communicated on paper and systematically distributed to members and potential members, which makes the transference of these elements to young people very difficult. The culture of memory, "the stuff" of Granny, has diminished considerably. The importance of books, like this one or Karida Brown's *Gone Home: Race and Roots through Appalachia*, is weakened when cultural recollection is lost in just two generations. The number of chapters of the Eastern Kentucky Social Club is at an all-time low, and the membership rolls of the individual chapters are heavily populated by elderly people who are over sixty years old on average, primarily those who remember what it was like growing up in the coal camps.

What makes the Eastern Kentucky Social Club unique?

Blacks in central Appalachian coal towns in the mid-twentieth century were the visual and literal opposites of the stereotypical images of poor Whites. Throughout the area, one could easily find many relatively impoverished Black neighborhoods with stinking plumbing that ran straight from clapboard shacks into the creeks. But President Lyndon Baines Johnson did not come to the Georgetown section of Harlan, Kentucky, and stand in front of a few Black people and tell them about his War on Poverty. Instead, the photo that defined Appalachia visually was taken on the porch of the White Fletcher family in Inez, Kentucky, one hundred miles north of Harlan County.

Living while Black in central Appalachian coal-extraction zones in the twentieth century has not been the image of a crystalline waterfall. Despite the times when they comprised the total populations of isolated hillside nooks and along the ridges and in the valleys of forested spaces such as Tom Biggs Hollow in Letcher County, Kentucky, Blacks were more like the fabled trees that fell in the woods when no one was around.

The greatest challenge, indeed, the very survival of the

Eastern Kentucky Social Club, will be met when its leadership deliberately raises and answers the following questions:

1. What are our greatest challenges as an organization?
2. What is it like to be us, and what (stuff) makes us unique and is worth protecting and preserving into perpetuity?
3. What are the mistakes we have made that must be avoided for the group to thrive?

Since Wagner and Obermiller published *African American Miners and Migrants: The Eastern Kentucky Social Club* in 2004, many of the people they interviewed have passed on, and the number of club chapters and their membership rolls have declined markedly. But fortunately, during the reunion of the club held in Detroit in 2019, short- and long-term planning was put squarely on the table when the leadership of the surviving chapters convened at its fiftieth annual gathering. For the first time, measurable goals about membership and results linked to specific to-do lists with dates and deadlines were introduced. Also, the millennials—and the powerful measure of their educational attainments and professional acumen—were unleashed. The generation born in the mountains that comprised the leadership of the club for the last half century took the role of mentors—some of them reluctantly—and gave way to the young ones with business and financial management expertise and sophisticated social media skills.

The new generation knows and appreciates their unique mountain heritage, almost as though it is a brand that sets them apart. A unique value proposition has emerged for the Eastern Kentucky Social Club: they know they must be intentional in terms of identity formation and building loyalty among those who have never slept a night in a coal-camp house or met their great-grandparents. Trust that was derived simply from living in the same location and interacting regularly is being replaced by business principles of organizational discipline, collecting data on the population, networking, and marketing. The chapters are actively talking about ways to compete in terms of growth, adaptation, and success. The Eastern Kentucky Social Club is effectively replicating the sense of community that characterized their ancestors' ways of being—surviving and thriving—back in the hills.

CHAPTER 16

Meditating on the Future at the Mountaintop

THE DOMINANT idea that has steered the direction of this book—growing up Black in a coal-company town beginning at the end of World War II—involved some very complex pictures, colors, and sounds: people and events seen, heard about, and especially felt at deep and lasting emotional levels. I have tried to convey some of those moods and emotions and to paint detailed descriptions of the codes that governed our streets, our family bonds, and those social rituals that framed our existence and our collective journey, the path of a century-long pilgrimage that began roughly at the turn of the twentieth century.

From the time I learned from my father how to bait my own hook, catch my own fish, and tell my own lies about the size of the fish I caught, I became aware of the many events that served specific community purposes. I did not have to wait for Black History Month to know what a sense of belongingness meant and that it was based on belonging to—or being in—this specific geographical location. Group cohesiveness was all around, and the activities that involved the elders who sharpened our focus on our traditions were ever present. Growing up in this environment is probably why I have never been attracted to mass-produced entertainment. After all, everybody knew everybody else's mama's nickname and how her rolls tasted. Blacks in Appalachian coal towns had some distinctive customs, beliefs, and practices. They're mostly all gone now.

Margaret Mitchell, writing in the classic *Gone with the Wind*, noted, "Land is the only thing in the world that amounts to anything." Black Appalachian coal-camp dwellers never owned land. But they did own their dreams, which amounted to everything they had, and in time, a great number of them lived out those dreams. Owning land *is* quite a big deal, but so are other important values, such as a sense of self-determination, social networking, community participation, cooperation, and mutual aid. Most of the people in my circle of life could not afford to own land: the coal companies were not selling it, even though they had stolen it for all practical purposes. I hope readers have observed and sensed the complexity of the clashes that occurred, how things fell apart, when the colored communities in central Appalachian coal towns were filleted like a fatted catfish, gutted, and eviscerated when the "colored" schools were tossed into the trash heaps of history through what was called "integration."

Beyond the mountains, in those places to which our people migrated, there was an equally pernicious dynamic afoot that was happening just as we got into the transformative 1960s, three generations ago. Our city cousins in the mid-1960s were also in the whirlwinds of structural and economic realignments. Richard Wright had written about them, had projected their likely futures, in his 1940 classic *Native Son*. Wright's ill-fated character Bigger Thomas could well have been born in Harlan County, Kentucky, in my mother's generation and migrated to Chicago's South Side in the 1940s. Many did from her generation. Save for the grace of God, there went Daddy, there went our family.

Favored by a fate—living conditions—that was much improved over Bigger Thomas's, I grew up in Black Harlan in a large extended family and within a circle of kith and kin who conveyed to me the various flavors of traditional Black Appalachian culture, its authenticity and distinctiveness. Chinua Achebe told how he wrote *Things Fall Apart* as "an act of atonement . . . the ritual return and homage of a prodigal son." Unlike Achebe, however, despite also having been blessed with a pretty good Western education, I had no misperceptions about my native culture, was never ashamed of it, and never suffered moments of tragic fate like Achebe's main character Okonkwo.

My fate and destiny were shaped inside a mold that was cast largely by Black people with positive self-images that held sway against the powerlessness that typified coal-camp culture. In so many words, my generation heard from the elders, "Just 'cause you're in a coal camp don't mean the coal camp is in you!"

No one would ever, not for long, restrict my sense of agency, my personal freedoms, and my right and responsibility for self-determination. Most Black people in central Appalachian coal towns, at least until the 1980s, felt and acted the same way. Now that the coal camps are identified only as spaces where people *once* mined coal, the identity of the Black people—their qualities, beliefs, and social actions—in these spaces no longer has the institutional structures that were forged and made segregated Black communities relatively autonomous, which puts young people in the mountains today in a peculiar cultural vacuum. Not only that, over the past two generations, the wealth gap has widened, not to mention that there are few places to which they can migrate where things—opportunities—are better.

Loretta Lynn's hit tune "Coal Miner's Daughter," for whatever reason, did not conjure up an image of my mother, and nor did Tennessee Ernie Ford's "Sixteen Tons" paint a likeness of my father. Films like Barbara Kopple's award-winning documentary *Harlan County, USA*, came a bit closer by presenting the central Appalachian coalfields as more diverse and inclusive spots than books like Harry Caudill's *Night Comes to the Cumberlands* or Paul Taylor's *Bloody Harlan* or John Hevener's *Which Side Are You On?* None of these forms of media touched the subject of race in Appalachia to any significant degree, let alone delve into stories of individual Blacks in coal towns.

By contrast, the 2010 book *They Say in Harlan County: An Oral History*, by Professor Alessandro Portelli, changed all that. Professor Portelli was in and out of Harlan County for most of three decades, spending considerable time in the same bedroom and eating in the same kitchen that I grew up in, interrelating and intermingling intimately with my family and friends. Portelli writes:

> In 1986, Bill Turner, a brilliant African American scholar, invited me to stay with his family in Lynch. I fell in love with the wisdom of his father, Earl, and the generosity of his mother, Naomi. It took me half an hour in Lynch to shed some of my more naive expectations. I had expected poverty, and here I was in a former "model" company town. Not that my notions of class struggle were all wrong. A neighbor sported a cap with the slogan "God, Guns, and Guts Made the UMWA," referring to the United Mine Workers of America; another dangled visions

of guerrilla warfare in a looming confrontation with the company, a situation that seemed custom-made for a naive radical like me.

But the dominant tone was pride: pride in the living they had achieved through hard work and hard struggles, in the well-kept homes and cars, in the elegant brick church on the corner, in the education received in the old black schools, in the success of friends and relatives who had migrated north. And I was introduced to Willetta Lee and the aptly named black community her mother, Mrs. Mattye Knight, had helped create: Pride Terrace.

That the friend I came to call Sandro made note that "pride" was the dominant sound he heard in Harlan County speaks volumes for me, especially in answer to the question I have been asked often and that I've tried to answer in these pages: "What did growing up in a town like Lynch do for you?"

In *They Say in Harlan County*, Portelli dove deeply into the layered and complex history including the area's settlement and enslavement, the launch of industrialization in the form of corporate-owned coal-mining camps, the recruitment and arrival of foreign immigrants and Blacks from the Black Belt South to work the coal mines, labor strife, the mechanization of mining, the out-migration of foreign immigrants and Blacks beginning in the immediate post–World War II period, and mountaintop removal. Portelli did not so much write about these subjects as he craftily allowed his "subjects," those he interviewed—like my grandparents, parents, brothers, and neighbors—to do the talking; he let them tell their stories. Portelli's mastermind as an oral historian and storyteller comes through in his ability to weave the voices of people into his reference points in the history of the text, the way he narrates the connections between what different interviewees are saying. I hope I have done the same thing in this book. In every Black community in the central Appalachian coalfields, the oral tradition was the channel on which we witnessed the stories of the simple joys our people sometimes found in life as well as what they overcame—their trials and hardships and all manner of cruel treatment based simply on being the color of coal.

When I have asked Black people who were born and raised in central Appalachian towns like mine during the times that I was raised, "What did growing up in a town like Lynch do for you?" they have most often responded using some variant of expressions involving empathy, honesty, openness, patience, pride, reciprocity, respect, stability, and trust.

While growing up in Lynch in the 1950s and 1960s, and from what I am told by some who grew up in similar towns—like nearby Big Stone Gap, Virginia—I intermingled with a critical mass of my neighbors who appeared, most of the time, to be happy, relaxed, comfortable, and relatively optimistic, even if they were not satisfied with their conditions. Arthur Saxton, in his 2018 memoir *Growing up Colored, Negro, Black in the Gap*, recounts such experiences from his native Big Stone Gap, which is less than a half hour from where our father grew up—in southwest Virginia, neighboring the town of Appalachia. Saxton recounts the lives of dozens of people, Black adults—parents—who genuinely and sincerely cared for each other and for their children. Compassion and kindheartedness were at every turn in the Black communities, a consciousness of kind that I have rarely observed since living outside the mountains, now more than a half century ago. It's like time has been flying in reverse, things worsening rather than improving.

From the time of World War I through the early 1960s, the

chief commercial investor in Lynch and the sole employer of its working class—US Steel—personified the supreme successes of the American corporate and capitalist system. What does the loss of this strong community—in the context of race and class struggle—mean for future generations?

The arrival of corporate-owned coal mines to the central Appalachian backwoods at the turn of the twentieth century transformed forever the isolated and pristine homesteads occupied by the few White settlers who had forcibly replaced the Indigenous people. Since coal has declined as the main source of employment, a new set of changes is being wrought in the region. The situation is nothing new: the quantity and quality of neighborhoods and communities are reduced when industrialization comes as well as when it goes. The loss of a sense of community, and the loss of connections within neighborhoods, is harmful to families and children. Disaffection, hostility, distancing, social helplessness, and a swarm of psychological implications sets into community life, and the quality of community is lowered. Is there a decline among residents in the pride of living in and identifying positively with central Appalachian coal towns? Without a doubt there is, and civic participation has weakened extensively.

In mid-August of 2019, I stood on the railroad tracks with roughly eighty coal miners in Harlan County—men and women, only three African Americans—who were blocking trains loaded with coal from moving out of the hollow because their employer, the coal giant Blackjewel, LLC, which is one of the largest coal companies in the United States, had made an emergency bankruptcy filing and closed shop, sending hundreds of workers home, their paychecks bouncing and their bank balances underwater with automatic deductions for house payments, cars, utilities, and the like laying on the line. These workers—the majority of whom were high school graduates, many of them high school dropouts—were accustomed to making $60,000 to $90,000 a year. The funeral-like atmosphere was tangible.

Such scenes—strikes and layoffs—are nothing new, but something about this scene indicated that this group could well be the last generation of coal miners in Harlan County that will be employed by the traditional economic monoculture to which they have become accustomed to for a century. As of March 2019, nearly 4,000 people worked as miners in the eastern Kentucky coalfields, down from 15,147 just a decade prior.

Those left jobless as of July 1, 2019, in Harlan County when Blackjewel and Revelation Energy, based in Houston, left the area represented more than a quarter of the eight hundred or so miners in the county, less than thirty of them African American. George Massey—sixty-seven, African American, born and raised in and a lifelong resident of Lynch, senior deacon at Mount Sinai Baptist Church, retired coal miner, United Mine Workers of America disciple, and a lifelong family friend who worked with my father and my brother Irvin—expressed, even if in somewhat cynical tones, the future of the many people blocking the railroad tracks that day, those who relied on the promise that President Donald Trump made three years earlier that he would revive coal:

> Man, it ain't 'bout Trump's foolish promises or what nobody else in Washington tells these people; it's about whether these coal miners will give in to the fact that coal jobs—in the amounts that our fathers and grandfathers had them—are gone! They had betta' get retrained and do something else to make a living, or they can just wait until the cows come home! And there ain't many cows

> in these here mountains! But there is a lot of politicians talking bull! The main one is Trump, up there telling us he is going to bring coal back.

George was referring to programs that have popped up throughout the region, such as the retraining courses funded by federal agencies like the Appalachian Regional Commission, that are designed to requalify coal miners to become electricians, IT supporters, welders, utility linemen, allied health professionals, fiber optics workers, and other skilled workers in jobs that are driven by the green economy that relies on renewable energy resources. George knows the difference between a renaissance and a requiem.

Black people in central Appalachian coal camps who choose to, or have to, remain—and those who return—have a rich history on which to rely, a history deeply rooted in a dogged determination to stay alive and to thrive, despite the odds and those challenges over which they have no control.

In a way, all people in Appalachia's former coal camps are canaries now. Their futures are indistinguishable from the destiny of the working class throughout the United States. As Professor Ron Eller observed two decades ago, "We are all Appalachians." Nothing I ever witnessed that reflects the fusion of fates—"We are all Appalachians"—matches the expression of commonality that followed the murder of Mr. George Floyd on May 25, 2020. Predominantly White crowds of young people poured into the streets of places as disparate as Big Stone Gap and Pennington Gap in Virginia, Morgantown in West Virginia, and my home county of Harlan and Corbin in Kentucky. These scenes of multiracial solidarity with the Black Lives Matter movement—from Lookout Mountain of Tennessee to Black Mountain in eastern Kentucky to Negro Mountain in West Virginia and to the far

Last four Black coal miners in Lynch: Patsy Tinsley, Ricky Holt, Jerry Massey, and Drena Smith. William H. Turner Collection.

northern endpoint of the Appalachian Trail, the White Mountains in New England—took my breath away.

Those who kept their hopes alive by working the mines of central Appalachia breathed a lot of "bad air," but they survived—and many thrived—by drawing in courage and faith and exhaling hope to the future generations. As a direct result of growing up in an industrial town, one where planning, hard work, and ingenuity transformed a wilderness into a relatively bountiful human beehive that sustained life—and hope and faith—for legions of otherwise rootless Black people, I developed an industrial-strength sense of optimism and positivity. Even the trees that were felled a century ago to make the homes we lived in have been replaced, and life has been renewed. Similarly, I believe, and hope, that yet another Harlan Renaissance—another recovery, an additional regeneration, and an extra special revival—will arrive in the once vibrant coal towns of central Appalachia. This is America, and despite its warts and scars, it is still ground zero for people of hope and faith who possess the determination, the perseverance, and the pluck necessary to survive the down cycles and the changes and to flourish and succeed into the great beyond. Central Appalachia is still home to many Black people, natives to the area, and they, and their heirs, are not going anywhere. After all, where is there to go? Appalachia's fortunes are America's riches and the other way around. Appalachia is mainstreamed, finally.

Notes

This is a selected list of published sources I consulted for this book. Quotes from unpublished sources and from my own memory are not cited here.

ACKNOWLEDGMENTS

xiv **"Being black held me back"** William Earl Turner, quoted in Bob Hill, "Black Home in Appalachia: A Return to Roots Deep in Eastern Kentucky," *Courier-Journal Magazine* (Louisville, KY), June 28, 1987.

xvii **I also listened quite attentively to women** Edward J. Cabbell, "History Uncovers the Role of Black Appalachian Women," *Mountain Life and Work* 58, no. 9 (1982): 4–7.

xix **kinky, curly, or nappy hair was "bad"** William H. Turner, "Hair Weaves and the Legacy of Madame C. J. Walker," *Winston-Salem Chronicle*, October 31, 1996.

INTRODUCTION

5 **The influx of Blacks—primarily from central Alabama** Ronald L. Lewis, "From Peasant to Proletarian: The Migration of Southern Blacks to the Central Appalachian Coalfields," *Journal of Southern History* 55, no. 1 (1989): 77–102, htttp://www.jstor.org/stable/2209720.

6 **"Lynch is the melting pot"** Rose C. Fields, "What I Found in Lynch, Kentucky," *Success*, March 1926, 58–61, 114–19.

14 **"The number of Negroes"** John C. Belcher, "Population Growth and Characteristics," in *The Southern Appalachian Region*, ed. Thomas R. Ford (Lexington: University Press of Kentucky, 1962), 37–53.

14 **Many White-lens views that focused on Appalachia** C. Ray Hall, "The Hillbilly's Burden," *Courier-Journal* (Louisville, KY), September 9, 1995.

15 **an assault on the integrity and self-determination of Blacks in Appalachia** William H. Turner, letter to the editor, *Lexington Herald-Leader*, August 19, 2016, http://www.kentucky.com/opinion/letters-to-the-editor/article96771592.html. See also William H. Turner, "Affrilachia as Brand," *Appalachian Heritage* 39, no. 4 (January 2011): 27–30. I have gone on record several times—in writing and presentations—to provide counterpoints to Frank X Walker's claim that he (literally) "unearthed" Black people in Appalachia: e.g., he put in writing on his website, "I have accepted the responsibility of challenging the notion of a homogeneous all-white literary landscape in this region" (https://www.frankxwalker.com/).

17 **"History is a clock"** John Henrik Clarke, "Why Africana History?," Department of Africana and Puerto Rican/Latino Studies, Hunter College, 1997, http://www.hunter.cuny.edu/afprl/clarke/why-africana-history-by-dr.-john-henrik-clarke.

17 **The experiences of Blacks in Appalachian coal towns have benefits** William H. Turner, "Eastern Kentucky Coalfields, Workplace and Home for Many Kentucky African Americans," in *The Kentucky African American Encyclopedia*, eds. Gerald Smith, Karen Cotton McDaniel, and John A. Hardin (Lexington: University Press of Kentucky, 2015), 157–60. See also William H. Turner, "Blacks in Appalachia—A Thematic Essay," in *The Encyclopedia of Southern Culture*, eds. Charles R. Wilson and William Ferris (Chapel Hill: University of North Carolina Press, 1989), 139–41; Dwight B. Billings and Kathleen Blee, "African-American Families and Communities," in *Encyclopedia of Appalachia*, eds. Rudy Abramson and Jean Haskell (Knoxville: University of Tennessee Press, 2006), 155–56.

CHAPTER 1: ALEX HALEY—THE TAPROOT

21 **"*Roots* is a study of continuities"** James Baldwin, "How One Black Man Came to Be an American: A Review of 'Roots,' " *New York Times*, September 26, 1976, https://archive.nytimes.com/www.nytimes.com/books/98/03/29/specials/baldwin-roots.html.

23 **C. Eric Lincoln and John Hope Franklin** John Hope Franklin, *From Slavery to Freedom: A History of African Americans* (New York: Knopf, 1947); C. Eric Lincoln, *The Black Muslims in America* (Grand Rapids: Wm. B. Eerdmans, 1994).

CHAPTER 2: BETWEEN ALEX HALEY, W. E. B. DU BOIS, ED CABBELL, AND THE AFFRILACHIAN POETS

32 **"It is a peculiar sensation, this double-consciousness"** W. E. B. Du Bois, *The Souls of Black Folk* (Chicago: A. C. McClurg, 1903).

34 **That Blacks in Appalachian coal camps are both Black *and***

Appalachian Wilburn Hayden Jr., *Appalachian Black People: Identity, Location and Racial Barriers* (Toronto: 91 South, 2015).

34 **"No, they don't because that is superseded"** Alex Haley, quoted in Ann Hawthorne, "Alex Haley at Home in the Hills of East Tennessee," *Appalachia* 25, no. 1 (1992): 33–40.

38 **The Black Appalachian Commission—founded in 1969** Edward J. Cabbell, "Black Invisibility and Racism in Appalachia: An Informal Survey," in *Blacks in Appalachia*, eds. William H. Turner and Edward J. Cabbell (Lexington: University Press of Kentucky, 1985), 3–10.

40 **"Appalachian values"** Loyal Jones, *Appalachian Values* (Ashland, KY: Jesse Stuart Foundation, 1984).

40 **"I, too, Am an Appalachian"** Edward J. Cabbell, "I, Too, Am an Appalachian," performed by Edward J. Cabbell, 1970 (West Virginia Public Broadcasting, 2018), video, https://www.pbslearningmedia.org /resource/009e877b-b092-4aa5-8efc-f9f6adbafca9/i-too-am-an -appalachian/. Reprinted by permission of Melissa Rolan.

42 **"is as a voice of the African-American Appalachian experience"** Edward J. Cabbell Papers, 1969–88, A&M.0217, West Virginia and Regional History Center, Morgantown, West Virginia.

42 **"Affrilachians"** The Affrilachian Poets, accessed October 12, 2020, http://www.theaffrilachianpoets.com/.

42 **"forged a space for himself"** Theresa L. Burris, "Claiming a Literary Space: The Affrilachian Poets," in *An American Vein: Critical Readings in Appalachian Literature*, eds. Danny L. Miller, Sharon Hatfield, and Gurney Norman (Columbus: Ohio University Press, 2005), 315–52.

44 **"It's a great term"** Sylvia Bailey Shurbutt, quoted in Chelsea DeMello, "New Anthology of Appalachian Writers to Be Released," West Virginia Public Broadcasting, April 29, 2014, https://www.wvpublic.org /news/2014-04-29/new-anthology-of-appalachian-writers-to-be -released/.

44 **Fact check: Effie Waller Smith** Henry Louis Gates Jr., ed., *The Collected Works of Effie Waller Smith* (New York: Oxford University Press, 1991).

46 **"I recently became a board member"** "Frank X Walker: A Conversation with CX Dillhunt and Drew Dillhunt," Verse Wisconsin Online, 2012, https://www.versewisconsin.org/Issue110/prose/walker.html.

47 **"focuses on poetry"** "Home," Old Cove Press, accessed October 12, 2020, http://oldcove.com/.

48 **"UK Professor Gurney Norman, a white man"** Frank X Walker, quoted in Quraysh Ali Lansana, "Soul in Them There Hills," *Black Issues Book Review* 3, no. 2 (March/April 2001): 50–51.

49 **"I don't write/live in Appalachia"** Shayla Lawson, quoted in Shaina D. W. Taylor, "Gender, Race, and Place: Plurality and Diversity in the

Writings of Affrilachian Women," Student Papers, Carter G. Woodson Project, Marshall University, https://www.marshall.edu/woodson-dev/plurality-and-diversity-in-the-writings-of-affrilachian-women/#_ftn56.

49 **The Appalachian region, as defined** "About the Appalachian Region," Appalachian Regional Commission, accessed October 12, 2020, https://www.arc.gov/.

49 **"turned to poetry to relieve"** Theresa Burris, "Claiming Literary Space," in *An American Vein: Critical Readings in Appalachian Literature*, eds. Danny L. Miller, Sharon Hatfield, and Gurney Norman (Athens: Ohio University Press, 2005).

54 **"support research efforts to collect untold oral histories"** "Great Smokies African American Experience," Friends of the Smokies, January 13, 2020, https://friendsofthesmokies.org/blog/great-smokies-affrilachian-cultural-experience/.

55 **"a 'Geechee girl' from South Carolina"** Shaina D. W. Taylor, "Gender, Race, and Place: Plurality and Diversity in the Writings of Affrilachian Women," Student Papers, Carter G. Woodson Project, Marshall University, https://www.marshall.edu/woodson-dev/plurality-and-diversity-in-the-writings-of-affrilachian-women/#_ftn56.

55 **"Being an Affrilachian poet"** Nikky Finney, quoted in Quraysh Ali Lansana, "Soul in Them There Hills," *Black Issues Book Review* 3, no. 2 (March/April 2001): 50–51.

55 **"highlights the archived experiences"** The Affrilachian Memory Plays, 2018, https://affrilachianmemory.wixsite.com/website.

55 **"considers himself a third- or fourth-generation"** Akhira Umar, " 'We're Here': Affrilachian Poets Make Visible the African Americans in Appalachia," March 17, 2020, http://www.kykernel.com/lifestyle/were-here-affrilachian-poets-make-visible-the-african-americans-in-appalachia/article_548beae8-68a2-11ea-a0dc-43ed6436c238.html.

60 **"confirms the contributions and historical presence"** Affrolachia, accessed October 12, 2020, https://www.affrolachia.com/.

CHAPTER 3: BLACK MOUNTAIN MANTRIPS AND WOMAN TRIPS

72 **"This prison will not be bothered by a recession"** Hal Rogers, quoted in Sam Adler-Bell, "Appalachia vs. the Carceral State," *New Republic*, November 25, 2019, https://newrepublic.com/article/155660/appalachia-coal-mining-mountaintop-removal-prisons-fight.

72 **In Kentucky, for example, the incarceration rate in 2015** Prison Policy Initiative, "Kentucky Profile," https://www.prisonpolicy.org/profiles/KY.html.

CHAPTER 4: WHAT'S IN A NAME?

85 **Theodore G. Bilbo of Mississippi** Pierre Tristam, "Sen. Theodore G. Bilbo's Legacy of Hate," Common Dreams, July 17, 2007, https://www.commondreams.org/views/2007/07/17/sen-theodore-g-bilbos-legacy-hate.

97 **Such Africanized names were extremely popular** Elisabeth Pearson Waugaman, "Our Evolving Black American Naming Traditions," *Psychology Today*, March 1, 2015, https://www.psychologytoday.com/us/blog/whats-in-name/201503/our-evolving-black-american-naming-traditions.

CHAPTER 5: BLACK FOLK DONE LOST THEIR STUFF

107 **"to train Negro teachers and preachers"** Paine College, "History of Paine," https://www.paine.edu/web/about/history.

114 **"Lift Every Voice and Sing"—called "the Negro National Anthem" at the Lynch Colored School** Faith Karimi and A. J. Willingham, "What Makes 'Lift Every Voice and Sing' So Iconic," *CNN*, September 10, 2020, https://www.cnn.com/interactive/2020/09/us/lift-every-voice-and-sing-trnd/.

124 **Johnson Publishing Company sold an equity stake . . . Viacom Inc. purchased Black Entertainment Television** Lynne Marek and Todd J. Behme, "JP Morgan Unit Buys Stake in Ebony Owner Johnson Publishing," *AdAge*, July 6, 2011, https://adage.com/article/media/jp-morgan-buys-stake-ebony-owner-johnson-publishing/228565; Leon Lazaroff, "Time to Acquire Remaining Essence Communication Shares," *Chicago Tribune*, January 5, 2005, https://www.chicagotribune.com/news/ct-xpm-2005-01-05-0501050193-story.html; Skip Wollenberg, "Viacom Acquires BET," *ABC News*, January 6, 2006, https://abcnews.go.com/Business/story?id=89100.

126 **I salute Kentuckians for the Commonwealth** Bill Turner, "Hallowed Hills: Protect Black Mountain, Towns from Strip Mining," *Lexington Herald Leader*, January 31, 2011, https://www.kentucky.com/opinion/op-ed/article44077320.html.

134 **Deacon Belton's enunciations and pronunciations** John Baugh, *Out of the Mouths of Slaves: African American Language and Educational Malpractice* (Austin: University of Texas Press, 1999).

141 **"The mountains may be high"** James T. Cone, *The Spirituals and the Blues* (Seabury Press, 1972; reprt., Maryknoll, NY: Orbis Books, 1992), 4.

CHAPTER 6: THE COMMON NARRATIVE OF BLACK APPALACHIAN COAL-CAMP FAMILIES

148 **The Ninety-Second Infantry Division was formed** "The 92nd Infantry

Division," 92nd Infantry (Buffalo Division), World War II Association, April 25, 2012, http://92ndinfantry.org/.

150 **Lynch and Benham were situated at the easternmost** Rose C. Fields, "What I Found in Lynch, Kentucky," *Success*, March 1926, 58–61, 114–19.

154 **Truth is, Dad's was a southwest Virginia dialect** Troy Smith, "How to Speak Southern Appalachian," Tennessee WordSmith, December 30, 2015, https://tnwordsmith.blogspot.com/2015/12/how-to-speak-southern-appalachian.html.

CHAPTER 7: BLACKS MOVING BETWEEN CENTRAL ALABAMA AND CENTRAL APPALACHIA

159 **Mr. Ben came to Lynch to work for US Steel in 1920** Ronald L. Lewis, *Black Coal Miners in America: Race, Class, and Community Conflict, 1780–1980* (Lexington: University Press of Kentucky, 1987).

165 **Most coal camps in eastern Kentucky, southwest Virginia** "Coal Camp Documentary Project," Appalachian Center and Appalachian Studies Program, University of Kentucky, accessed October 12, 2020, https://appalachianprojects.as.uky.edu/coal-camps.

CHAPTER 8: CLOSE-KNIT CENTRAL APPALACHIAN COAL-CAMP BLACK COMMUNITIES

172 **The most well-known Black person in the United States . . . was Booker T. Washington** History.com Editors, "Booker T. Washington," *History Channel*, December 13, 2019, https://www.history.com/topics/black-history/booker-t-washington.

185 **At the VFW Club, the adults gathered and drank alcohol** Alex Crevar, "Driving the Juke Joint Trail," *New York Times*, May 19, 2013, https://www.nytimes.com/2013/05/19/travel/driving-the-juke-joint-trail.html.

CHAPTER 9: ON TRASH-TALKING AND SIGNIFYING ALONG LOONEY CREEK

187 **Two words carried the most emotional explosiveness—*Black* and *nigga*** Robert H. Decoy, *The Nigger Bible* (Chicago: Holloway House Publishing, 1972).

188 **When I was ten, I got my first real sense** Elijah Anderson, *The Cosmopolitan Canopy: Race and Civility in Everyday Life* (New York: W. W. Norton, 2011). Anderson explains his provocative phrase "a nigger moment" that "occurs when others are too quick to make assumptions based on race, too quick to link a person to poverty or crime based on the color of his or her skin."

189 **"Black people can be out having a good time, and then along comes a bunch of niggas!"** Chris Rock, *Bring the Pain*, directed by Keith Truesdell, aired June 1, 1996, on HBO.

193 **I often heard, in response to an incredulous or unbelievable statement** Elijah Anderson, *Code of the Street: Decency, Violence, and the Moral Life of the Inner-City* (New York: W. W. Norton, 2000).

199 **Despite the widespread use of homosexual slurs and the maltreatment** Delroy Constantine-Simms, *The Greatest Taboo: Homosexuality in Black Communities* (New York: Alyson Books, 2001).

CHAPTER 10: IN A COAL MINE, EVERYBODY IS BLACK; OUTSIDE, NOT SO MUCH

210 **Most of the White people in Appalachian coal camps** William Goodell Frost, "Our Contemporary Ancestors in the Southern Mountains," *Atlantic*, March 1899.

211 **if Africans had not been enslaved in America, these coalfield Whites** James C. Klotter, "The Black South and White Appalachia," *Journal of American History* 66 (March 1980): 832–49, https://doi.org/10.2307/1887639.

213 **The town was built as a circle** George D. Torok, *A Guide to Historic Coal Towns of the Big Sandy River Valley* (Knoxville: University of Tennessee Press, 2004), 287.

215 **3,500 White people showed up to witness the hanging of Floyd Frazier** Mable Green Condon, *History of Harlan County* (Nashville: Parthenon Books, 1962).

216 **Blacks were notably absent in parts of Harlan County** Chris Kenning, "In Former 'Sundown' Town Shadowed by Racist Past, Advocates Seek Allies for Racial Justice," *Courier-Journal* (Louisville, KY), September 14, 2020, https://www.courier-journal.com/in-depth/news/2020/09/14/former-kentucky-sundown-town-shadowed-by-racist-past/5607254002.

218 **In Corbin that year, virtually all the African Americans of the town** Kristy Owens Griggs, "The Removal of Blacks from Corbin in 1919: Memory, Perspective, and the Legacy of Racism," *Register of the Kentucky Historical Society* 100, no. 3 (Summer 2002): 293–310.

220 **A family that emigrated into eastern Kentucky from Syria** Margaret Buranen, "All in the Family: Dawahare's Celebrates 100 Years in Business," Smiley Pete Publishing, March 2, 2012, https://smileypete.com/business/2012-03-02-all-in-the-family-dawahares-celebrates-100-years-in-business/.

220 **The presence of Eastern European immigrants** Kenneth R. Bailey, "A Judicious Mixture: Negroes and Immigrants in the West Virginia Mines, 1880–1917," *West Virginia History* 34 (January 1973): 141–61.

227 **rhythm and blues and rock and roll music** Reginald Stuart, "Rise of Radio's 'Black Music' Source," *New York Times*, July 12, 1982, https://www.nytimes.com/1982/07/12/us/rise-of-radio-s-black-music-source.html.

CHAPTER 11: SCHOOL INTEGRATION WAS WORSE THAN A KICK IN THE HEAD BY AN ALABAMA MULE

236 **all parents present were given a list of *What the Teachers Expect of the Parents*** This document is in the author's possession.

253 **There was considerable loss when these schools were desegregated** Raymond Wolters, *The Burden of Brown: Thirty Years of School Desegregation* (Knoxville: University of Tennessee Press, 1992).

253 **the United States did not really abolish slavery, but simply repurposed it** Marian Wright Edelman, "The Cradle to Prison Pipeline: America's New Apartheid," Child Watch Column, Children's Defense Fund, February 6, 2009, https://childrensdefense.org/child-watch-cikynbs/health/2009/the-cradle-to-prison-pipeline-americas-new-apartheid.

256 **school was a centering point** Josh Moss, "Where Are All the Teachers of Color?" *Harvard Ed. Magazine*, Summer 2016, https://www.gse.harvard.edu/news/ed/16/05/where-are-all-teachers-color.

257 **Most of the White teachers seemed stiff and pretentious** Lindsey E. Jones, "Why Black Teachers Matter," *Black Perspectives*, African American Intellectual History Society, October 13, 2016, https://www.aaihs.org/why-black-teachers-matter/.

257 **The rate of Black students who went to college dropped off precipitously** Rod Paige, *The Black-White Achievement Gap: Why Closing It Is the Greatest Civil Rights Issue of Our Time* (New York: AMACOM Books, 2010).

262 **Blacks traded the relative degrees of independence** Eugene Robinson, *Disintegration: The Splintering of Black America* (New York: Anchor Books, 2011).

CHAPTER 12: THE PRINCIPAL OF THE WHITE SCHOOL BECAME A LIFELONG FRIEND

275 **I stood in for Muhammad Ali** Tom Eblen, feature writer for the *Lexington Herald-Leader,* reflected on the significance of the author's speech in a column: "50 Years Ago: How a Murder and a Speech Were Wake-Up Calls for Segregated Lexington," April 4, 2018, http://www.kentucky.com/news/local/news-columns-blogs/tom-eblen/article207486124.html.

CHAPTER 13: NOT BAD FOR SOME COLORED KIDS FROM HARLAN COUNTY, KENTUCKY

279 **Bernard Bickerstaff** Glenn Nelson, "Becoming Bernie: Sonics Coach Bernie Bickerstaff's Basketball Roots," *Pacific NW Magazine*, April 24, 1988.

280 **"I am who I am because of the influence of those in that community"** David Cobb, "Bickerstaff Boulevard: The Grizzlies Coach's Road to NBA, Sports History in Memphis," *Commercial Appeal*, February 22,

2019, https://www.commercialappeal.com/story/sports/2019/02/22/nba-coaches-j-b-and-bernie-bickerstaff-make-history-memphis-grizzlies/2842731002/.

282 **There are many high-achieving Appalachian African Americans** William H. Turner, "Black Hillbillies Have No Time for Elegies," in *Appalachian Reckoning: A Region Responds to Hillbilly Elegy*, eds. Anthony Harkins and Meredith McCarroll (Morgantown: West Virginia University Press, 2019).

284 **"Gallows humor is an index of strength"** Antonin J. Obrdlik, " 'Gallows Humor'—A Sociological Phenomenon," *American Journal of Sociology* 47, no. 5 (March 1942): 709–16.

284 **"stubbornly ingrained cultural"** *and* **"poor and under-educated"** Erin Keane, "Amy Adams Will Probably Win Her Oscar for 'Hillbilly Elegy' and That's a Damn Shame," *Salon*, April 6, 2019, https://www.salon.com/2019/04/06/amy-adams-probably-will-win-her-oscar-for-hillbilly-elegy-and-thats-a-damn-shame/.

295 **When cities like Detroit began to show signs of desertion** Danielle DeRuiter-Williams, "The Critical Nexus: Deindustrialization, Racism and Urban Crisis in Post-1967 Detroit," *McNair Scholars Journal* 11, no. 1 (2007).

297 **"I've been to the mountaintop"** Dr. Martin Luther King Jr., "I've Been to the Mountaintop," address delivered at Bishop Charles Mason Temple, Memphis, Tennessee, April 3, 1968, King Papers, Martin Luther King Jr. Research and Education Institute, Stanford University, https://kinginstitute.stanford.edu/king-papers/documents/ive-been-mountaintop-address-delivered-bishop-charles-mason-temple.

CHAPTER 14: KING COAL LEAVES THE THRONE

298 **cotton was plunging from its throne** Crandall A. Shifflett, *Coal Towns: Life, Work, and Culture in Company Towns of Southern Appalachia, 1880–1960* (Knoxville: University of Tennessee Press, 1991).

298 **Alabama-based Google data center is in an Appalachian Regional Commission–designated county** Jerry Underwood, "Google Kicks Off Construction on $600M Alabama Data Center," Made in Alabama, April 9, 2018, https://www.madeinalabama.com/2018/04/google-kicks-off-construction-on-alabama-data-center/.

301 **Fully half of the Blacks in . . . Counties in eastern Kentucky** *2020 Kids Count Data Book: 2020 State Trends in Child Well-Being* (Baltimore: Annie E. Casey Foundation, 2020).

301 **"One group of Appalachians who are consistently overlooked"** James G. Branscome, "Annihilating the Hillbilly: The Appalachian's Struggle with American Institutions," *Journal of the Committee of Southern Churchmen* (Winter 1971): 40.

302 **"It's a common theme"** Ronald D. Eller, *Uneven Ground: Appalachian since 1945* (Lexington: University Press of Kentucky, 2013), 191.

304 **When work disappears, when the company leaves the town** William Julius Wilson, *When Work Disappears: The World of the New Urban Poor* (New York: Vintage Books, 1997).

305 **no coal-mining work anymore** Michael Sainato, "The Collapse of Coal: Pandemic Accelerates Loss of Coal Jobs in Appalachia," *Guardian*, May 29, 2020, https://www.theguardian.com/us-news/2020/may/29/coal-miners-coronavirus-job-losses.

309 **"more than 1,300 people attended"** "Summit 19," Save Our Appalachian Region (SOAR), 2020, https://www.soar-ky.org/.

310 **"systems of racism and economic injustice" through "celebrate the many shade and melodies of our existence"** The STAY Project, accessed October 12, 2020, https://www.thestayproject.net/what-is-black-appalachian-young--rising.html.

CHAPTER 15: THE GRAYING OF THE EASTERN KENTUCKY SOCIAL CLUB

316 **The annual gathering of the Eastern Kentucky Social Club is framed** Gary Hendricks, "Memorial Day Reunion Draws Kentuckians Back to Their Roots," *Atlanta Journal-Constitution*, May 28, 1992.

CHAPTER 16: MEDITATING ON THE FUTURE AT THE MOUNTAINTOP

323 **"an act of atonement"** Chinua Achebe, "Named for Victoria, Queen of England," *New Letters* 40, no. 3 (Fall 1973).

324 **"In 1986, Bill Turner, a brilliant African American scholar"** Alessandro Portelli, *They Say in Harlan County* (New York: Oxford University Press, 2011).

328 **Those left jobless as of July 1, 2019, in Harlan County** Michael Sainato, "Laid Off and Owed Paid: Kentucky Miners Blocking Coal Trains," *Guardian*, September 18, 2019, https://www.theguardian.com/us-news/2019/sep/17/harlan-county-coalmine-train-protest.

329 **"We are all Appalachians"** Ron Eller, quoted in Bill Bishop, "When It Comes to the Economy, 'We are All Appalachians,' " *Daily Yonder*, March 30, 2009, https://dailyyonder.com/when-it-comes-economy-we-are-all-appalachians/2009/03/30/.

330 **Those who kept their hopes alive by working the mines** William H. Turner, "The Canaries in the Coal Mine Were Black," *Now & Then: The Magazine of Appalachia* 34 (Winter 2017): 16–20.

Index

Page numbers in *italics* indicate illustrations.